AF560831

J.B. Priestley

A Traveller in Time

R.K. Kulkarni

Published by

ATLANTIC

PUBLISHERS & DISTRIBUTORS (P) LTD

7/22, Ansari Road, Darya Ganj,
New Delhi-110002
Phones : +91-11-40775252, 23273880, 23275880, 23280451
Fax : 91-11-23285873
Web : www.atlanticbooks.com
E-mail : orders@atlanticbooks.com

Branch Office
5, Nallathambi Street, Wallajah Road,
Chennai-600002
Phones : +91-44-64611085, 32413319
E-mail : chennai@atlanticbooks.com

ISBN 978-81-269-1645-0

Printed in India at Nice Printing Press, A-33/3A, Site-IV, Industrial Area, Sahibabad, Ghaziabad, U.P.

Dedicated to

My late mother, Banutai
Whose sacrifice hewed the way for me to walk
And whose spirit gave me wings to fly

Observations by Scholars

I have gone through the work very carefully. I am simply mute with delight. I admire your perseverance in assimilating the Time theories, stream of consciousness theories, in understanding Bergson, Jung, Virginia Woolf, etc., and presenting the whole spectrum in a lucid and graceful style. Even congratulations raised to nth power are not adequate for your *Priestley*.

—Late Dr. H.T. Sasnur
Bijapur

The study of Dr. Kulkarni's work on J.B. Priestley was highly educative and rewarding; in fact, the study was a 'feast' for my mind. By his thorough analysis of Priestley's works, the author has assigned to Priestley, a rightful place in the firmament of Time writers. The words "to understand Time is to understand life itself" will always be ringing in my ears.

Dr. V. Gopalan
Retd. Principal and Professor of Sanskrit,
Chennai

Foreword

Time is a given with which we start our journey through the world, and in which our departure from the world is marked. Yet, there is nothing more mysterious than Time; perhaps, only God is.

The past—our boyhood, youth, prime and advancing years—lives within us as memories, as consciousness, as a seed grown into a spreading tree. But they too cease to be, with our exit from the world. We live on, nonetheless, as part of other people's memories until those living monuments too are knocked out. Maybe, our genes give us a fresh lease of life through being transmitted to our children and our children's children. But all that is beyond our cognitive territory. For all we know, we pass this way but once, and that's that.

Man has invented other modes of defeating death and outlasting the earthly termination of life. He has invented photography and he can script his biography in print and film, which give him a new dimension of survival. We live in the works we leave behind.

But Time does not cease with our ceasing. It will flow on like a river (as it has done from before the 'beginning of recorded time') to join the sea of eternity. I have a (layman's) guess. Time was created with the creation of the sun (But when did that take place? Nobody knows). Time cannot have been in existence in primordial darkness. With the sun came light, day and night. And man for his convenience of reckoning, hacked time into seconds, minutes, hours and days. But why did he have to have a week of seven days and a year of three hundred and sixty-five days? That was a creation of man's 'meddling (read, order- imposing) intellect'.

Time is at once a simple proposition and also something that bogs our imagination. It is an enigma, a riddle. How long does the present time stretch? It could be a moment that is already slipping into the past; it could be a longer bandwidth when the action is stretched over a long period. And, you know, time lost cannot be regained. But Einstein spoke of the speculative possibility that if one travelled at more than the speed of light, one could arrive at yesterday! But do men and events hover in mid-air there, like astronauts in a spaceship, under conditions of zero gravity?

Futurity, again, is a big question. Though part of it is predictable, part of it is totally unpredictable. Our dreams and fancies are not controlled by clock time. They travel at the speed of lightning. Lately, we have begun to speak of 'real time', as against virtual time, the time actually taken by an event to happen or an action to mature and take effect.

We have, accordingly, different ways of looking at time (Einstein spoke of time being relative). So there is clock time or empirical time, which is temporal and has a linear movement. It is segmented into past, present and future. Another view of it is that it is an entity that had no beginning and will (conceivably) have no end (unless we believe in Apocalypse and a second creation) which we may call timeless Time. A 'world time', too, has been posited, of which I can have no conception, unless we term it as Cosmic Time.

Now, J.W. Dunne and Peter D. Ouspensky had their own theories. According to Dunne, Time consisted of a series attuned to each one of us as an observer; it therefore stretched in an endless series. Ouspensky held that Time had a cyclical movement. He posited that those who are after comfort and pleasure continue to live the same kind of lives, circulating through the cycle, and those who live virtuous lives can break out of circular Time and escape from eternal recurrence into spiralling Time. And it is principally on these theories of Time, plus those of Indian philosophers, that J.B. Priestley developed his own. But more than that, he 'fleshed' out these theories and their implications through the plots and characters of his novels and plays.

It is only a brave-hearted critic, of the kind that Dr. R.K. Kulkarni is, who with a rare power of penetration into abstruse theory and complicated literary articulation, undertook to analyse and interpret the oeuvre of Priestley's Time works—short stories, novels and plays, numbering nearly forty. The stuff of these Priestleyan literary configurations are patently 'cavaire to the general'. Only Dr. Kulkarni, who took it up as a challenge, could essay the task and bring it to speedy fruition. Even I, nominally his old guru, hesitate to tread into the dense jungle where Dr. Kulkarni ventured forth like an expert botanist. I compliment him on the successful accomplishment of the task he had undertaken. With his book in hand, no student of Priestley need look around elsewhere as he/she has a knowledgeable guide to lead him/her by the hand. Kudos to Dr. R.K. Kulkarni!

Dr. G.B. Sajjan
(Retd. Principal and Professor of English)

J.B. [illegible]
century, [illegible]
misjudged [illegible]
just and [illegible]
with a [illegible]
hardly [illegible]
plays a[illegible]
present [illegible]
of all his [illegible]
enduring [illegible]

This [illegible]
accoun[illegible]
backgro[illegible]
chapter [illegible]
fifth chap[illegible]
Priestley [illegible]
sixth chap[illegible]
chapter [illegible]

The [illegible]
English [illegible]

Preface

J.B. Priestley was a major British writer of the twentieth century, but unfortunately he is a forgotten figure today. Often misjudged as a mere entertainer, Priestley has not received a just and due recognition as a serious Time-writer endowed with a poetic vision, from literary critics, and consequently, hardly any comprehensive critical work, putting all his Time plays and Time novels into focus, has appeared so far. The present book fills this gap and makes a thorough critical study of all his Time works with a view to bringing out his solid and enduring contribution to British drama and fiction.

This book has seven chapters. The first chapter gives an account of various perceptions and dimensions of Time as a background to the study of Priestley's Time works. The second chapter is about Priestley and his age, while third, fourth and fifth chapters deal with the early, middle and final phases of Priestley's development as a Time writer, respectively. The sixth chapter is on Priestley's technique of writing, and the last chapter highlights his achievements as a writer.

The book shall be useful to students and teachers of English literature, and researchers in this field.

R.K. Kulkarni

Acknowledgements

I am thankful to all the writers and critics I have consulted and referred to in this book.

I am deeply indebted to Dr. C.R. Yaravintelimath, my teacher, who happily combines in him "sweetness and light" and who provided valuable guidance from time to time. I am extremely grateful to Dr. M.K. Naik, my teacher and a doyen among Indian English literary critics, for suggesting very useful books and articles on Time and the Time theme. I always cherish the sacred memory of my late teacher Dr. H.T. Sasnur who inspired me with a vision and a purpose for life and took a keen interest in my pursuit of Priestley.

I simply cannot express in words what I owe my teacher Dr. G.B. Sajjan, a recipient of *honoris causa*, a rare master of English, who patiently and minutely went through the entire original draft and brushed it up, lending it the benefit of his critical eye and perfect pen. I am beholden to him for writing an insightful Foreword to this book.

I am thankful to Dr. R.S. Chulki, my friend and colleague, with whom I have usefully discussed the subject of this book. My hearty thanks are also due to Dr. A.R. Kulkarni, Retd. Professor (Mumbai University), the late Kannada litterateur Shri Raghavendra Khasnis (Bangalore), Dr. Sanjay Deshpande (Solapur), and Prof. R.G. Kulkarni (Dharwad).

I respectfully remember my late father-in-law Shri L.H. Desai, a keen student of literature himself, who heartily helped and encouraged me in all my academic endeavours.

Also I warmly thank all the members of my family, especially my wife Manjula for her co-operation and my sons Raghavendra and Raveendra and my nephews Vijendra and Sanjay for their interest and involvement in the publication of the work.

Also my thanks are due to Mr. Vishwas Nitsure for his efficient and diligent typing of the manuscript.

Last but not least, my obligations are to the Atlantic Publishers and Distributors (P) Ltd., New Delhi, for bringing out this book in good time with the professional skill and aesthetic sense.

R.K. Kulkarni

Contents

John
century,
critic,
figure of
experimen
fiction, Pa
to a prec
He was
achievem
was a do
Bergson's
of this pe
fiction, H
leading
Time-har
still in th
Eliot we
poems;
plays abo
audience
theories
Time no
the soluti

Prestor
writers
treated the

1

Introduction

John Boynton Priestley, a major writer of the twentieth century, was a versatile writer—dramatist, novelist, essayist, critic, biographer and autobiographer—and a towering public figure of his time. A prolific professional writer and a lifelong experimenter with the form and technique of drama and fiction, Priestley wrote at varying levels, from the plain thriller to a profound philosophical probing into the mystery of Time. He was a unique Time-traveller. The best part of his literary achievement is found in his Time-plays and Time-fiction. Time was a dominant force in the 1920's and the 1930's; Henry Bergson's *durêe* had a powerful influence on the major writers of this period. If Henry James had been the pioneer of Time-fiction, H.G. Wells was the father of science-fiction. The leading lights of the English literary scene of the time were all Time-haunted writers: James Joyce and Virginia Woolf were still in the arena of 'stream-of-consciousness' fiction; Yeats and Eliot were expressing their sense of Time's mystery in their poems; Lord Dunsany and James Barrie were out but still their plays about the Time element were not out of the mind of the audience. As a writer greatly influenced by various Time theories and views, Western and Eastern, Priestley regarded Time not as a mere artistic technique but as a Sphinx riddle, the solution of which was a key to the happiness of man.

Priestley stands distinguished from other English Time-writers in three respects. He is the only English writer who has treated the Time theme in two major forms, viz. drama and fiction. Primarily a writer with a poetic vision, Priestley has made into art the Time theories like J.W. Dunne's Serial Time, Ouspensky's Recurrent Time, and Jung's Collective Unconscious, whereas others have not creatively employed any metaphysical theory of Time. Another speciality of Priestley is that he is the only non-Bergsonian English Time-writer; while the others have treated the Time theme psychologically he alone has handled it philosophically.

Priestley's contribution as a philosophical Time-writer is solid and significant. But it is surprising that he was not seriously taken in his own life-time; he was often misjudged and taken in some quarters simply as an entertainer, "a Jolly type with a pipe."[1] Even today English academic criticism has denied him his rightful and legitimate place. Therefore, an attempt has been made here in this book to map out how various views and theories of Time have shaped and sustained these works, and to answer thereby the critical charges undeservedly levelled against him, as also to assign to him his just and rightful place among the canon of English writers of Time-plays and Time-fiction.

A critical account of the nature, perceptions and dimensions of Time is quite necessary to the proper understanding of Priestley's Time-works.

To think of Time is to think of man's existence, of the World and the Universe. Time is as old as the creation; perhaps older even. What is it that we call Time? We are unable to speak of it in definite terms although we experience it. St. Augustine's cry of helplessness is well-known: "What is time? Who can simply and briefly explain it?... Yet what is more familiar and well known in conversation than time?... What, then, is time?...if nobody asks me, I know; but if I try to explain it to one who asks me, I do not know."[2] Certainly one cannot explain Time simply and briefly. However, we have different definitions of Time coming from different thinkers, philosophers and scientists. The best known definition of Time from the ancient Greek World is by Plato: "A moving likeness of Everlastingness."[3] To Aristotle it is "movement so far as it admits of enumeration."[4] Alexander, who considers Time to be the generator of change and novelty, observes: "Time is in truth the abiding principle of impermanence which is the real creator."[5] If Schopenhauer defines Time "as the possibility of opposite states in one and the same things", [6] Bergson speaks of Time as 'duration' which is "the continuous progress of the past which gnaws into the future"?[7] To Locke "Time is a perpetual perishing."[8] A.G.E. Blake's observation is "Time is representative of conditions under which we exist, not only as bodies, but also as mind."[9] If Kant thinks of Space and Time as "organs of perception", Eddington, the famous physicist, treats Time merely as "a symbol". If the mathematical concept of Time is analogous to the time in geometry, infinite in length and infinitely divisible, to C.H. Hinton, it is the fourth dimension. All these definitions suggest the complexity of the nature of Time. Therefore, it is imperative to take into account how Time is popularly viewed, and how it is academically considered in all its aspects.

Time is invincible and destructive. The familiar images of Time are that it is a Master Conqueror, Greedy Devourer; Relentless Harvester. It is universally believed that Time attacks and destroys everything. Things and beings come into this world, grow old, decay and vanish into thin air. This experience of mankind finds a very powerful expression in the language of poets:

"Fair daffodils we weep to see
You haste away so soon"[10]

"Golden lads and girls all must,
As chimney sweepers, come to dust."[11]

Time is considered a fast-fleeting universal Bird, a Forward-flowing River, a mercilessly rotating wheel and so on and so forth. The popular proverb "Time and Tide wait for no man" speaks of this commonly felt transitoriness of time; nothing remains steadfast in Time, everything changes because Time rolls it on and changes it.

Time is believed to be irreversible. An event will not happen again. A thing done cannot be undone. You can't kill a man twice. You can't unscramble an egg.

Generally Time is divided into past, present and future. But these divisions are not independent of one another. The past was once present and that which we call present is going to be past. Still Time is regarded as a thing in itself. If Time were an independent entity or a physical quantity—it is so considered in science—there could be certain indisputable characteristics of it. But our experience is such that we cannot hypostatize Time. Some call Time the 'Eternal Now'. How can we locate this 'now-ness' when our efforts to catch it meet with a miserable failure? Scientists view it as an interval between two events. But we are not sure whether events take place in Time or Time exists only as a background and events take place against that backdrop.

Time is too abstract and elusive a concept to be fitted into the Procrustean bed of any formula or definition. The complexity and paradoxical nature of Time perforce throws up a plethora of questions that stare us in the face: Does Time subsist in its own right? Is Time absolute or relative? Is it eternal or ephemeral, real or unreal, cyclic or linear, spiral or serial? Is Time one or many? Is it divisible and measurable? What do we mean by 'long time' and 'short time', 'good time' and 'bad time'? Man—especially modern man—cannot wish away these irksome and challenging questions hurled at him by Time the Sphinx.

Time is differently viewed in different fields of learning and literature.

Logically speaking, Time can never be wholly grasped; it is both a percept and a concept. Time is too elusive to be perceived in its passing. Time as perceived is not the same as conceived. Time perceived is only that much of it which is related to the content of an event. Perceptual cognisance of Time is limited in character, while conceptual Time is unlimited in character. We never see Time in abstraction from events; for perception something should happen. "We are not directly aware of events without duration, still less of moments of empty time."[12] Temporal succession or order of events gives us an awareness of 'earlier' and 'later'. This phenomenon of 'happening' is pivotal to our thinking of Time as divided into past, present and future, which are not exclusive, independent divisions and are not the essential attributes of Time. Past, present, and future are not definite and indisputable attributes of Time like the redness of a red rose or hardness of a raw apple. Logic has its own relentless way of judging things in the light of its governing principle of 'cause and effect'. But Time defies logicality: there is something alogical about it. Logic demands certainty which is certainly not in Time; it involves change. Riddled with contradictions Time has an element of contingency, something that may so unexpectedly happen.

The psychologist deals with sense-perception; he distinguishes between sensation and perception. We recognise material objects as such and such, because our past experience enables us to do so and find a meaning in them. Thus time past and time present meet at the point of perception, and make the experience meaningful. The psychological present, in William James's phrase, 'the specious present', is not just an extentionless glimpse of the world at an instant; in its terms only we see changes. All change takes 'time' and it takes place within the specious present. Wildon Carr observes: "The moment of experience has no distinction of past and present, but it has distinction of before and after."[13] Psychology as the science of mind treats a moment of Time as having duration; 'duration' is felt because of our consciousness which is a key to our experience of Time. This moment of experience is not a durationless point; it is, however, not the same as a point in the mathematical line of time denoted by 't'. James calls our attention to the nature of the specious present when he says that it is "no knife edge, but a saddle-back, with a certain breadth of its own on which we sit perched and from which we look in two directions into time. The unit of composition of our perception of time is 'duration' with a bow and a stern, as it were—a rearward and forward-looking end."[14]

The present becomes past in a mysterious way. The specious present contains both immediate perception and immediate memory. Each succeeding instant is so related to the immediately preceding one that the welding of the two makes the present the past. In the psychological experience of Time the key factor is memory; it is memory that links the past to the present by conjoining the immediately previous instant with the present instant. However, a sharp line of demarcation cannot be drawn between perception and memory. Therefore, according to James, the feeling of past time is a present feeling. Our attention is both retrospective and prospective. The retrospective attention enables us to recall or relive the past and the prospective attention is a watching, a waiting for what is to come. Time may be viewed like a river flowing backwards —the future flowing into the present and the present into the past, the past being gathered into the ocean of eternity.

Our notions of past and future emerge from our awareness of the present moment receding fast. But the awareness of the 'present' is formed only in contrast with the past and the future. Time is described as irreversible. Then what is the psychological view of this Time's irreversibility? The idea of irreversibility is connected with our concept of the 'passage of time'. Men like A.E. Burtt lay stress on the present which alone is the source of 'time-flow' and 'time-growth'.

As against this view is Bergson's observation about the past: "The past in its entirity is prolonged into the present and abides there actual and acting."[15] If Burtt's time has a backward-forward passage, Bergson's has a passage from the backward to the forward direction. Bergson's time is the continuous progress of the past towards the future.

Psychological time is subjective and it is contrary to objective time, i.e. clock-time. The psychological term 'duration' is not identical with the physicist's 'duration' as time-interval. The 'longness' or 'shortness' of time is the result of how the time-lapse is felt; the duration of an event is subjective: people make different estimates of duration in different situations. If we are passing through painful or anxious or boring situations our attention is made conscious of the slow passage of time which makes us weary of it; then we feel that time is 'long'. Likewise, excited states of mind make us feel that time is dragging dead slow. On the contrary, when we are passing through states of joy and happiness time appears too 'short' and 'fleeting'. "Time travels in diverse paces with diverse persons."[16] Thus, it points to the fact that subjectively experienced time is not subject to clock-time, and on the other hand it is the content of our experience of an event that determines the estimates of the time-interval.

Psychologists refer to 'associations' and 'dissociations' of thoughts and actions. Normally our thoughts and actions keep pace. If they are dissociated we find the time spent or passed either longer or shorter. The specious present is connected with the succession of ideas in our mind. If the succession is retarded by something like a tedious job or the spell of a drug on the mind, we feel time is ticking slowly. De Quincey's experience under opium-trance, narrated by him in *Opium-Eater,* is an example of how a drug acts on the mind, giving the feeling of slow-moving time: "Space swelled, and was amplified to an extent of unutterable infinity. This, however, did not disturb me so much as the vast expansion of time; I sometimes seemed to have lived for seventy to a hundred years in one night; nay, sometimes had feelings representative of a millennium passed in that time, or however, of a duration far beyond the limits of any human experience."[17] Dreamers pass through long and complicated situations spreading over a long time, in a few seconds. In some cases long period of time, even a life-time, flashes by like lightning.

Time is treated merely as a symbol in physics and denoted by 't'. Physicists recognise the 'passing away' of time as its essential character and their view is that intervals of time do not exist at the same time; past and present are continuous and the past is remembered. Strictly speaking, time cannot be measured but only 'experience' regarding its 'order' can be measured. Physical time symbolized by 't' is not identical with Time as conceived by metaphysicians. Modern physics cannot think of time in isolation from space. A space-Time continuum is essential to our understanding of the physical world. The three dimensions of space and the one dimension of time make one bound and according to physicists everything exists, every event takes place, in this four-dimensional bound.

All objects of our experience have a magnitude called extensity because of which they extend in space and, similarly, they possess another kind of magnitude called protensity because of which they endure in time. Just as we recognise the position of an object of our view in relation either to the right or to the left of another, we see a single specious present to have precedence over, or succession to, another. It is believed that all the material points take their places in a single three-dimensional series of geometrical points, and likewise all the events in the history of the world fall into their places in a single series of moments. The three coordinates of space and one coordinate of time make this space-time continuum. Because of this relation between space and time we have come to spatialize time and temporize space. Modern physics, especially Quantum physics, has accepted this inseparable relation since the Newtonian classical theory of absolute time has been disproved and pushed to the wall by Einstein's theory of relative time. Newton theorised that "Absolute, true and mathematical time, of itself, and from its own nature flows equably without relation to anything external."[18] According to him time was an independent substance, uniformly flowing. In fact our idea of time comes from sequence of events whereas absolute time of Newton's conception was independent of events. This Newtonian absolute theory reigned supreme for nearly two centuries until Alfred Einstein put forth his theory of relativity of time.

In fact Einstein's theory of relativity had been anticipated by Leibniz. Even Aristotle, with his concept of time as a numbering process based on motion involving a perception of 'before' and 'after', did think of something other than temporal time or only one time. C.H. Hinton in his book *What is the Fourth Dimension*?, published in 1887, treated time not as a line but as a dimension. He assumes that the past and the present coexist; matter extends [endures] in time-dimension. The present, according to him, is a three-dimensional view of the four-dimensional world. Thus Einstein had forerunners but none had explained and established the relativity of time with clarity, conviction and mathematical accuracy as did Einstein in his special theory and general theory.

Thus the idea of absolute time was exploded by the relativity theory. Einstein proved that the greatest velocity in the universe is that of light. He says, "If I travel faster than light, events will happen in reverse order for me."[19] He is not suggesting a possibility but stating a hypothesis. His *General Theory* (1911) showed that mass affected the rate of time. For example, if the earth had been larger, time would have been slower on it. Thus Einstein established two things: (1) Time is relative to the observer and (2) Time is relative to mass. Today our awareness of the space-time continuum is due to Einstein's adding of the fourth dimension of time to the three dimensions of space. "It is worth noting that Relativity admits of 'seeing ahead' in Time, in the sense that what is future to Jones may be present to Brown."[20] In other words, the date of an event is relative to the position of the observer. An event may be present to Brown, while the same event will be future to Jones who is at a remote distance from Brown.

Literature, like music, is a time-art as it involves temporal factors. A work of literature, as Wyndham Lewis observes, "can only be apprehended, as music can be apprehended, in time, not in space".[21] Literature deals with both aspects of existence: temporal succession (objective time) and the self that experiences subjective time. It presents what Goethe calls "duration within change".[22] Time in Literature is subjective; it is time in experience, in opposition to time in nature which is objective. If the objective pattern of events or facts constitutes a man's biography, the subjective pattern of significant associations, or time in experience, constitutes that man's self or identity. There is a dynamic fusion of temporal elements in works of literature, especially in modern literature, which is keenly Time-conscious. The Time-fiction of the twentieth century does away with linear time. Since the ordinary modalities of time—past, present and future—are indistinguishable in experience, it calls our attention to the infinite possibilities present in any moment in the life-span of an individual. The 'stream-of-consciousness' fiction points to a timeless co-presence of temporal elements in fantasy and imagination and dreams. Literature uses dreams and fantasies because they are "experiences suitable for conveying both the quality of duration and the quality of dynamic disorder and association".[23]

Time appears in various forms in literature. The views and theories of Time propounded by modern thinkers and philosophers like Freud, Jung, Bergson and J.W. Dunne have considerably influenced the fiction, poetry and drama of the twentieth century. As a result, we have 'timeless time', *durêe,* 'cyclical time', 'time-shifts', 'epiphany', etc. Years and ages may be telescoped within a few hours of fictional time as in *Ulysses* or 'the moment' may occupy hours of the reader's time as in *Mrs. Dalloway.* "During a few hours of reading, one imaginatively lives through a period of time that may stretch for anything from centuries to minutes."[24] Cyclical time is used in the treatment of mythical themes because mythical figures are timeless human prototypes. Proust, Thomas Mann, James Joyce, Dorothy Richardson, Virginia Woolf, Thomas Wolfe, William Faulkner, J.B. Priestley and many more Time-haunted writers have perceived time as being other than linear and depicted it as such. The various techniques of time representation in modern literature have been prompted by a deep-felt desire to depict the timeless reality of life.

There are mainly two types of Time: (i) Time temporal and (ii) Time eternal. Temporal Time is a temporal succession or order of events and we have this type of Time, running as a straight line, in history. Science too held this view till the discovery of the relative character of Time by Einstein. The Christian concept of man's life, as a journey towards perfection from 'Original Sin' at birth (both individual and racial) till his redemption, put man on the straight road of Time and of history, and Time came to be linear.

Timeless Time has a much older history. This type of Time needs to be understood with reference to 'eternity' which has been a recurring theme of discussion in all religions and philosophies of the world. Therefore, it is necessary to examine the important concepts and theories of Time from Heraclitus to modern metaphysical thinking in the West and from Egyptian mythological lore to the Vedantic writings of India in the East. Priestley's Time-works are to be viewed in the light of the various views and theories of Time with which he was thoroughly acquainted.

As the long hours do pass away,
So doth the life of man decay.[25]

This philosophical motto, inscribed on an old-time sundial, speaks of temporal time or clock-time which is believed to be merciless a tyrant 'tick-tocking' everything to extinction and everybody to his grave. It is this passing time that is personified in the popular image of Time as Tyrant, Destroyer, Insatiable Devourer, Ever-Flying Universal Bird, Ever-flowing Stream, and so on and so forth.

The conventional popular view of Time is linear. This is the historical concept of Time and for long science too went the same way. This line of thinking holds that all the events of the world fall in their places in a straight line. Past, present and future are its divisions and the measurable divisions like years, months, days, hours and so on are attempts to fix in time our experiences in a temporal succession; everything is contained in this single-track 'holdall' of time. Man spent centuries in inventing and improving different kinds of measurement of time in different periods of history and this fact speaks of the tyranny of temporal time that has held man in thrall for ages!

The views, first, of the Western thinkers and then, of the oriental philosophers, on temporal time are discussed in the following pages.

The first great advocate of life as a flux was Heraclitus, a Greek philosopher of the fifth century B.C. His is the negative view of life which states that nothing stands, everything that comes into being disappears into nothingness. The world is a 'perpetual flow'. "You cannot step twice into the same river; for fresh waters are ever flowing in upon you."[26] This kind of attitude to life is a result of looking only at the temporal aspect of passing time. Aristotle's definition of Time as the number of motion binds Time to motion; motion is unthinkable without object and hence his view of Time is basically temporal. In one sense his view is psychological, because Time as a 'number' presupposes a soul or mind that counts. But this philosopher believes in becoming; becoming involves changes; change means a moving entity, that is, temporal time. If Plato's view of Time as the Image of Eternity is metaphysical, Aristotle's is a physical view. "It seems that he thinks of time as so many hours or days or years."[27]

The Aristotlean view of Time as 'number' was rejected by the Epicureans and the Stoics who shared some common ground in their ideas of Time. They conceived of the cosmos and Time as a continuum; moving synchronously with the cosmos, which was moving in a circle, Time was one and whole and circular.

The Roman World clung to the idea of cyclical time and the recurrence of all things for a long time. When the Roman Emperor Constantine embraced Christianity, chronological time became important owing to the rise of Christian History.

With the triumph of Christianity the two old ideas of eternity and recurrence of history through time cycles vanished. The mythical belief in Eternal Great Time, which had lent people an imaginative living for centuries, disappeared and the Christian started journeying on the straight road of Time and of history towards the much-longed-for redemption, to be delivered from Original Sin at the end of Time which would end at some future date at God's will.

The Middle Ages were an age of faith. The Scholastics established a scale of cosmic structure, a hierarchy of forms: God was the transcendent cause, the omnipotent at the top, which from without preserved the creatures and their individual existence. The medieval Christian did not feel that his existence was one thing and his endurance as a creature in time another. The world was a world of abiding things. How did things abide? This question had its answer in the cause that had created all existences: the creator caused them 'to be' and 'to endure'. Creation and preservation were two faces of an indivisible act of the creator. The man of this period recognised two tendencies in himself: a tendency towards 'nothingness' and a tendency towards the continuance of his existence. If the first tendency made him feel that he was a transient being, the opposite tendency made him feel that he was a permanent being.

The Christian conception of Time in the middle ages was different from the ancient Greco-Roman pagan conceptions and had no hint of modern conceptions. The age believed in a double continuity: the permanent continuity of the substantial form—the 'true self of things and beings—and the successive continuity of change. To them Time was not a kind of duration absolutely different from permanence; it was an incomplete permanence. All becoming in the natural world and spiritual world depended on the determination of God. The permanent continuity of the substantial form sustained the moving continuity of Time, and Time unrolled itself in such a mobile way that the successive moments could not be distinguished. This moment of Time was not a passive one like life-denying futile 'perpetual flow' of Heraclitan time; this had a definite goal to reach. "Even in his body the Christian of the middle ages felt a continuous orientation towards a spiritual perfection. Time had a direction. Time finally carried the Christian towards God."[28] All of man's bodily and spiritual actions were achieved only through Time. Any act of the human spirit—the act of feeling, of thinking, of enjoyment—was brought to perfection through Time; then it achieved its transcendental quality and lasted in duration. The Christian of this period believed that he was a 'fallen creature' but he would, through his good deeds, get liberated from Original Sin by God's grace. He was sure of realizing himself in Time through divine succour. Thus Time in the Middle Ages was not exclusively temporal; it did have a higher level and duration which would take man to the door of Eternity. In fact medieval man was more concerned with Eternity than with Time; he was not Time's fool or slave. The Arthurian legends are a proof of how imagination reigned supreme in the age. Medieval man believed in the magic land of Time which was to him "really a kind of outpost of Eternity in this world".[29] Most medieval writers attempted to put their characters out of Time so that they wandered in Eternity only to come back eventually to the real world.

The Maya civilization that flourished between the third century A.D. and the ninth was obsessed with Time. They regarded Time as eternal in the sense of unending rectilinear passing time. They believed in Time carrying gods who would succeed in a cosmic relay-race. Theirs was a unidirectional track moving from the past to the present; it was an endless race.

The Newtonian theory of Absolute Time had its influence on the Realists and Materialists of the seventeenth and eighteenth centuries. Though everything else underwent a sea-change with the dawn of the modern Age the Newtonian idea of Time survived and influenced the popular mind. With the advent of the Industrial Revolution clock-time was markedly felt. The smooth natural rhythms of work, to which man in the West was accustomed for centuries, were upset by the mechanical work introduced by the Industrial era. Work in the factories and mills tied the worker to the mechanical passage of time, which was notably felt as he was perforce made to be aware of the divisions of time as hours and minutes measuring his working time. Man was driven relentlessly along the ever-speeding flight of time.

Evolutionists like Gentile and Croce advocated the importance of history and the Time-process. They asserted an ideal of progress through Time which they held to be an indispensable factor to the realization of the highest values of the human race. Philosophers like Plato, Plotinus and Spinoza do not attach any value to temporal time because to them the ultimate reality, which is timeless, is all in all. But Hegel, the great German philosopher, distinguishes his philosophical approach to the universe from that of all these metaphysical thinkers. To him the Time-process or historical process is indispensable to the realisation of the Eternal. Man as a superior being is, however, not so at birth. The evolution of man as a creature endowed with consciousness and freedom is unthinkable unless it is to be had through the temporal time process.

Plato said that God created Time; Time to him was an illusion which was cyclical in process. Christian philosophers believe in the creation of Time by God but not in the concept of its cyclical movement; to them Time is linear and this line is going to end at some date in future. That is, they believe not in the recurrence of the past but in the coming of the future. The world and the soul were not created within the limits of Time, but Time was created along with them. It is for this reason that the life of the soul in this world is inseperably connected with Time. The Christian view of history is that it "is a sequence of creative moments in which something new enters the world and determines the future".[30] The time movement, which may be called empirical time or temporal time, cannot be dismissed as unessential to the realisation of the 'soul' of man. The origin of Time temporal and Time Eternal can be traced to the Vedic mantras, and both these types of Time have appeared from time to time in different systems of Indian philosophical thought.

The first reference to temporal time is found in the *Maitri Upanishad*: "There are, assuredly, two forms of the Brahman: Time and the Timeless. That which is prior to the sun is the Timeless [a-kāla], without parts. But that which begins with the sun is Time, which has parts. Verily, the form of that which has parts is the year."[31]

This Upanishadic text speaks of two times: Time with a form, which is temporal time, and formless time, which is timeless Time. This view is an advance on older Vedic view, which regarded it as a primordial power. The kāla spoken of here is measurable and hence it has the year as its form; this is empirical time which is also called clock-time.

Buddhism holds that nothing remains, everything changes; that is, nothing 'is', everything 'becomes'. It is a philosophy of change which recognises the transitoriness of everything and every being. This philosophy is one that negates everything except Nirvana, the supreme peace, to be attained after being liberated from the wheel of Time. It believes in the doctrine of Karma but not in the attainment of the eternal state of God after liberation from the Time wheel. Its sense of liberation is one of release from the Time wheel, but not a release into the blessed life of heaven. Buddha does not believe in the immortality of the individual self or personality continued after death. According to Buddhism Time is one and is basically temporal, which idea is pictorially expressed in these images: "The flame of a lamp appears to be the same though it changes from moment to moment. The Stream of water appears to be the same, though it changes every moment. All objects of the world are undergoing destruction every moment. But they appear to persist owing to illusion".[32] This illusion is not the Platonic illusion of Time as the 'Image of Eternity' but one which is called life, here and now. Buddha offers no heaven and no hell. "As he proposes a theology without a deity, so he offers a psychology without a soul; he repudiates animism in every form, even in the case of man. He agrees with Heraclitus and Bergson about the world, and with Hume about the mind. All that we know is our sensations; therefore, so far as we can see, all matter is force, all substance is motion. Life is change, a neutral stream of becoming and extinction; the soul is a myth...."[33] Accordingly there is no such a thing as immortality in any sense that implies the continuance of the individual after death.

According to Jainism there are two types of Time: Real time [Kãla] and empirical time [Samaya]. Real time is one, eternal, infinite and devoid of varieties. Empirical time has a beginning and an end, and it is divisible into seconds, minutes, hours, days, etc. Real time is absolute, while temporal time is relative. Empirical time is the auxiliary cause of change, movements and modifications and so also of temporal priority and posterity of substances in the world.

Of the six Hindu philosophical systems two, namely, the Sãmkhya and the Vaisesika, treat Time as the temporal succession of events.

The Sãmkhya is the oldest of these systems of knowing. This system holds that Space and Time are not independent realities; they are generated from ether. While space consists of coexistent points, Time consists of moments. One eternal Time cannot exist and be divided into past, present and future; one eternal infinite Time is only an intellectual construct. Moments alone are real. Moments follow a definite sequence and sequence is succession of events occuring in moments. The sequence of momentary events is known as Time.

The Space-Time continuum is an important idea in the Sāmkhya system. This is a philosophy of becoming, of the evolutionary process. All this takes place in temporal time, or world-time. "Every phenomenon of cosmic evolution is characterized by activity, change or motion [Parispanda]. All things undergo infinitesimal changes of growth and decay. In the smallest instant of time [Kşana] the whole universe undergoes a change."[34]

Temporal time finds systematic treatment in the Vaisesika School, which is basically an atomistic philosophy. It is a scientific approach to the understanding of the universe. Kanada is the foremost exponent of this theory. The Vaisesika School recognises Time as: "posterior in respect of that which is Posterior, 'simultaneous', 'slow', 'quick'—as such [cognitions] of the marks of Time."[35]

This philosophical school regards Time as a force causing change in all things and beings; it is the cause of all movement; it acts on things and creatures not from the inside but from the outside. Time is a ubiquitous, independent reality. It gives the ideas of past, present and future.

The popular notion of Time in India is that it is an all-destroying merciless demon. Time is called Kãla-Purusa, 'Kãla-Bhairava', meaning a terrible deity, a demon-dancer. Father Time of the West could be called Kãla-Purusa. Shankara, the founder of Advaita [non-dualism], has a prayer addressed to Time, wherein he praises Time as a terrible god with a trident, penetrating and pervading everything. Here Time's tyranny over humans is brought out vividly and the wrathful demon is sought to be appeased; the human world has no other way than to accept Time's supremacy, and hence, the need to praise and worship 'Kãla'. It is a popular belief in India that after death one is gathered to Time; the dead enter the world of Yama, Lord of Death. Time and Death are regarded as the same power. Hence it is said "O Time, Salutations to thee."

All these ideas about Time flow from the fact that men observe the phenomenon of change taking place in the objective world through temporal time; this change or becoming is an empirical truth. Consequently, people think that Time is a tyrant. The tyranny of Time, however, can be vanquished if we look beyond temporal changes—the phenomena of birth, growth decay and death.

Eternity is a timeless dimension to human experience. Although our life is inextricably linked to the temporal order of the external world, there is something in us, a part of our individual self, which rebels against this order. This idea finds a unique expression in W.H. Auden's poetical lines:

And all our intuitions mock
The formal logic of the clock.[36]

In moments of intense feeling and perception each of us feels that he is in a timeless state where he finds and feels the 'whole' of himself. Such moments, such 'rings of light' have produced the best in men, which we come across in the enduring works of art and literature, science and philosophy, religion and ethics. The concept of timeless Time or the Eternal is a time-old concept. We find it recognised as such, as well-expressed in the philosophical writings of both the West and the East. Time Eternal or timeless reality is recognised in two ways: as a metaphysical idea of Time as cyclical or circular and as a psychological concept of Time as duration. It is worthwhile examining first how this view of Time as a timeless reality has been treated both in terms of metaphysics and psychology by different thinkers of different lands in ancient days as well as modern times. Then a critical resume will be attempted of the philosophical theories and views of Time as established by modern Time-theorists and thinkers which have influenced the writing of J.B. Priestley.

The idea of the eternity of Time can be traced back even to the thinking of primitive man. When primitive man started, after thousands of years of a wandering life, to live a settled life of tillage he must have felt the necessity of keeping temporal time. Perhaps after a few thousand years there came a stage when he started thinking of the good and the evil powers of nature; there followed his worship of the phenomena of nature leading to their deification and the emergence of the pagan's pantheistic religion. Then his mind must have begun thinking of supra-mundane things.

Fear of death and the curiosity to know what would happen after death led primitive man to the belief that the dead lived on in some other place. About this belief Will Durant says, "The Kurmis encouraged themselves in war by the notion that all the enemies they slew would attend them as slaves in the after life."[37] This belief in reincarnation means a belief in man's return to the earthly life through Time; this was a belief in Great Time or the Time Cycle. This Time cycle felt by primitive man should not be taken in the sense of the Time Wheel of the Heraclitan philosophy or of the Karma doctrine. But, certainly primitive man's religion contained the embryo of the philosophical views and concepts of Time developed in later periods of man's history.

Western Views

The first great philosopher of the Occident, who advocated ideas of the Time cycle and immortality of the human soul was Pythagoras. His quest was for that which is timeless; his mathematical reasoning is combined with mysticism. His doctrine of emanation results from the concept of 'Being' not 'Becoming', as the Ultimate Reality which manifests itself in circular order of Time. This idea led him to the idea of immortality of the soul through birth and death. His doctrine of reincarnation is an affirmation of his belief in the eternal cycle of Time.

Parmenides [500 B.C.]: He does not believe in flux; flux is an illusion; there is something indestructible in the universe and that is unchanging and eternal. He also does not believe in the past; for everything is eternally present. His contention is that that which is commonly regarded as past must, in some sense, exist. "If memory is to be accepted as a source of knowledge, the past must be before the mind 'now', and must therefore in some sense still exist."[38] He attaches no value to temporal time; his quest is for the timeless reality. He seeks that timeless reality which exists in the human mind. His concept of memory as a source of knowledge, making the past a part of the present, anticipates the modern psychological concept of Time as 'duration'. Empedocles, another pre-Platonic philosopher, also believes in eternal Time, which is cyclical.

Plato, of the fourth century Greece, was the fountain-head of all Western metaphysical thought. His was the well-known system of Ideas. He defined Time as "the moving image of eternity". He held that God created the universe as an image of the eternal; but to bestow the everlastingness of the eternal to its fullness on this copy was impossible. "Wherefore he resolved to have a moving image of eternity, and when he set in order the heaven, he made this image eternal but moving according to number, while eternity itself rests in unity; and this image we call Time."[39] According to Plato's theory of creation, Time and the heavens came into existence at the same instant. God made the sun; the days and nights followed; days and nights growing into months and years created knowledge of number, and human beings were given the conception of Time. His theory of creation and Time speaks of the inseparability of the universe and Time. His theory that eternity rests in unity and Time is its moving image suggests two things: that eternity is 'being' and Time is 'becoming' or change; that eternity is beyond temporal time, which is to say that eternity is timeless. Then, is not Time eternal? If Plato thinks it to be so, in what sense is it eternal? Alfred Weber, discussing this point at length, comments, "The universe cannot be eternal like the creative Idea; hence God makes it eternal, so far as this is possible; that is, he creates endless time."[40] Thus in Plato's view Time is eternal in the sense that it is endless. He believes in the immortality of the soul; the immortality of the soul speaks of the eternity of Time or timelessness. He too believes in Time circles. Life invariably and universally produces death, and death produces a new life, by the pre-existence of the soul, which is demonstrated by his doctrine of metempsychosis. To be freed from the body, he clarifies, was to be out of Time's cycling or the wheel of birth and death.

Aristotle assumes that, like Space, Time exists only as the condition of motion. It is a measure of motion; and it is potentially infinite. This idea suggests the Aristotlean concept of temporal time. This view, involved in the Aristotlean definition of Time, has already been discussed. But he also speaks of the necessity of a soul to count the number, which goes to show that he did have a psychological grasp of Time as well. Thus, it is apparent that Aristotle was aware of both objective time and subjective time—the latter being of psychological character. As a psychological concept, time is 'duration', the mind's part being most important in it. Thus Aristotle too believed in the eternity of Time as conceived by the mind.

Plotinus of the third century A.D., the author of *Enneads,* was the founder of Neoplatonism.

Plotinus speaks of his experience of 'ecstasy' when he felt himself lifted out of the body; he recounts those transcendent moments, severing him from the spatio-temporal existence, when he could be in contact with the highest order. He believes that the universe emanates from the Absolute as light emanates from the sun. The universe and Time together emanated. The activity of the universe, which manifests itself everywhere, is the activity of Time; Time is creativity itself and the universe is the content of Time.

This great spiritualist and mystic refutes Aristotle's views on Time. He argues that Aristotle's definition, binding Time to motion, helps us understand the measurement of Time but not Time. Plotinus's argument is that Time is a thing in itself and that rest and motion are within Time and not the other way round. Time is identified with the creative activity of the soul. According to him Time is to be sought in our soul, not outside; we understand it if we look inward. Plotinus stands at the end of the Greek Age and the beginning of Christendom.

St. Augustine of the fourth century A.D. was a rare combination of philosopher, mystic and spiritualist, and his views on Time are strikingly original.

The saint's views are summed up by Bertrand Russell as follows: "Time was created when the world was created. God is eternal in the sense of being timeless; in God there is no 'before' and 'after', but only an eternal present. God's eternity is exempt from the relation of time; all time is present to Him at once. He did not 'precede' His own creation of time, for that would imply that He was in time, whereas He stands eternally outside the stream of time. This leads St. Augustine to a very admirable relativistic theory of time."[41] Augustine says that neither past nor future exists; only the present 'really' is. The present is only a moment, and time can only be measured while it is passing. Nevertheless, he thinks that there is the past time and the future but they are conceived as present. He identifies past with memory and future with expectations; memory and expectation are both present facts. According to him there are three times [Russell quotes from *Confessions*]: "a present of things past, a present of things present, and a present of things future".[42] The saint's argument is that Time is subjective and it is in the human mind. This theory of Time, it is plain, was a great advance on anything to be found on Time in Greek philosophy. Augustine anticipates Kant's subjective theory of Time.

Augustine's concept, as we have noted above, is not merely metaphysical but psychological. In his account of Augustine's contribution to the knowledge of Time, Eric Frank Writes, "Augustine was the first to free himself from [the Pan-Psychist views of time] these fantastic ideas. In his analysis of time he drew the consequences resulting from his fundamental change of view and sought the source of our time consciousness in a stratum of man's existence which is different from the world."[43] Though he holds that time moves in a linear order—as a Christian he believes in its onward movement towards future—he is of the firm conviction that man can, even while still in body, catch a 'glimpse' of that 'eternal light' in moments of contemplation and intense feeling. This speaks of his belief that man can realize himself in world-time uniting his temporal existence with the timeless reality.

As noted before, the Medieval Age was concerned more with eternity than with time. Most of the Schoolmen followed Plato and Augustine in their views on this question. The view of eternity held by the age finds its best expression in the words of Meister Eckhart: "In eternity is no before and after: the happenings of the past millennium and the future one, and now, in eternity are all the same. God's doing of a thousand years ago and now and a thousand years to come are but one single act."[44]

The Renaissance brought about a shift in the outlook of the European on the world and human life: God was no longer outside or above His creation; He was not the transcendent cause but the indwelling power which, from within, sustained and continued the 'universal motion' by which things and beings fulfilled their temporal destiny; God, the supreme power, sustained the whole universe only in its becoming; it was all cosmic becoming.

Renaissance man never thought that he was just a helpless plaything in the hands of God or Destiny, but very much an individual soul with an abundant potentiality for action: he had a free will, a will to choose or act; in this sense, he was a creator of his own destiny. His unfettered spirit did not bother about the temporal limitations of his bodily existence; its actions were timeless. He viewed Time as Creative: it was by Time that everything was brought into this world; he did not, therefore, hate temporal time. Rabelais says, "[For] by time there have been and shall be brought to light all things which were hidden."[45]

Reformation man was possessed of a keen awareness of two durations: temporality, the time of his bodily existence, and eternity as relating to the soul or the spirit of his being. The first was only the shadow of a duration. Each moment of his existence is discontinued but God renews the operation of the moment—before for each new instant; that is how the divine will is moving the just soul of the 'fallen creature' towards redemption in fulfilment of the divine promise. Each earthly moment of the just is joined to an eternal moment; the duration of the redeemed is eternal; eternity has no movement, but temporality moves and its order is linear. Thus the Reformation Christian had a sense of two durations.

The seventeenth century offers an altogether different philosophy of life, and a human psychological study. The concept of existence was one of continued creation; existence and duration were no longer identical, every moment dies and a new one is created and creation is the gift that keeps the creature's existence continuous. The idea of continued existence gets a unique place in the thinking of this period. Man's existence, every creature's existence, is confined to the instant; thus the existence of man is not a duration but is perpetually prolonged from moment to moment. What matters is the moment that stands totally isolated from the past and the future; it is a 'naked moment': Descarte's 'pure moment'. The state of that moment is unique. "All his past life, all his future destiny are found to be erased or suspended. Nothing remains except the gift of actual existence; then in a new instant, the same gift, and the same consciousness of that gift. Duration is a chaplet of instants. The creative activity alone permits passage from one bead to another."[46] For the first time human existence here is seen to be apprehended by the mind to be outside any specific duration. Existence is one thing and endurance or duration is another. The creative act sees nothing but the creativity of the moment. This understanding of existence gave the age its joyous feeling about the unity of the soul. The Cartesian moment of intuition or 'pure moment' gave a new look to the subject of Time and human existence; this view is basically sustained by the psychology of the human mind.

The eighteenth century found the dominance of materialism with the advent of the Industrial Revolution. This was an age of reason, and radicalism; God, as creator and preserver of existence, was absent. The place of God was taken over by feelings and sensations. No ontological necessity was felt to connect the Creator and the Creature. The sole necessity for the affirmation of the creature's existence was psychological. The more intense the sensations are, the more one will feel his present existence; the multiplicity of such sensations will lead one to sense one's duration. Thus the durational eternity of Time was established by the psychological studies of the period; the eternity of Time as conceived by the philosophers of an earlier period had now been replaced by another concept, the psychological concept of the eternity of Time, termed durational eternity. "It is as if to exist meant to live two lives at the same time; the life lived day by day; and the life lived before and beyond the day or the moment; a life which lengthened into duration."[47]

The Romantic Age of the early nineteenth century gained considerably from this concept of psychic time or duration. Psychic time, or time durational, is 'inward looking' and 'inward life'. The romantic writer felt that he was no longer only a 'creature of sensation' but one capable of seeing 'before and after'.

Much earlier than the psychological writers of the twentieth century like Proust, the romantic writers—especially the poets—attempted to rebuild and relive in a moment vast periods of reminiscences. Theirs was a bold attempt to put the self in the immobile moment of consciousness and to bring the past and future to the centre of the moment; thus they experienced the sensation of 'eternity in an instant': it was a way of feeling the 'duration' in a single moment, of making the moment more significant and more colourful and richer. The romantic writer binds the actual moment of experience to the past by memory and to the future by his intuitive feeling of presentiment. The past surges up and the future flashes into the moment in which the romantic writer found the enchantment and value of living. "The past, together with the whole train of its emotions, surges up in the moment and endows it with a life that is not momentary. One seems then to relive instantaneously, all at once, a long period of his existence."[48] Mozart is said to have 'heard' his music all at once. That was how psychic time or 'duration' gave a sense of the eternity of Time to nineteenth century man.

The nineteenth century conceived of Time as essentially a continuous motion, a becoming, which is always future. "Human time and cosmic time are then both continuous."[49] Instead of placing psychic time in opposition to clock-time, as was done by eighteenth century man, nineteenth century man sought to telescope the two times into a sole continuity. Then at the end of the century came Henri Bergson with his epoch-making views on Time and human life, which call for an examination in detail.

The modern age believes in continuous creation not by God but by the mind. Psychology has given the age a new philosophical outlook on human existence. The present is considered the generative act of Time. Every new moment eludes the grasp of consciousness and becomes transformed into a thing of the past. Every moment kills itself giving rise to a new one. We may say that time kills itself and creates itself. This is the paradox of existence: life coming out of death. This paradox of life, which is, in fact, the paradox of Time, is metaphorically expressed in words of the French writer Eluard: "I am my mother and my child at each point in the eternal."[50]

Oriental Views

It is timeless Time that has attracted the attention of most oriental philosophers and thinkers of ancient times, more particularly those of India from the Vedic age to the medieval Vedantic period. The oldest civilization of the East was Egypt and it was the first civilized society to think about the mystery of Time; the Egyptians were fascinated by the recurring character of Time which they witnessed in the life of nature and of man.

The Egyptian myths possess enough evidence to show that the Egyptians were aware of the eternity of Time or timeless Time. Ra, the sun-god, was their highest god; different gods represented different forces of nature. The myth of Osiris speaks of Osiris as the god of the Nile and also of justice; his wife Isis, the Great Mother, was the goddess of the black soil of the Delta. Their union—the Nile river watering the delta—which was yearly celebrated, symbolized perennial fertility and life; the myth, built around the ebb and flow of the river, is symbolic of life and death, 'creation and destruction' taking place through the cycle of Time. The Egyptians believed in Great Time, which contained past, present and future. To them, Time was not linear, but cyclical; and the past was not dead but, in fact, Time was one eternally moving cycle. They believed in the immortal vital spirit called 'Ka'. "What distinguishes this religion above everything else was its emphasis on immortality. If Osiris, the Nile, and all vegetation might rise again, so might man."[51]

J.B. Priestley writes in his *Man and Time* that to the Egyptians Time appeared in three ways and hence there were three gods; one who brought storms, sickness and sudden death; one who gave life; and the Third, uniting the opposites, represented the godhead. They believed in the eternity of Time, in its eternal cycle. "Great Time" was a "God of Millions of Years".

The Egyptian Book of the Dead has a dialogue between the deceased and the god Thoth. The deceased asks the god how long he should live, and the reply is that he should live for millions and millions of years. "This Egyptian, it could be said, would live for millions of years because he would return again and again to Time, in one shape and personality after another, until finally purged of all desire for any further existence on this earth."[52] This view of Time comes very near to the Hindu view of it. The latter differs in that it is logically rooted in the cause-effect dialectics of the Karma doctrine.

Time is an important factor to reckon with in the metaphysical thinking of every religion of India, which has necessarily a distinctive cosmology and a philosophical system. In his *Man and Time*, Priestley observes "I must also admit that in any account of man's ideas of Time, India must be given a prominent place. Its speculative thought has been Time-haunted. Time is the villain in its huge cosmological drama."[53] From the Vedic seers to the medieval Vedantic philosophers every metaphysical school in India has tried to catch this villain, Time, by its forelock but it has remained an elusive and mysterious spirit. Therefore, worthy of notice are the bold attempts of these explorers on the 'Waters of Time'.

Time has been an integral part of Indian philosophical approaches to the understanding of the Ultimate Principle of the universe; the Doctrine of Karma, which is common to all these approaches including Buddhism and Jainism, hinges on Time as an ever-rotating wheel.

The earliest reference to timeless Time in Indian writing is found in the Atharva Veda. The sacred text speaks of Time:

"Him the inspired poets mount."[54] The analogy of Time to a horse is significant. The horse of Time is moving everywhere in the universe, unchecked and uncontrolled. The inspired poets, that is, seers, alone are capable of mounting it, which means, they alone are able to understand what really Time is and how to conquer it: to them Time is timeless, eternal Time. Such sages are free from the tyranny of temporal time. This concept anticipates modern thoughts regarding Time.

The Upanishadic concept of Time is an advance on the Vedic thought. Time is a key factor in the cosmology of Upanishadic thinking and the spiritual experience of the ancient Indian mind. These books of wisdom teach that the intellect is inadequate to grasp the complexity of creation and only our 'intuition', 'the inward seeing of mind', can help us know the meaning and mystery of life.

The Upanishadic cosmology—whether conceiving of the universe as an emanation of Brahma or His creation—has Time as an integral part of it. Stanzas 14 and 15 of the *Maitri Upanishad* describe Time as having a form as well as being formless too: Time is both temporal and timeless. Time temporal or world-Time is called Kãla which is measurable, and timeless Time is formless, which existed prior to the sun, that is, before creation, and is called 'a-Kãla' [Time not divisible]. To the seeker of knowledge there is a secret spelt out in the lines:

> Whoever reverences Time as Brahman, from him time withdraws afar.[55]

This utterence of the Rishi may safely be taken to mean that he who realises timeless Time as the very Brahman frees himself from the cruelty of Kãla. When he grasps the truth that Brahman is above and beyond temporal or this-world time, the terrors and illusions born of his living enslaved to empirical, passing, time, will vanish. Timeless Time is formless, infinite and eternal. Here it is necessary to note that Kãla [temporal time] is not to be confused with 'a-Kãla', Timeless Time, but Kãla, rightly understood, frees us from the shackles of Mutability.

Puranic cosmology does not treat the creation as a thing created at a point in time. The cosmology described in the Puranas is mainly the cosmology of Time:

> There is no creation in the sense of Genesis; the world is perpetually evolving and dissolving, growing and decaying, through cycle of cycle, like every plant in it and like every organism. Brahma—or, as the Creator is more often called in this literature, Prajapati—is the spiritual force that upholds this endless process.... Each cycle or Kalpa in the history of the universe is divided into a thousand 'mahayugas', or great ages of 4,320,000 years each; and each 'mahayuga' contains four 'Yugas' or ages, in which the human race undergoes a gradual deterioration.[56]

A Kalpa, a world cycle, is the equivalent of one day in the life of Brahma at the end of which Pralaya or total annihilation takes place, and then Brahma will begin another day. A Kalpa consisting of 4,320,000,000 human years is just one day of Brahma's! Mind-boggling, surely, are these vast circlings of Time. Fantastic as these details are, they, however, help us to know how the ancient Indian mind pictured the infinite, endless, eternal Time through cycle after cycle.

The Puranic myths are a record of how in the far-off times immemorial the Indians were aware of different levels of consciousness connected with their experience of time. Prof. Mircea Eliade's book *Images and Symbols* tells us a number of mythological tales dealing with Time-concepts and views of ancient times. Priestley cites, from the book, the story of Narada, a hermit and devotee of Lord Vishnu, to illustrate how the ancient Puranic thinkers thought of relative times and degrees of illusion and reality; the story throws a flood of light on their thinking of human consciousness at different levels. The story tells how, under the maya or illusion wrought by the Lord, Narada felt that he had spent just half an hour, when away from Him, whereas in actuality, he had spent twelve years. The story highlights the contrast between human time and celestial time by presenting a period of twelve years of passing time as just equal to half an hour of supra-terrestrial time. It calls our attention to that dimension of human experience which is outside the familiar chronological time; it is time subjective, or psychological time. Thus the puranic literature is seen to take for granted not only cyclical time or eternal circularity of Time but a relative notion of Time including psychic time and its durational character. The Narada story, like the story of Rip van Winkle, adumbrates an idea which may be said to anticipate Einstein's relativity theory of Time. Some myths of India show that Time is a creative force, a truth grasped by modern metaphysical thinkers like Bergson and Alexander. Prof. John M. Malveille of the university of Colorado, USA, who read a paper at the International seminar on "Kãla/Time" in New Delhi in 1991 dwelt upon the symbolic meaning of Indian myths and observed: "the myths of India are threaded with insights about the fragile and uncertain nature of time."[57]

The Yogic concept of Time is that the ultimate Reality, the supreme state of the soul is timeless; the essence of man's life is not cribbed, cabinned and confined by temporal time. Patanjali, the founder of the Yoga system, speaks of Samadhih, the ecstatic condition, which breaks all connections with the outer world; this Yogic condition lifts the soul from its temporal connections and while in that state a soul shoots out of passing time into the timeless eternity. Dr. Radhakrishnan quotes, in support of this yogic concept, an identical view of Schelling's: "In all of us there dwells a secret marvellous power of freeing ourselves from the changes of time.... At that time we annihilate time and duration of time; we are no longer in time, but time, or rather eternity itself, is in us. The external world is no longer an object for us, but is lost in us."[58] This transcendental view of Schelling and the Yogic view of Patanjali come from depths of the same kind of experience and thought.

The *Gita* view of Time is well-known. Lord Krishna declares—"Time am I." The meaning is that God is above the temporal time order: Time with its process of change and succession, is not an illusion or appearance; it is a reality. Time, according to this philosophical poem, is not antithetical to eternity; eternity is Time in a different form. "Eternity does not mean the denial of time of history. It is the transfiguration of time. Time derives from eternity and finds fulfilment in it. In the *Bhagavadgita* there is no antithesis between eternity and time. Through the figure of Krishna the unity between the eternal and the historical is indicated. The temporal movement is related to the inmost depths of reality."[59]

Lord Krishna's words "Time am I" should not be interpreted to mean that God is Time and Time God. God is above Time. God creates and destroys the world through Time, which is the prime mover of the universe. "God has control over time because he is outside of it and we also shall obtain power over time if we rise above it. As the force behind this, He sees further than we, knows how all events are controlled and so tells Arjuna that causes have been at work for years and are moving towards their natural effects which we cannot prevent by anything we can do now."[60]

The Advaita School of Shankara holds that Time is as unreal as everything else, except Brahman. However, the endless, or the eternal shows itself continuously in Time. Shankara speaks of the cycle of birth and death and this cycle is the Time cycle only, which is an eternal process. The creatures of the world can attain the eternal only when they break out of the circle of Time.

Ramanuja's qualified non-dualism holds that Time is a reality. It is a form of all existence, an object of perception, the cause of transformation of Prakriti and its mutations. A very brilliant discussion of Time, however, is to be found in the writings of Venkatanatha, a thirteenth century pundit of the Ramanuja school. According to him time is co-existent with God. The production of time at a point in time is logically inconceivable because such a view presupposes the existence of time. Therefore, time is beginningless and eternal in the sense that that which is not a created thing is not subject to destruction. Time is directly perceived as quality of all perceived things. The present cannot be separated from the past and the future; in fact, the past and the future are simply modes of experience of things conceived as 'before' and 'after', 'earlier' and 'later'. These views anticipate a lot that came centuries later from the Western metaphysicians like Kant and Bergson.

The Dvaith (dualism) of Madhva too accepts Time as real. In fact, this school holds that everything is real, and that nothing is unreal or illusory in the universe. Time is an uncreated eternal factor. To Madhva Time, like Space, is a thing to be intuitively perceived. Madhva's unique contribution to Hindu philosophy is his concept of Saksi, the witnessing self or the inner sense of self. This concept of Saksi has something of Dunne's serialism. We cannot think of experience at any level without its reference to time. In fact, our experience of time and that of the world around us go together, move inseparably. Madhva values intuition as fundamental to our perception of Time. His views also have a lot of similarity with those of modern European metaphysicians like Kant, William James and Alexander.

The Doctrine of Karma is common to all the Indian philosophical schools and approaches. It involves Time. Karma or action is of three kinds: (a) Prarabdha—deeds done in the past whose consequences have begun to operate in the present life; (b) Samchita—those done in the past whose consequences have to be expiated in some future life or stored deeds; and (c) Agami—those produced in the present life or in some future life.

The Karma doctrine assumes that every act is followed by its consequences which are of physical, mental and moral character; that the consequences of a person's acts cannot be worked out in this life and therefore a future life is inevitable for their fruition. It also believes that the happiness or suffering of a man in this world may be due to his acts in the previous existence or the ones in the present birth. How is it that a man's Karma is carried from birth to birth? What is it that survives the body after death? The Upanishads and the *Gita* have answered these queries: A jiva holds itself in two forms of the body—the gross body and the subtle body. Death is the extinction of the gross body, but not of the subtle body which consists of *manas* (mind), the five senses of knowledge, the five tanmatras or subtle elements, *Pran* (subtle breath), merit and demerit. When the gross body drops, the soul is accompanied by the subtle body. It is the subtle body that becomes the basis for consciousness and goes into the making of one's personality; it is the carrier of Karma to the body in the next birth. This is the modus operandi of rebirth and the passing on of Karma.

"Though our bodies may be shattered to dust, still there is something in us which survives; and it is this which determines our future life. The knowledge we have gained, the character we have formed, will pursue us into other lives. The moral and pious rise, while the immoral and impious sink in the scale. The nature of the future life depends upon the moral quality of the past life."[61] The Karma doctrine is a daring and original attempt in the direction of solving the mysteries of life and death and finding an answer to the question why there exist inequalities in the lives of men in this world. Rhys David says, "The history of the individual does not begin with his birth. He has been endless generations in the making."[62] This idea finds a unique metaphorical expression in a sloka of the *Mahabharat*: "As a calf finds its mother among a thousand cows, so does the deed previously done follow after the doer."[63] Karma is not fate. Fatalism breeds a mindset of meek acceptance of whatever one is, and therefore it is inimical to any kind of human progress. The Karma doctrine believes that man can influence his future destiny. It allows man the freedom of will to evolve and develop.

The law of Karma does not apply to the knowers of Brahman, who are real yogis. Of such yogic state the *Brahma Sutra* says: "when we attain liberation, the chain of work is broken. We become superior to time."[64] That is the way to release onself from the cruelty of time, the way not to feel the 'icy hand' of passing time and that is also how man can attain a timeless state, real eternity.

Men in different ages and lands have been haunted by Time and they have realised that they are not slaves of Time. But temporal time, which is a condition of our living, cannot be denied its due recognition because it cannot be wished away. That also is one way of understanding our existence. In his book *Science and the Common Understanding* J. Robert Oppenheimer, a well-known physicist, makes the following significant observation: "These two ways of thinking, the way of time and history, and the way of eternity and of timelessness, are both parts of man's efforts to comprehend the world in which he lives."[65] It is to be seen how these views and theories relate to those of modern thinkers on Time.

Time and Modern Thinkers

A short but critical resume of the well-known modern Time theories and views especially of J.W. Dunne and Ouspensky is necessary as a prolegomenon for a fuller and better understanding of Priestley as a Time-writer.

Immanuel Kant, an eighteenth century German philosopher, holds that space and time are a priori intuitions. Space is the form of the outer sense and time of the inner sense. "Space and time are original intuitions of reason, prior to all experience; this is the immortal discovery of Kant."[66] Sense-perception depends on a priori ideas of space and time, which are not images corresponding to external objects. "There is no object called space, nor an object called time. Time and space are not objects of perception, but modes of perceiving objects, instinctive habits, inhering in the thinking subject."[67] The most original of Kant's teachings is that Time and Space are subjective. He shows that Space and Time are the eyes of the mind, the organs which reveal to it its inexhaustible content. The thrust of his argument is on the perceiving capacity of the mind which is central to everything. Kant as an idealist does not believe in the reality of Time but he values it as a mode, as an organ, of perception.

Henri Bergson, the famous metaphysician of France, who appeared in the closing years of the nineteenth century, created a big change in the philosophical outlook of the people as regards the world and human existence. To Bergson, Time is not a mode of perception but a great creative force, the essence of life and of all reality. He distinguishes between clock-time or scientific time and real Time which he calls duration. Duration is the vehicle of perpetual novelty; it is something that pulsates through our very being; indeed, it is our very being. True Time is duration which is the creative principle, elan vital. His conception of Time as duration is not the same as mathematical time. According to him mathematical time is really a form of space. Time which is the essence of life is what he calls 'duration'. In duration our states melt into one another. Russell's explanation of duration catches the true spirit of Bergson's view: "Pure duration is what is most removed from externality and least penetrated with externality, a duration in which the past is big with a present absolutely new. But then our will is strained to the utmost; we have to gather up the past which is slipping away, and thrust it whole and undivided into the present. At such moments we truly possess ourselves, but such moments are rare. Duration is the very stuff of reality, which is a perpetual becoming, never something made."[68]

Bergson's *Time and Free Will* establishes the imperative need of understanding the psychic nature of man's existence. Man's free will operates only in duration, in timeless Time, when he is fully his own self. It is in rare moments that he can choose to act, because his will is then free from externality of any kind. Bergson's Time is creative; it directs the course of life on this planet; it directs and shapes the evolution of life. This speaks of the eternity of duration, the timeless psychic time.

McTaggart, a twentieth century idealist philosopher, argues that time is unreal and full of contradictions; his arguments are directed towards showing that "these contradictions are not resolvable, but essential and ultimate, as long as we continue to use the notion of time. He assumes that nothing which is self-contradictory and impossible to thought can exist, and hence he concludes that time does not exist."[69]

The three important points of McTaggart's argument are: [a] time, though not itself real, is really an appearance; [b] things appear to us as in time as the result of our misperception of time that it is a thing in itself; and [c] temporal appearance is important and inescapable.

J.W. Dunne, a great Time theorist, is known for his theory of serialism of Time. He approaches the Time question with care and scientific detachment. He holds that Time is multi-dimensional and endless and that it leads to immortality. He takes a longer and closer look at Time; his is not a mystical approach. He recognised "the displacement of time" in some dreams and that led him to study the true nature of Time. His theory of serialism showed that one could move from one kind of time to another without involving any mystical exercise or feat of superhuman skill or capacity.

Dunne's two books, *An Experiment with Time* and *The Serial Universe* present his metaphysical theory of Time, in all its details. His investigation of dreams establishes firmly: first, that a definite element of prevision or precognition can be discovered in our normal dreaming; secondly, our dreaming self cannot be entirely contained within passing time or clock-time; thirdly, the larger temporal freedom of the dreaming self is not the privilege of a very few special type of people, but is within the domain of common humanity. All his findings pointed to the conclusion that human beings are not necessarily the slaves of chronological time; they could be noble creatures with vast potentialities.

Writing about 'Times behind Times', he says, "Now, we have seen that if Time passes or grows or accumulates or expends itself or does anything whatsoever, except stand rigid and changeless before a Time-fixed observer, there must be another Time which times that activity of, or along the first time, and another Time which times that second Time, and so on in an apparent series to infinity."[70] He says that serialism in Time involves a serial observer.

C.H. Hinton had already held that matter extends [endures] in Time and ours is a three-dimensional sectional view of a four-dimensional reality, time being the fourth dimension. Dunne accepts this view but adds what was missing in Hinton's theory: recognition that anything moving in Time takes time over its movement.

Explaining Dunne's serialism, Priestley writes, "He believes that each of us is a series of observers existing in a series of Times. To Observer One, our ordinary fully awake sharp selves, the fourth dimension appears as Time. To Observer

Two, which is the self we know in dreams when the first observer is not functioning, the fifth dimension would appear as time. This second observer has a four-dimensional outlook and this fact explains the fantastic scenery and action characteristic of dreams, in which everything seems to be fluid, incidents have no proper beginning or ending, houses melt into woods. Dunne says this is because we try to interpret in our ordinary three-dimensional fashion these strange images gathered by our four-dimensional selves, who have to work during sleep without the sharp focus and business-like attention of the first observer. Now Dunne holds that the dreaming self, now moving Time Two, has a wide length of Time one, the fourth dimension, stretched before it, and so contrives to telescope into the fantastic narratives of dream both images from the past and images from the future."[71]

Dunne's theory of serialism holds that the future can be seen, and because it can be seen, it can be changed, too. The question is: how can it be changed if it is solidly laid out? If it does not exist, it cannot be seen; if it is there solidly fixed, it cannot be changed. This dilemma has its answer in the postulation of "intervention" or "interference" by Observer 2 in the future of Observer 1. Observer 2 has an access to the 'future' brain states as well as the past brain states of Observer 1. While Observer 1 is asleep, Observer 2 happens to see what lies ahead in Time—whatever happens in a precognitive dream. Observer 2's experience becomes, for Observer 1 on waking, a remembered dream. If there is an undesirable or tragic happening in the dream (in Observer 2's experience) that is avoided or altered by Observer 1 in Time 1, the fourth dimensional time of actualisation. This 'intervention' seems to settle the old quarrel between free will and determinism.

According to Dunne's theory, the past is not dead and gone; it has not been destroyed; it still exists not as a dim memory, but in all its colour and hum. It exists along the fourth-dimensional track, not as a ghostly memory, but as solidly real in its eternal Present. This idea frees us from the tyranny of ticking time.

Priestley says that all of Dunne's talk about the waking self and dreaming self and man's existence in multi-dimensional Time is part of his solid faith in human immortality. Discussing, in brief, two other works of Dunne's, *The New Immortality* and *Nothing Dies,* Priestley writes, "We are here, he (Dunne) insists, immortal beings. It is true that we 'die' in Time 1 when our Observer 1 reaches the end of his journey along the fourth dimension. And then all possibility of intervention and action in Time 1 comes to an end. This limits Observer 2's experience (through Observer 1's brain-states) of Time 1, but it does not involve the death of Observer 2 who exists in Time 2.... He has to begin learning all over again as his four-dimensional focus moves along the fifth dimension or Time 3. People and things will be the same and yet not the same. We catch glimpses, though confused and distorted, of this after-death mode of existence in our dreams."[72] That is, Observer 2 in Time 2 survives the death of Observer 1 in Time 1. After death, Observer 1's Time 2 becomes Observer 2's Time 1.

Some of Priestley's very important plays are written against the background of Dunne's serial theory of Time and hence a rather lengthy discussion of the theory and its implications here is quite in order.

No less important, however, is Ouspensky's spiral theory of Time for a proper understanding of some of Priestley's works. A brief analysis of Ouspensky's views as expressed in his *A New Model of the Universe* is presented here.

Ouspensky, a Russian Time theorist, and a leading exponent of Gurdjieffs esoteric school of Time, expounds his theory in his book *A New Model of the Universe.* He believes that Time, like space, has three dimensions and only three and the universe has, in all, six dimensions, three of space and three of Time. The three dimensions of space and one dimension of Time, which we call world Time, are known to us. But the fifth and sixth dimensions—the remaining two dimensions of Time—are unknown to us.

The fifth dimension is eternity, not in the sense of a four-dimensional single-track time extended to infinity, but the eternal 'Now', or Timelessness. The past exists along this dimension; along it runs the perpetual 'now' of any given moment. What, then, is the sixth dimension of the universe, which is the third dimension of Time? It is the line of actualisation, it is our spirit or power of imagination.

The most important part of Ouspensky's theory is the idea of 'Eternal Recurrence'. His ideas regarding the nature of human life and re-incarnation have found a telling expression in Priestley's words:

> He holds that Time has a wave-like movement, that the line of the fourth dimension is circular. We think of Time and life running along a straight line, on which the birth and death of any person could be indicated by two points, the length of line between them being the life of that person. That is an illusion, according to Ouspensky. Our Time is far more personal than that. It may coincide to some extent with other Times, those of other people, the greater Time of the race or the world, but it is our own. There cannot be any of this Time for us outside the circle of it that we open at birth and close at death. The movement round this circle is Eternity. When a man dies, he immediately enters the same life from the other end, is born again in the same house, of the same parents, on the same day and year, and everything will happen as before. The only difference, he argues, is that there may be an inner development one way or the other. Some people, those comfortable creatures of custom we all know, live identically the same lives over and over again. Others such as madmen, suicides, criminals, go through the same tragic performance with a dwindling inner life until at last there is nothing vital left in them.[73]

Both Dunne and Ouspensky believe in the eternity of Time. Dunne's theory is based on a careful study of the human mind, of human consciousness. Ouspensky is an esoterist, half philosophical and half scientific. Together they have greatly influenced the writing of Priestley.

NOTES

1. David Hughes, *J.B. Priestley: An Informal Study of his Work* (London: Rupert Hart-Davis, 1958), p. 101.
2. M.F. Cleugh, *Time and Its Importance in Modern Thought* (London: Methuen & Co. Ltd., 1937), p. 5.
3. *Ibid.*, p. 26.
4. *Ibid.*, p. 231.
5. *Ibid.*, p. 141.
6. *Ibid.*, p. 281.
7. E.W.F. Tomlin, *Western Philosophers* (London: Hutchinson & Co. Ltd., 1969), p. 267.
8. A.G.E. Blake, *A Seminar on Time* (Charles Town USA: Claymont Communications, 1980), p. 80.
9. *Ibid.*, p. 11.
10. Robert Herrick, "To Daffodils", *English Verse* ed., G.C.F. Mead and Rupert C. Clift (Cambridge: Cambridge University Press, 1939), p. 110.
11. William Shakespeare, *Cymbeline* (New York: Signet Classics, 1968), p. 132.
12. James Hastings, ed. *Encyclopaedia of Religion and Ethics,* Vol. XII, 2nd edition (Edinburgh: T & T Clark, 1934), p. 334.
13. M.F. Cleugh, *Time and Its Importance in Modern Thought* (London: Methuen & Co. Ltd., 1937), p. 18.
14. *Ibid.*
15. Will Durant, *The Story of Philosophy* (London: Ernest Benn Ltd., 1946), p. 388.
16. William Shakespeare, "As You Like It", *The Complete Works of William Shakespeare,* ed. B. Hodek (London: Spring Books, 1961), p. 222.
17. Quoted by M.F. Cleugh, *Time and Its Importance in Modern Thought*, p. 34.
18. J.B. Priestley, *Man and Time* (New York: Aldus Allen Book, 1964), p. 85.
19. M.F. Cleugh, *Time and Its Importance in Modern Thought*, p. 64.
20. J.W. Dunne, *An Experiment with Time* (London: Faber and Faber Ltd., 1934), p. 107.
21. A.A. Mendilow, *Time and the Novel* (New York: Humanities Press, 1972), p. 24.

22. Hans Meyerhoff, *Time in Literature* (Los Angeles: University of California Press, 1960), p. 17.
23. *Ibid.*, p. 26.
24. A.A. Mendilow, *Time and the Novel* (New York: Humanities Press, rpt. 1972), p. 71.
25. J.B. Priestley, *Man and Time,* p. 24.
26. Bertrand Russell, *History of Western Philosophy* (London: George Allen and Unwin Ltd., 1954), p. 63.
27. *Ibid.*, p. 229.
28. Georges Poulet, *Studies in Human Time,* Eng. trans. Elliott Coleman (Baltimore USA: The Johns Hopkins Press, 1956), p. 6.
29. J.B. Priestley, *Man and Time,* p. 165.
30. Eric Frank, *Philosophical Understanding and Religious Truth* (New York: Oxford Univ. Press INC, 1945), p. 70.
31. R.E. Hume, trans., *Thirteen Principal Upanishads* (London: Oxford University Press, 1934), p. 433.
32. Jadunath Sinha, *A History of Indian Philosophy,* Vol. II (Calcutta: Central Book Academy, 1952), p. 411.
33. Will Durant, *The Story of Civilisation,* Part-I (New York: Simon and Schuster, 1942), p. 434.
34. S. Radhakrishnan, *Indian Philosophy,* Vol. II (London: George Allen and Unwin Ltd., rpt. 1946), p. 277.
35. Theos Bernard, *Hindu Philosophy* (New York: Philosophical Library, 1947), p. 56.
36. Quoted by Theodore Ziolkowski, *Dimensions of the Modern Novel* (Princeton: Princeton: University Press, 1969), p. 196.
37. Will Durant, *Story of Civilisation* , Part-I, p. 67.
38. Bertrand Russell, *History of Western Philosophy*, p. 71.
39. *Ibid.*, p. 166.
40. Alfred Weber, *History of Philosophy,* trans. Frank Thilly (New York: Charles Scribner's Sons, 1925), p. 69.
41. Bertrand Russell, *History of Western Philosophy*, p. 373.
42. *Ibid.*, p. 374.
43. Eric Frank, *Philosophical Understanding and Religious Truth*, p. 81.
44. Quoted by M.F. Cleugh, *Time and Its Importance in Modern Thought*, p. 79.
45. Georges Poulet, *Studies in Human Time*, p. 10.
46. *Ibid.*, p. 14.

47. *Ibid*., p. 25.
48. *Ibid*., p. 27.
49. *Ibid*., p. 30.
50. *Ibid*., p. 36.
51. Will Durant, *The Story of Civilisation,* Part-I, p. 202.
52. J.B. Priestley, *Man and Time,* p. 148.
53. *Ibid*., p. 171.
54. William Whitney, Eng. trans., *Atharva Veda Samhita,* Vol. II (Delhi: Motilal Banarasidas, 1962), p. 987.
55. R.E. Hume, *Thirteen Principal Upanishads*, p. 433.
56. Will Durant, *The Story of Civilisation,* Part-I, p. 513.
57. John M. Malveille, "Myth of History", Excerpt from *Span* Feb. 1991, p. 39.
58. Quoted by S. Radhakrishnan, *Indian Philosophy*, Vol. II, p. 360.
59. S. Radhakrishnan, *The Bhagavadgita* (London: George Allen and Unwin Ltd., 1948), p. 274.
60. *Ibid*., p. 280.
61. S. Radhakrishnan, *Indian Philosophy,* Vol. II, pp. 646-47.
62. Quoted by Sir P.S. Sivaswamy Aiyer, *Evolutions of Hindu Moral Ideas* (Calcutta: Calcutta University, 1935), p. 138.
63. S. Radhakrishnan, The *Brahma Sutra* (London: George Allen & Unwin Ltd., 1960), p. 194.
64. *Ibid*., p. 530.
65. J. Robert Oppenheimer's observation from his book *Science and the Common Understanding* quoted in Reader's Digest. Dec. 1990, Bombay, p. 66.
66. Alfred Weber, *History of Philosophy*, p. 357.
67. *Ibid*., p. 359.
68. Bertrand Russell, *History of Western Philosophy*, p. 824.
69. M.F. Cleugh, *Time,* p. 149.
70. J.W. Dunne, *An Experiment with Time*, p. 133.
71. J.B. Priestley, *Midnight on the Desert* (London: William Heinemann, rpt., 1947), pp. 253-54.
72. J.B. Priestley, *Man and Time,* p. 260.
73. J.B. Priestley, *Midnight on the Desert,* pp. 275-76.

2

Priestley and His Age

Priestley declares, "Politically and socially I am a radical; culturally I am a conservative. I really belong to the avant-garde of the 1880's—say 1886, the date of Faure's second piano quartet."[1] But his works largely reflect the ethos of the 'anxious 1920's' and the 'serious 1930's'. His creative writing after the Second World War acquired a maturity and richness of vision which was not the result of any magical phenomenon; it had its roots in the twenties and attained fruition in the thirties. Therefore, it is essential to take a bird's-eye-view of the period between the two World Wars.

The effect of the First World War was disastrous, with a million men from Great Britain and her empire killed or wounded. Time-honoured social and political institutions received a fatal blow; the old values and traditions of British life lost their meaning. The War-time hope of a bright future, of the birth of a 'new Jerusalem in England's green and pleasant land', had melted into thin air.

Economically and commercially Britain suffered a terrible setback; her national debt increased enormously; she lost her pre-War world markets. The twenties witnessed endless agitations and strikes in the industrial sector. Unemployment posed a grave problem. The labour government of Lloyd George and the conservative government of Baldwin failed to deliver the goods. The older generation of people felt like helpless spectators of a waste land all round them; and the young felt as if they were moving in a rudderless ship on a trackless sea. This period—particularly the early twenties—is called the Jazz age also. The general atmosphere of the times was marked by decadence. The young took to drinking and dancing—dancing a mad swirling round and round without aim—to forget the purposelessness of their existence; they ran after fun and pleasure, having no interest in anything serious like religion, philosophy or politics. The war had "Shattered Great Britain's national confidence and produced doubt, uncertainty and confusion."[2] It created a neurosis among the youth who revolted against humbug and hypocrisy; a sense of loss, disenchantment and frustration swamped their minds. A cultural crisis and spiritual void gripped the age. Wilson Knight sums up the post-War mood in these words: "...patriotism and heroism were soiled values; cynicism, light or bitter, was rampant...."[3]

The 1930's witnessed a more serious situation both at home and abroad. As a consequence of the First World War there had come into existence communism in Russia and totalitarianism in Italy, and capitalism in Britain had taken a back-seat owing to the prominence of socialism. The home economy and foreign trade, already hit hard by the failure of the Versailles Treaty, suffered a further crisis because of the 1929 Wall Street Crash. All of which led to conditions of depression with its attendant misery throughout Britain. Poverty and social unrest were aggravated in spite of Ramsay McDonald's social reforms. If mass unemployment caused desperation among the youth, mass-production methods robbed the English working classes of their bread and pride.

The thirties saw New England, which was basically an Americanised England, with a rat-race for money and 'admass' assailing people's psychology and purse. An unusual development in the political sphere was people's sharp political polarisation: they swore either by Labour Politics or by Conservative policies. "Young men and young women 'got politics' as their grandparents were accustomed to 'get religion'."[4] This situation led to an ambience of political bitterness and vendetta. Though air-travel, television and radio made people feel that any foreign country was their next-door neighbour, quarrels and cross-purposes at home disrupted the social fabric. Money became a universal god of adoration, killing men's love of human values.

The European scene grew still worse: cruelty, murder and oppression became the order of the day. The Nazi and Fascist forces in Germany and Italy stalked brazenly. "...The god of war, overthrown in 1918, was mounting his throne again, not only in Germany but also in Japan."[5] After his invasion of Poland and Czechoslovakia in 1939 Hitler plunged Europe into the bloodiest war ever known to history. England too was perforce dragged into it.

All these and many more events of this period between the two World Wars influenced Priestley's mind and art. A look at Priestley's life and career is necessary for a just and correct understanding of him as a Time-writer.

A creative writer needs to be approached not only in terms of the historical context but also with reference to his biography. Similarly the distinctive character of his work owes as much to the inherent qualities of his personality as to the men and forces that helped shape that personality.

John Boynton Priestley was born on 13 September 1894 at Bradford in West Riding of the county of Yorkshire, England. His father was a teacher. His school days were neither joyful nor boring; he studied English and History with interest. After his matriculation he became a junior clerk with Helm and Company, Swan Arcade, a wool firm at Bradford.

As a 'Swan Arcadian', Priestley's was a carefree life, a sort of dandy phase in his career. A first-hand knowledge of men and affairs in the office and the wool market was a boon to his curious and creative mind. He was always a lover of books and a friend of book-lovers. This period of colourful dreams nourished by his wide and voracious reading filled him with the ambition of becoming a professional writer so as to live with independence. He began to scribble for pleasure and print in the local journals and papers, but the adolescent productions of this period were not of great literary value. His serious writing started only after the First World War.

The First World War broke out in 1914, and Priestley joined the Army. He was not a military type, and was, naturally, disgusted with the huge engine of destruction the war was. Three times he had a narrow escape from death. He spent four and a half years in the British Army, first as a soldier and then as an officer. When he came out of the 'idiotic war' after demobilisation, and emerged into 'civilian daylight', he found himself a divided young man who could not reconcile the comedy and the tragedy of war, but had learnt a good deal from the war, 'a great book of men'.

Priestley joined Cambridge University on an ex-Army Grant for a degree course. He regarded the opportunity Cambridge gave him of wide reading as a much greater gift than the degree of Arts the University gave him in 1921. Dismissing all thought of regular employment, he moved to London to start as a freelance writer. For several years he worked as a reader to John Lane's book firm, the Bodley Head; he could read scores of manuscripts and recommend for publication the deserving ones. Literary London came to life for Priestley in a big way. He had the benefit of a close association with the brilliant and delightful circle of writers and scholars, young and old. It was in the late twenties that he acquired a firm place as a professional writer. He had published volumes of essays before and began to write novels now. *The Good Companions* (1929) was a 'gold gusher' and a 'giant jackpot' that made its author famous overnight. His first play *Dangerous Corner* came in 1932 and established him as a first-class playwright. As a writer of fiction and drama he moved from strength to strength, from fame to fame, and never looked back.

Priestley's literary output was, both qualitatively and quantitatively, astoundingly prolific. Over a period of seven decades he produced more than one hundred and fifty books, creative and reflective together.

In the late Nineteen Thirties and early Forties Priestley ran his own production company called the London Theatre, which produced his plays like *Time and the Conways* and *Eden End*. He did not like razzle-dazzle side of the theatre world. He preferred “the legitimate stage to be quiet, solid, bourgeois”.[6] Once out of necessity he acted too—he had a total involvement with the theatre.

During the Second World War Priestley was an all-rounder—playwright, novelist, critic of his time, orator and public figure. He was a war-time hero with his ‘rumbling but resonant voice’ addressing the English-knowing world on the BBC in the programme called ‘Post Scripts’ several times a week, especially during the Blitz period. As such he was the English nation’s conscience-keeper, too. He crusaded, with his mighty pen, against the Nazi cult and Fascist forces. The general public rightly regarded Priestley as “a very solid character who would be the last to panic in an emergency”.[7] He was such an adorable public figure that “people would stop him in the street, crowd round in pubs just to touch him”.[8] During this darkest period of Britain’s history Winston Churchill’s and Priestley’s were the only two heroic voices. “When most people were too astonished to find words, theirs were the only voices.”[9]

Priestley was a member of the 1941 committee, a kind of Left Wing ginger group and also a member of the Common Wealth, a new progressive political party formed during the war. He made an attempt to get into Parliament, too, but was unsuccessful. He was interested not in active politics but in the fate of his people, which was being shaped by the politics of the time. He joined CND—Committee for Nuclear Disarmament—and remained a lifelong active member of the movement. He threw his considerable energies into it in the fifties and sixties. He raised a battle cry against the N-Bomb.

Priestley stood like a firm rock in the face of ups and downs in politics, society and literature in his time. He received many honours in his lifetime—he was Vice-President of the Conservation Society; elected to the Council of the Royal Literary Fund; was on the U.K. delegation to the Second General Conference of the UNESCO in Mexico City, Nov. 1947. He was the guest of honour at the fiftieth anniversary reception of the Poetry Society on the 22nd May 1959 held in the Grocer's Hall. He was closely associated with the P.E.N., and delivered the Herman Ould Memorial Lecture for it.

Though the English literary world did not concede Priestley the recognition he richly deserved, the British public paid him rich tributes on several occasions for his contribution to life and literature. The BBC broadcast on 14th September 1969 a Birthday Salute in 'Omnibus' on his seventy fifth birth anniversary. Sir Neville Cardus, Lord Snow, Michael Foot, Pamela Hansford Johnson, and Alan Dent offered birthday greetings on the occasion. "The speakers paid tribute to his tough adventurousness of mind, his gusto and aggressiveness and generosity of thought."[10]

He had received honorary degrees from American Universities and was now honoured by Bradford University in his old age. The greatest of the honours he received was the Order of Merit.

Even in his advanced age Priestley was interested in national and international affairs. He was concerned with the survival and progress of mankind; he was interested too in the survival and promotion of the true and lasting values in literature and other arts. He kept sound health, of body and mind, even in his advanced eighties. He is aptly called 'The Last of the Sages' by John Atkins, who ranks him with Wells, Shaw and Chesterton. Indeed Priestley was a sage who could see life steadily and saw it whole, and put his wisdom and experience embalmed in the large corpus of his works. Such a giant writer, public figure and "a hydra of letters"[11] passed away on 14 August, 1984.

Priestley is an intensely personal writer. Especially his works with the Time theme or the element of Time as a recurring motif show Priestley as a man with a very personal experience of, and attitude to, life. He was a lifelong dreamer, a visionary, a seer of the kind that Wordsworth was. The deeply meditative part of his personality is reflected in his intense concern with the solution of the problem of Time for mankind's sake. Even as a child he had been a dreamer, a meditative type. As a kid of four he had an intuitive feeling of the presence of some unique treasure on summer mornings of which he writes, "Somewhere, not far out of reach, it was waiting for me and at any moment I might roll over and put a hand on it."[12] This visionary stuff grew stronger and richer with the years. But he was never a sentimental soul. He was a happy blend of coolheadedness and a fiery romantic imagination.

Priestley was born with a love for music; he played on the piano and sang; had earned a prize, when a boy, for singing at a variety concert at Bradford. In his teenage, being fond of 'huge doses of orgies of sound', he was fascinated by the music-halls. As he grew older his taste became finer and he acquired a technical knowledge of music. He is all praise and admiration for the power and glory of the Ninth Symphony of Beethoven whom he regards as the noblest of all wizards because he 'projects his dreams to the sky'. Music is a powerful experience in his works, especially in his Time-works, where he too 'projects his dreams on to the sky'.

Priestley was a good connoisseur of painting; he was a watercolourist himself. Another art he loved with all his heart was that of the theatre. At Bradford he was a 'stage-struck' teenager. His fascination for the stage made him a lifelong lover of the theatre. He believed that the theatre is a bridge between the two mysteries of the work-a-day reality and the reality outside it.

Likewise, love of nature was in his blood and it was the strongest motive force behind his journeys in his native country and abroad. His was primarily the heart of a poet. Oak Creek in Arizona, an enchanting green valley, filled him with a thrill of joy. He danced with delight, as Wordsworth did at the sight of a rainbow, when he watched the Bright Angel Creek in the changing colours of twilight. The Grand Canyon was a revelation to him! It lifted the romantic in him to ecstasy and he wrote, "It is all Beethoven's nine symphonies in stone and magic light."[13] As a lover of the simple life amidst nature he felt a dislike for the busy mechanical life of industrial cities like London, Liverpool and New York.

Also, Priestley loved to travel widely. Besides an ardent desire to see the ever-changing scenes and sights of nature he had an insatiable curiosity to know different peoples and civilisations not only in Europe but also in Africa and Asia. His sharp observing eye never missed even the smallest detail of things and men wherever he went. He was a great humanitarian. His liberal socialism, advocacy of individuality, love of liberty and freedom stemmed basically from his deep concern for man. He saw the good of humanity in the good of man: if man could be at peace with himself, the whole of mankind could automatically be happy and peaceful. His staunch upholding of individuality did not run counter to the social order or community life which, he admits, is essential because otherwise men will be brutes. But his contention is that an exaggerated importance given to the vast social pattern is likely to take away the best from men as individuals, and they should, therefore, fight against narrow 'isms' and regimentation of any type which will surely kill the spirit of man. The greatest thing for Priestley was life. He had a zest for life and its good and beautiful things; he therefore hated any life-contracting system or ideas, be it religion, politics or literature. He was a sportsman, a good eater; his pipe was a lifelong companion. He was not a fastidious person. He says, "I have enjoyed books, music, pictures, but without despising music-halls and football matches."[14] Like Shakespeare, his favourite literary genius, Priestley believed in moderation. Both puritanism and hedonism were repugnant to his nature. Though a thinker, he was never opposed to healthy emotions and sentiments. Through his writings, he sought to restore the balance lost between religion and science, the world within and the world without, the intellect and emotions. His science admits of religion, which is the inner piety of man, and therefore never dogmatic; and his religion is not antagonistic to science, which is not just a mindless apotheosis of Matter.

Some people thought that he was aggressive and peevish. But this was far from the truth: he was a warm-hearted, amiable and generous man. He represents John Cowper Powy's ideal view of life which combines, in Priestley's own words, "scepticism of everything with credulity about everything".[15]

Just as the inherent qualities of Priestley's head and heart moulded him as a man in a distinctive way, his personality as a writer was greatly influenced by certain persons and events.

The first influence on Priestley was the personality of his father, a teacher, who was unselfish, brave and most honourable. Priestley inherited from his father a love of knowledge and human values, and a practicable attitude to men and things. Again, liberal socialism and a moderate view of everything came to him from this Victorian teacher. His father's friends, mostly teachers, made an impressive company in the Priestleys's house; their loud and heated talk interested the boy Priestley. Though he did not like all their talk about education, he liked the visitors who later found a place in some of his works. Priestley was greatly impressed by Richard Pendlebury, a teacher who taught him English in his Bradford school: he owed him immensley as regards his love of writing and English. Pendlebury's discussion of literature was full of life, and his talk had glints of humour and a cutting edge. Writing about this teacher's gifts, Priestley says, "I can see and hear him again, quite clearly, across years that changed all human history; and if his influence on me was greater, as indeed it was, than that of all the professors and lecturers I heard later in Cambridge and the critics I met in London, that was because I sat in a classroom at the right time, with a teacher who loved good writing."[16]

The library in his father's house filled the boy Priestley with a passion for reading. Of all the books that impressed him most as a child was *The Triple Alliance,* a children's story book (by Harold Avery, whom he calls a magician from a distant land) which brought him a world of wonder, adventure and joy that remained ever-green in his adult mind. Then the novels of Charles Dickens came to him like a treasure trove. He recalls how he used to get lost in the stories of the master novelist, sitting in a corner, in a small rocking chair, poring over *Nicholas Nickleby* or *David Copperfield*. Dickens became a lifelong companion and a seminal shaping force for Priestley. As for his childhood friends, he remembered, with warmth, a school-fellow called Harold Thorlaw, whose parents, he recalls, were another name for hospitality itself.

Priestley's Arcadian period—from 1910 to 1914—was really an important period which he calls a Golden Period in his life. This was the period when his personality began to take shape and he felt deeply and intensely about a number of things and dreamt of depicting in literature the beautiful and happy life he enjoyed at Bradford. These four years made such an imprint on his mind that nothing of it could be disturbed even by the catastrophe of the First World War. On the contrary, the period remained throughout his life 'a sunlit plain', standing out of the black and terrible road, to which he would go back time and again for solace and inspiration. About it he says, "Nobody, nothing, will shift me from the belief, which I shall take to the grave, that the generation to which I belong, destroyed between 1914 and 1918, was a great generation, marvellous in its promise."[17] Priestley's Time-plays and novels like Bright-Day and *Lost Empires* are like an after-glow of this bright Edwardian period. Priestley recalls the impressions of two musical programmes of this period. The first was a concert—a catchy light piece of the time—named 'In the Shadows', which, he says, still dances in his head. He says, "Nothing would bring back, so quickly and truly the time, the scene, the moods of my youth, than the sound of 'In the Shadows'."[18] He calls that old musical ditty his equivalent of Proust's *Madeleine*. Even more profound was the effect of ragtime, a performance in the Empire one evening given by three Americans: Hedges brothers and Jacobsen. He felt that the song sounded out a prophetic message; it was a foreshadow of the future caught in the mirror of the present. This is how he describes it:

> Out of those twenty noisy minutes in a music-hall, so long ago, came fragmentary but prophetic outlines of the situation in which we find ourselves now, the menace to old Europe, the domination of America, the emergence of Africa, the end of confidence and any feeling of security, the nervous excitement, the frenzy, the underlying despair of our country.[19]

It was this ragtime that inspired Priestley to write a topical skit entitled *The Secrets of the Ragtime King,* which appeared in 'London Opinion' and fetched him a guinea. He felt proud of his first 'breakthrough in print and money'.

Priestley started his literary career as a poet in his Arcadian days. He speaks of an exceptional girl typist who had a typing agency near his office and typed out his poems. The adolescent poet was more than in love with this girl for sometime. Describing his association with the girl, he recaptures, after five decades, a sensuously powerful image of her as "a saucy dark lass, like the woman Shakespeare seems to have loved and then hated, with raven curls, bold eyes, a white skin".[20] This beautiful dark girl haunted his imagination, and has appeared in some of his fictional works like *The Magicians, Look After the Strange Girl,* etc.

The Arcadian period set its stamp on Priestley for another reason also: he spent his days happily in the company of writers and book-lovers. He formed a friendship with James A. Mackereth, a poet who had come from the Lake Country to work in a Bradford Bank. Priestley was greatly impressed by this poet's attitude to life: he took a poetical view of everything. It was a rich repast for the young poet to be in the company of this older poet; he visited his house frequently, travelling down miles to see him and discuss literature. Talk and tobacco, tea and cake with this poet opened young Priestley's "mind then to that sense of unlimited possibilities, both in this life and some other, which has been described so often by the romantics."[21] Mackereth's company and then a brisk walk under the stars lifted him into that 'blessed mood' in which 'the heavy and weary weight' of earthly existence is lightened.

In 1914, a few months before the outbreak of the First World War, Priestley felt along with the whole generation, that he was moving towards something unknown to the conscious self; that they were soon to be at war; deep in their unconscious, which has a wider 'now' than consciousness knows, already the war was on, a world ending. There was nothing rational and conscious behind his joining the Army.

Some mysterious force prompted him to plunge into the stream. What he says about that unknown force is worth noting:

> ....I went at a signal from the unknown.... There came, out of the unclouded blue of that summer, a challenge that was almost like a conscription of the spirit, little to do really with King and Country and flag-waving and hip-hip-hurrah, a challenge to what we felt was our untested manhood.[22]

The two World Wars affected Priestley differently. Commenting on his soldiering and suffering in the First World War he observes that there was an indirect contribution from his soldiering life to his literary life, though he wrote nothing directly about the war as others, like Sassoon, Aldington and Hemingway, did. He found no 'deeper reality' in the war, as the war-writers of the time did. On the contrary, it appeared a vast piece of imbecility owing to its being wholly masculine. But he could never throw away the wound of his generation's fate—the best were sorted out for slaughter—which lent an elegiac quality to such of his works as have Time as a haunting idea. He expresses what he felt about the Second World War in these words:

> Now and then I remember with nostalgia the England of the Second World War, when my nation had a bright image of itself and the rat-race was not yet on; but never those four-and-a-half years of the First War.[23]

Priestley, the Time-haunted writer, was considerably influenced by four Time-theorists in the main, namely, McTaggart, J.W. Dunne, Carl Jung and Ouspensky. He met the first three in the flesh. He has placed on record his deep debt to these thinkers. McTaggart, an idealist thinker, was a philosophy lecturer in Cambridge when Priestley was studying there. Priestley was greatly impressed by his flawess and highly ingenious arguments. His admiration for this teacher and philosopher is expressed thus: "His presence was delightful: he had a curious high voice, a large moon-baby face with spectacles on the end of his nose.... He was one of the great originals of Cambridge."[24] Priestley was one of the early reviewers of J.W. Dunne's *An Experiment with Time* which had a lasting influence on him as regards his views of Time. He admired the intellectual integrity and courage of this great explorer of Time, a retired military engineer whom he met twice, first when this old theorist was invited to explain his serialism to the cast of *Time and the Conways* and then not long before the war one night when Priestley discussed his views of Time with him. About him he writes, "Those of us who are Time-haunted owe him an enormous debt."[25] Also Carl Jung proved a powerful influence on Priestley. Jung's theory of the unconscious which Priestley calls "one of the great liberating ideas of this age"[26] profoundly coloured his ideas of human personality in the thirties when he was in his forties. Priestley met Jung several times after the latter's seventieth birthday in 1945, when he was at Zurich, to write about this giant German for the BBC Ouspensky's theory of Eternal Recurrence and Intervention gave Priestley a new pair of eyes to look at the mystery and problem of Time. Priestley's quest for reality led him to study dreams. His probing into dreams was an integral part of his lifelong probing into Time and consciousness. Therefore, it is essential to consider what he thinks of dreams.

Priestley, throughout his long life, was interested in knowing the meaning and purpose of man's life in this world. Therefore, he took up studying consciousness at different levels which he found pivotal to his quest for that knowing. His quest led him to study dreams which opened up for him new dimensions of reality; they gave him a peep into that reality of consciousness which is alien to our understanding of reality. He recognised the Dream-Time nexus quite early.

Priestley, ever since his childhood, had been in the habit of flickering between the world of dreams and the waking self. Talking about dreams, he says, "I am one of the dreamers. My dreaming self is as important as my waking self."[27] Further he observes that dreams are our night life, and that the real life of a man is his waking life plus his dreams. He was more and more fascinated by dreams from his late twenties onwards. He was profoundly impressed by Dunne's analysis and explanation of various dreams in *An Experiment with Time* where the theorist calls attention to the 'displacement of time' in dreams. As a Time-haunted writer Priestley was haunted by dreams and the behaviour of Time in dreams.

Priestley discusses in detail four types of dreams: Ordinary dreams which everybody experiences almost every night; dreams containing universal experience; dreams giving a peep into the world of another reality; and dreams of wisdom which ancient sages and saints experienced.

Commenting upon the nature of his own dreams, he says that he has experienced some impersonal stuff, some kind of experience belonging to someone else's life. They were not of the common stuff, woven of fears and joys of the past or the present or things and desires suppressed in waking life, but of a peculiar character surging up in dreams; they were mostly unconnected with his actual earthly living. He never felt that his dreams were nothing but idle fantasizing of his waking life. Even as a child he found dreams to be real; they left too deep an impression on him to be shaken off by the objective world around him. Speaking of the significance of his dreams, he says:

> Then I began to suspect that in our dreaming there is a clue, a clue not only to our inward nature but also to the enduring nature of life itself. At the very moment we seem to lose the real world we are beginning to find it.[28]

Priestley wrote three essays in the Nineteen Twenties—then he was writing a weekly essay—which are mostly about his dreams. In *Rain Upon Godshill* and *Man and Time* he gives a detailed account of his own dreams and dreams of others to show how Time behaves in dreams and how reality needs to be caught outside passing time. Two of his dreams are worth considering for the precognitive element they contain. The essay *The Strange Outfitter* describes how he once found in an outfitter's shop the outfitter and a tall woman sitting together, both of them wearing large masks, and that those masks had 'movable mouths'. He found outside the shop a whole crowd of people dancing and singing, all wearing masks. Years later in the production of *Johnson Over Jordan* all the people in the

Second Act had to wear masks specially designed to have 'movable mouths'. He thinks that possibly the dream had come true. In the other dream, which he dreamt when he was a school-boy, he saw an uncle of his, whom he had rarely seen, appear suddenly in a doorway and glare at him angrily. He woke up, shivering with fright, and the dream remained thick in his memory. Years afterwards, during the First World War he was home on leave and was having a drink in a crowded bar. The uncle he had seen in the dream was staring at him angrily exactly the way he had done in the dream, and came across to reproach him angrily about something that was no fault of his. Priestley could not dismiss dreams such as these as mere coincidences.

Priestley was capable not only of precognitive dreams but also of such as contained someone else's experience which he calls Type Two dreams. In one dream he was a younger man, a student or something of that kind; he crept into a room where there were a number of tiny models of some military or naval invention; he had just taken one of those things when two uniformed officers rushed in, and as he was running out of the opposite doorway one of them fired several times at him, wounding him severally and as he staggered out into the street he could feel his life ebbing out. Commenting on this dream Priestley says that undoubtedly his consciousness had re-lived somebody else's last moments. Though he was actually wounded during the First World War he was never wounded thus and never in his waking life had felt life ebbing away as he experienced it in the dream. He felt in that dream a terrible sense of reality. He observes, "it is as if the wires of experience were crossed. Or that my consciousness, or some part of it, suddenly went flowing into the channel of somebody else's experience, thus making me live—or, rather relive—an episode or two from another autobiography."[29] This dream, he asserts, points to an individual's consciousness being turned to a fellow being's or universal consciousness. Such dreams as this draw our attention to timeless orders of life which cannot be apprehended by the positivists to whom linear time is the only time. The Third Type of dreams that he describes contain a glimpse of some entirely new order of reality. In these dreams we apprehend, through the same five senses, things far remote in Time and space; the dreamer feels that he is nearer waking life than his sleeping self; these dreams afford a glimpse of some higher multi-dimensional order of life. He cites an ecstatic experience he had when he went through the effect of nitrous oxide at a dentist's. He gulped the gas, lost consciousness and suddenly had a vision, which, he says, penetrated to the very heart of all things. He was convinced that the gas released some part of his mind which looked farther and fared better; the mind under the influence of that gas experienced a rare ecstasy.

In *Man and Time* Priestley examines a sample of the many hundreds of letters he received following his appeal on the BBC television programme 'Monitor' in 1963. He shows how some dreams contain Future signals, and help the dreamers avert unpleasant happenings by giving them a foreknowledge of those events. Here are cited two such premonitory dreams from a variety of dreams the letters narrated. Sir Stephen King-Hall, a well-known writer and naval officer, had a dream of his ship meeting with a disaster; he could avert the tragic event in actual life. The other dream was one narrated by Dr. Louisa E. Rhine as an example of 'Precognition and Intervention'. A woman had a dream of her visit to a creek; she had her baby with her and taken some clothes for washing; she left the baby and the clothes down there and went back home to bring a cake of soap; on her return she found that the baby had drowned and the body was floating. Some days afterwards she happened to go to a creek; she had her baby with her and had forgotten the soap, as in the dream, for washing the clothes; remembering the dream, she took the baby along with her while going back home to bring the soap; thus the woman averted the tragedy. Priestley brings out clearly from the examples how the dreaming self—Time Two or Observer Two in Dunne's language—has a wider length of Time One and how through the intervention of precognitive dreams unhappy occurances can be averted or their course changed.

The Fourth Type are the dreams of wisdom in which things are not out of focus but are more sharply observed than in waking life. These are rare dreams and they connect our mind with some infinitely richer and greater mind, give the wisdom of life, a brilliant peep into the nature and meaning of life. He narrates at length the dream of birds which he considers the wisest dream ever he had and changed his outlook on life itself. In the dream of birds, Priestley saw life operate along three different dimensions. There were all kinds of birds, a vast river of birds; but in a mysterious way the gear was changed, time speeded up; Priestley saw generations of birds, come quickly into life, procreate fast, and then were all struck by death. Again the gear was changed; time went faster still; no movement of birds could be seen; there appeared one vast plain sown with feathers. But along this plain a 'white flame' passed, and, in a rocket-burst of ecstasy, Priestley realized that the white flame was the flame of life. He ends the description of this dream of wisdom with the following words:

> I had never felt before such deep happiness as I knew at the end of my dream of the tower and the birds..., I have not been quite the same man since....[30]

This is the vision of a sage, a Rishi. The dream lent Priestley a profound insight into life; he came to realize the nature of being which knows no temporal succession; this dream gave him the realization and wisdom which only a yogi can attain and possess owing to his entering a timeless state of living. The ecstasy and the wisdom that Priestley obtained dramatically changed his outlook on life and things.

This discussion of the influence of dreams on Priestley makes it clear that behind the comic side of Priestley, the popular entertainer, there was a seriously contemplative metaphysical thinker. The influence of dreams has been closely examined, because it is an integral part of Priestley's lifelong quest for the right understanding of life through the right understanding of Time. Priestley's exploration of dreams has a close bearing on his endeavours to understand Time and its problem.

The best part of Priestley as a writer is revealed in his Time-works. His thoughts and ideas about Time are found mainly in two sources: two autobiographical books *Midnight on the Desert, Rain Upon Godshill,* and two speculative books *Man and Time, Over the Long High Wall,* and some essays form the first source; and his Time plays and some fictional works are the other source. The views and theories of Time he discusses in the first source are creatively presented in the plays and fictional writings in which Time is a dominant idea. The distinctive quality of Priestley's career as a writer is his Time-philosophy, an obsession he carried right from his teenage to the grave; Time is the most powerful recurring idea in most of his writings. It is his firm belief that life is not snuffed out by death and there is something in us that is not wiped out by Time. Priestley's is an intuitive grasp of the problem and mystery of Time.

In *A Great Wall*—Priestley shows how the problem of Time lies across mankind's path like a formidable wall, and that a passage through the wall will lead mankind to real happiness. He had been haunted by Time's enigma since his early teens. In his late teens he was attracted by Indian Metaphysics, its discussion of Atman and Brahman, the Ultimate Reality which could be attained by escaping from the bondage of Time. He recalls how he was offered an opportunity to discover a door in the wall of Time:

> Perhaps I was offered then one of those 'favourable moments'—the discovery of the door in the wall where none can be seen—by means of which, if the opportunity is seized, the Indians believe we can begin to escape from the bondage of Time. I did not seize the opportunity, was bound again to the wheel, and perhaps this is one reason why I am writing this book *Man and Time.*[31]

In the twenties and thirties of this century it was very much the vogue among writers in England to treat Time in one form or another. Priestley, always a Time-haunted man, addressed himself more seriously to the subject. Though he could not realize his dream of writing a book on Time till 1964, when he published his magnum opus on the subject, viz. *Man and Time,* he had been seriously contemplating what had been said by thinkers like C.H. Hinton and others. He speaks of how again he felt Time like a wall across mankind's way to happiness:

> For several years I had had a hunch—I dare not call it anything better—that this problem of Time was the particular riddle that the Sphinx has set for this age of ours, that it was like a great barrier across our way and we were all squabbling and shouting and moaning in its shadow, and that if it could be solved there might follow a wonderful release and expansion of the human spirit.[32]

The conventional explanation of Time as one endlessly flowing river could not satisfy Priestley. His belief remained steadfast that if we could find a key to fit the lock of Time we might open a door into a new universe. This idea again finds itself metaphorically expressed even in Priestley's advanced age of seventy-eight in *Over the Long High Wall.* The book ends with the following description of modern man's anguish resulting from his illusory notion of Time, suggesting a way out:

> That is the world lying in the shadow of the long high wall, the passing time wall, which we have imagined into existence as our beliefs have shrunk and hardened, denying God the Creator, the Absolute, emptying the universe of higher levels of being and all far-flung adventures of the spirit, and refusing to accept the magical gift we possess—our consciousness.... I hope some readers will climb up and at least try to peep over it. I hope even more fervently that at least a few readers, with me all the way, will go in search of a wider view and a sunlit horizon—simply by walking through the wall.[33]

Priestley uses 'passing time' for clock time, a phrase borrowed from Maurice Nicoll's book *Living Time.* This passing time is the 'wall' he speaks of in the three passages quoted above. He firmly believes that we can have a peep over the wall and even a passage through it if we enlarge and enrich our consciousness. For him the pre-1914 Edwardian age was a 'sunlit horizon' for ever. A number of characters in his works are shown as capable of peeping over the wall. The men and women in the play *They Came to a City* go through the door of Time; Gregory Dawson in *Bright Day* and Richard Herncastle in *Lost Empires* peep over the wall of passing time and find that nothing of their past is lost but, on the contrary, it appears richer and deeper.

Priestley clearly makes out in his writings, discursive and creative, that the root-cause of our age's misery is the exaggerated importance we have given to passing time. The immense development of our modern technology has sharpened our attention to a fine edge, and the result is that we are more and more aware of divisions of time; that is, we are taking a short view of Time; to us Time is only a single track time ending up, for us, at our death. Priestley is at one with Time philosophers like Bergson, Dunne, and Ouspensky in the belief that it is this narrow, dogmatic view of Time as unidimensional that is responsible for the shrinking of our souls and minds; our age's fear of passing time compels men to do anything wicked and inhuman to achieve their goal, because they are, anyhow, going to be out, to be cancelled out by death. He, therefore, declares that this wrong attitude to life is born of a misconception of Time. There is a strong note of optimism behind his plea for reposing our faith in the eternity of Time. His eternity of Time is not the same as 'everlasting time' which has done much harm. "It means a non-passing time, another kind of time, existence not measured by clock and calendars, a level of being that cannot be analysed in any laboratory, belong to that kingdom of Heaven which most Orthodox Christians refuse to believe in within them, the great Here and Now we enter through the arts and love and friendship and acts of simple goodness."[34]

Priestley's intuitive speculations that Time was multidimensional were strengthened by his reading of F.A. Abbot's *Flatland* and C.H. Hinton's *New Era of Thought*. He was impressed by Hinton's idea of the fourth dimension as time; if Abbot's Flatlanders, beings with a two-dimensional outlook, found the third dimension of height as time, then for us with a three-dimensional outlook, the fourth dimension would be time. Dunne's Serialism, propounded in *An Experiment with Time* caught Priestley's imagination. The Serial theory of Time enabled him to understand in a better light the two puzzles of self-consciousness and Time which he had tried hard to grasp for long. To him there was always something bewildering about self-consciousness. When we observe something, we are conscious of our observation, and further we are conscious of the observation of the observation and so on. He found the same baffling mystery about Time.

Priestley learnt three important things from Serialism:

Our waking self, Observer One, has three-dimensional outlook and to him the fourth dimension is time; the self we know in dreams is Observer Two, and this observer has a four-dimensional outlook and to him the fifth dimension is time; Our dreaming self—Observer Two—has a wide length of Time One. Priestley appreciates the Dunnian serialism for yet another reason, and that is, it holds out a message of optimism in as much as it leads to the idea of Immortality. He observes:

> We are engaged, according to him (Dunne) in the process of learning how to live. On this theory the tragic brevity of life is immeasurably expanded and is no longer tragic.... There is more than sheer greed of experience in our hunger for immortality. This is something nobler than mere fear of death.[35]

Serialism with its idea of multi-dimensionality of life and consequently of Time is superbly grasped and picturesquely presented by Priestley as follow:

> On this view of Time, the Past has not vanished like a pricked bubble.... Then the past is the station we have just left, and the future is the station we are approaching. The Past has not been destroyed any more than the last station was not destroyed when the train left it. Just as the station is still there, with its porters, and ticket inspectors and bookstall and its noise and bustle, so the past still exists, not as a dim memory, but in all its colour and hum.[36]

This is Priestley's idea of the eternal present. He is opposed to the view that death is the end of our life. The view that Time is an unconquerable tyrant destroying everything creates pessimism and takes away all interest in, and respect for, life. To him human life is noble and beautiful. He firmly believes that our Time-One life—our "today"—is part of the ever-enduring, timeless drama of our existence, and is a preparation for our "tomorrow", the fifth dimension. Priestley's well-known plays, *Time and the Conways, Johnson Over Jordan,* and novels *Bright Day, The Magicians* and *Lost Empires* are based on serialism.

The idea of Enternal Recurrence, the nucleus of Ouspensky's theory of Time, hooked Priestley's imagination as an artist; he found in it an El Dorado of a highly imaginative quality. He was fascinated by the idea of some souls being capable of evolving themselves to such extent that they would be able to turn the circle of their Time into a spiral and finally swing out of it and escape from Time's wheel altogether. This idea is illustrated by the play *I Have Been Here Before.* Priestley shows his originality in adding the idea of 'Intervention' to the theory, which appears in the form of Gortler in the play.

Priestley accepts Ouspensky's fifth and sixth dimensions: the fifth dimension is one of the Eternal now or timelessness and the sixth dimension is the line of actualisation of other possibilities. Speaking about the fifth dimension, Priestley writes, "(But) intuitively and in imagination we are not so narrowly bound. In high moments of emotion, we seem to feel the timelessness, the Eternal now, of the fifth dimension."[37] The sixth dimension is of the spirit or imagination, which is the domain of unactualised possibilities. Priestley has an original approach to this idea. He theorises that imagination, a mysterious faculty, helps the artist actualise other possibilities in his works of art; it is the sphere of imaginative creations. In other words, the possibilities which have not been actualised in Time One are actualised in this dimension through the power of imagination and this dimension is significantly called an aggregate of "all times". The masterpieces of all great writers like Dante and Shakespeare, and of musicians and painters like Mozart and Michael Angelo come from this sixth dimension. At this level the will to create and the power to create are joined meaningfully and the combination results in wonderful creations of art. Priestley uses the idea of the creative imagination in the novels *Jenny Villiers* and *The Thirty First of June.*

Priestley does not believe in the divisions of Time—Past, Present and Future. He believes in eternity as non-passing time or eternal present as already discussed. He illustrates this idea by depicting in his works people who are capable of precognitive and retrocognitive power in them; these characters can travel in Time, backwards and forwards. The Old Man on the mountain and Mrs. Baro in *Saturn Over the Water* know what has been and will be anywhere in the world the moment they close their eyes and contemplate; they have come to possess wisdom through the conquest of Time. We have Dorothy and Jock in *Bright Day* who belong to this class of rare souls who have a smooth sailing in Time. Margaret in *Summer Day's Dream* 'sees' forward and tells the coming of foreigners to their farm. The old queer fellow Candover in *Let the People Sing* is also made of this stuff. The "indomitable trio" of magicians in *The Magicians* are a supreme embodiment of the apocalyptic view of life; they are yogic souls, capable of moving in a timeless dimension. To these and many more people in Priestley's play and fiction the past and the future are no barriers because they have knocked them down. Priestley's idea of the past and the future is clearly expressed in the following passage:

> The past is fixed. Go back to the right place along the time track and the Saxons are losing the Battle of Hastings.... But once allow any kind of interference, and clearly the future is in a different category. It is anything but fixed. That does not mean that it is nothing. It means that it is a realm of possibilities, some of which will be actualised.[38]

The knotty problem of the future has exercised Priestley's mind much more than the idea of the past. He discusses three views regarding it in his book *Over the Long High Wall.* One view believes that the future is not born, and is "uncreating nothing", a blank. The second view holds that it is fixed and the result is that it cannot be avoided; this is a fatalistic or deterministic view and according to this view an exercise of free will is an exercise in futility, an illusion. The third view is that a future can be created, at least partially. Priestley agrees with the third view. He is at one with Dunne in holding that when the future can be seen—at least by a few people—its unpleasant aspect can be avoided. This idea has been given an artistic rendering in some of Priestley's works. Priestley introduces the Dunnian idea of 'Intervention' and shows how unhappy and tragic events can be averted. Thus he seems to point to one possibility of settling the old quarrel between Free will and predestination.

Consciousness as well as Time had been treated in English fiction by writers of the 'Bloomsbury Group'. The treatment of the topic in the works of this class of writers generally known as the 'stream-of-consciousness' fiction-writers was psychological. But Priestley's approach is philosophical; he moves on the lines of Dunne and Jung. As a Time-philosopher —he was called so in his time—he has a philosophical message to deliver to mankind in addition to entertaining them with his art.

The problem of the self had occupied Priestley's mind for a long time. Dunne's Serialism helped him see the problem in better light. But it was in the thirties, with a flood of new light being thrown by Jung's theory of the unconscious, that he was able to see the question clearly in all its aspects; Jung's theory opened up a new world of awareness and wisdom for his Time-haunted mind. Very soon Priestley realised that consciousness was bound up with Time. It was his conviction that mankind could have all its problems solved through the right understanding of the inner life. He places his finger on the poverty of the inner life as the root-cause of all the unrest and fatigue, the anguish and misery, heat and passion of our present civilisation:

> In other words, the main line of progress runs through the consciousness itself. We have been trying for centuries to discover the clue to the mystery somewhere outside ourselves. We must, now, if only for a change, reverse this process and try to find the clue inside ourselves.[39]

The path of consciousness takes us into the deep-down depths of our being which is outside passing time. Priestley therefore says that on any cosmological scale the self is an illusion; it is not independent of the all-pervasive universal consciousness; the individual souls cease to be individual if we deeply think about them; they tend to dissolve into something else. This is an Advaita (non-dual) view of life and also the Platonic concept of "many merging into One". Each one of us does experience at some rare moments that he is part of a larger and mightier force, an infinite being. Accordingly, our consciousness is not personal and the universal consciousness can be reached only through our mind. But Priestley does not ignore the importance of the individual consciousness, because unless the individual personality is developed the universal mind or consciousness cannot be reached. Therefore, he is emphasizing the need to expand our consciousness. His belief is that by heightening and enlarging our consciousness we can liberate ourselves from the tyranny of Time and, then, we will see things "as really they are". If we explore the inner world at the deeper levels of consciousness we become less and less aware of ourselves and begin to move out of passing time. This concept of individual self-effacement is the theme of the play *Music at Night* in which the characters lose their entity under the influence of music, and linear time is expunged overall. Similarly, under the spell of some yogic trance people may go out of their individual consciousness and passing time. For example, Tim and Rosalia have the experience of going out of themselves and entering a new dimension when the old man operates his power on their minds. In support of this view Priestley cites the findings of hypnotic tests conducted by French hypnotists like Colonel de Rochas; a hypnotised mind also loses its conscious identity and moves into a much greater consciousness. Priestley takes personality as one small 'focal point' of the universal consciousness. No doubt he accepts the self not in the conventional sense of a separate individual identity imprisoned in a person but in the sense of a part however small it may be—of the supreme consciousness.

Whenever Priestley experienced a Time-shift he felt a 'quiver' or a 'shiver'. Some of his characters like William and Ramsbottom in *Music at Night,* Kay in *Time and the Conways,* and Joan in *Bright Day,* likewise, feel a shiver or a cold creeping through the blood, while they are entering another Time-order. In the thirties, Priestley thought Time played tricks but later he realised that there were different orders of Time, and that our consciousness dwelt among many dimensions.

Priestley is an intensely personal writer, and his explanation of these orders of Time comes from his genuine personal experience. The first order is that of passing time. When we are passing through a great danger or are contemplating works of art or certain aspects of life, things seem to be put into 'slow motion', and we, the observers, are detached from passing time, as if existing outside any sphere of action. This is the second order of Time. The third kind of experience, Priestley feels, does not withdraw us from action but flings us into it; we are turned not into detached observers but into creators working like men possessed by some power; our energy and creative will are harnessed to work; things seem to be put into 'speedy motion'. In fact in this experience there is an absence of self. These two fundamentally different kinds of experience belong to two different states of consciousness. There is also a Time element in these experiences. They are alike in that they appear in passing time; in both situations our mind seems to escape from passing time in two different directions, one out of action and the other into action. These two different kinds of experience are again alike in suggesting some Time-shift; they release the mind from an egocentric relation with passing time. Of these two experiences the second belongs to the third order of Time. Thus Time seems to divide itself into three; passing time (Time One), the contemplative 'slower-up' (Time Two) and purposeful, imaginative and creative 'speeder-up' (Time Three). Time One and Time Two have no alternative possibilities, which exist only in Time Three, the level (the Ouspenskian sixth dimension) where we come across the power to connect or disconnect the potential and actual. Priestley recalls how he experienced Time Three when he wrote *Time and the Conways* at breakneck speed. Cheveril in *Jenny Villiers* and Sam Penty in *The Thirty First of June* move into this world of creative imagination, the dimension of Time Three.

Imagination is not something of an escape from reality. Priestley is not one who cannot face life with courage. He emphatically says that imagination itself is reality of a higher order. Its creations are real and enduring, whereas the world we construct from our Time-One experience is artificial, thin and hollow. Imagination is essential to the human mind, because it keeps human beings human and noble. Priestley is lashing out at utility-oriented positivist philosophy when he remarks, "But an adult in whom imagination has withered is mentally lame and lopsided, in danger of turning into a zombie or a murderer."[40]

Priestley studied a number of *ESP*—Extra-Sensory-Perception—and telepathic cases as part of his broad enquiry into consciousness and Time, and his conclusion is that the findings of parapychologists in terms of the science of the mind do not carry us far but such things should be looked at intuitively to see if they can throw any light on our understanding of consciousness and Time. Priestley cites the example of an *ESP* case from the private lives of two people he knew. He calls it a good example of *FIP*—future-influencing-present. The *FIP* phenomenon finds an artistic illustration in the relationship of Richard and Nancy in *Lost Empires*. Several other *ESP* cases are dealt with in some of Priestley's stories included in the collection *The Other Place*. This goes to show how Priestley studied Time from all possible points of view.

Priestley elevates his ideas of Time to a philosophical pedestal by explaining the mystery of Time vis-a-vis the world of human consciousness. Really 'Time-thinking' becomes a philosophy when he connects it with different levels of consciousness in terms of different orders of reality. In fact his approach all along has been not one of psychology and logic but of the intuition of a sage.

Priestley recognises three levels of consciousness: the conscious, the unconscious (generally associated with Jung's theory of the 'Collective Unconscious'), and the super conscious. He relates this division to the temporal system: the ego and its field of consciousness belong to Time One; the unconscious belongs to Time Two and the super conscious to Time Three. But he cautions that we should not make watertight compartments of these divisions because we live, even here and now, in all three kinds of Time.

We cannot go beyond death in Time One; at death our portion of Time One ends; our body and brain cease to function. But our consciousness continues to exist in Time Two, taking with it our total experience in Time One. *Johnson Over Jordan* puts this idea effectively into dramatic form. Our life is not contained entirely within our conscious life in Time One. Intensely emotional moments, just like dream experience, enlarge and enrich our emotional landscapes, and we are lifted into Time Two. To move into Time Two, the realm of the unconscious, is a way of elevating our consciousness, of gaining a rich bonus from the unknown. The Time Two world is richly reflected in Priestley's plays and fictional works. The romantic moments in the life of Irina and Christopher in the English house in *Summer Day's Dream,* the thrill of joy experienced by Dawson in *Bright Day,* on hearing the 'schubert Trio' and again his delightful moments at seeing Stanley's picture in Mrs. Childs' house in the same novel, can be cited as examples of heightened emotions in Time Two. For Priestley, to be incapable of this kind of noble and emotional life is real death. He emphasises the need and importance of living meaningfully, that is living a life of enjoyment of good, noble and beautiful things like literature and arts, love and friendship, sights and scenes of beauty and sublimity in nature, because all this is going to be with us when we enter Time Two after death.

Priestley explains his concept of the third level of consciousness, namely super consciousness, in terms of Jung's "individuation", the process of transforming the one-sided ego into the broad-sided "self". He thinks that probably we move from personality to the essential self in Time Two, and later the self must take on its final shape and colouring, stretching to its full limits, to move into Time Three, the super conscious level. He observes, "We must become more completely ourselves before, in our existence only in Time Three, finally dissolving into selfless consciousness, as I appeared to do when ecstatically aware only of that white flame."[41] He wants us to make conscious efforts to expand and heighten our consciousness so that we will learn to live in Times Two and Three, and finally be able to reach the stage where we will dissolve into the universal consciousness which he calls 'selfless consciousness'. Priestley experienced universal consciousness in his dream of birds as a 'white flame'. Referring to the symbolic meaning of that dream which changed his whole attitude, he says that the 'white flame' did not become visible until after the second speeding-up of all the bird life in what may be called Time Three. He means that unless we have become completely ourselves in Time Three, that is, have attained the super conscious stage, even here and now, in our Time One we cannot experience the universal or supreme consciousness which is selfless and timeless. It is to be noted that Priestley's experience of the 'white flame' is very much the mystic experience of eternity that W.T. Stace describes in the following words: "Looked at from outside itself, the mystic moment is a moment in time. But looked at from within itself, it is the whole of eternity."[42]

On another level, the 'white flame', or universal consciousness, experienced by Priestley, is akin to the universal form of Being described in the *Gita* as the "mass of glory" shining all around, as "Time's universal conflagration"[43] seen and experienced by Arjuna who has been vouchsafed a divine vision by Lord Krishna. Priestley's experience of selfless consciousness may well be compared to Sri Aurobindo's "supraconsciousness" described as "an infinity above us, an eternal Presence or an infinite Existence, an infinity of consciousness, an infinity of bliss—a boundless self, a boundless light, a boundless Power, a boundless Ecstasy."[44]

NOTES

1. Gareth Lloyd Evans, *J.B. Priestley—The Dramatist* (London: William Heinemann, 1964), p. 8.
2. G.S. Fraser, *The Modern Writer and His World* (Baltimore USA: Penguin Book, 1970), p. 97.
3. G. Wilson Knight, *The Golden Labyrinth* (London: Phoenix House Ltd., 1962), p. 355.
4. A.C. Ward, *20th Century English Literature 1901-60* (Bombay-Calcutta-Delhi: B.I. Publications Pvt. Ltd., 1986), p. 14.
5. W.H. Hudson, *An Outline History of English Literature* (Bombay-Calcutta-Delhi: B.I. Publications Pvt. Ltd., 1978), p. 290.
6. J.B. Priestley, *Margin Released* (London: The Reprint Society, 1962), p. 198.
7. John Atkins, *J.B. Priestley—The last of the sages* (London: John Caldler, 1981), p. 8.
8. Susan Cooper, *J.B. Priestley—Portrait of an Author* (London: Heinemann, 1970), p. 7.
9. Davind Hughes, *J.B. Priestley—An Informal Study of his Work* (London: Rupert Hard-Davis, 1958), p. 162.
10. John Atkins, *J.B. Priestley,* p. 14.
11. Davind Hughes, *J.B. Priestley,* p. 185.
12. J.B. Priestley, *Delight* (London: Heinemann, 1949), p. 124.
13. J.B. Priestley, *Midnight on the Desert* (London: Heinemann Ltd., 1947), p. 287.
14. J.B. Priestley, *Margin Released,* p. 185.
15. J.B. Priestley, *Saturn Over the Water* (London: Heinemann Ltd., 1961), from Prologue p. XIII.
16. J.B. Priestley, *Margin Released,* p. 6.
17. *Ibid.*, pp. 132-33.
18. *Ibid.*, p. 58.
19. *Ibid.*, p. 64.
20. *Ibid.*, p. 24.
21. *Ibid.*, p. 34.
22. *Ibid.*, pp. 78-79.
23. *Ibid.*, p. 87.

24. J.B. Priestley, *Man and Time* (New York: Aldus Allen Book, 1964), p. 71.
25. *Ibid.*, p. 244.
26. *Ibid.*, p. 290.
27. J.B. Priestley, *Rain Upon Godshill* (London: Heinemann Ltd., 1939), p. 287.
28. *Ibid.*, p. 293.
29. *Ibid.*, p. 300.
30. *Ibid.*, pp. 305-06.
31. J.B. Priestley, *Man and Time,* p. 171.
32. J.B. Priestley, *Midnight on the Desert*, p. 245.
33. J.B. Priestley, *Over the Long High Wall* (London: Heinemann Ltd., 1972), p. 142.
34. J.B. Priestley, *Thoughts in the Wilderness* (London: Heinemann, 1957), p. 46.
35. J.B. Priestley, *Midnight on the Desert*, p. 259.
36. *Ibid.*, pp. 263-64.
37. *Ibid.*, p. 274.
38. J.B. Priestley, *Rain Upon Godshill,* p. 316.
39. *Ibid.*, p. 277.
40. J.B. Priestley, *Man and Time,* p. 297.
41. *Ibid.*, p. 308.
42. Hans Meyerhoff, *Time in Literature* (Berkeley and Los Angels: University of California, 1960), p. 60.
43. Edward J. Thomas, trans., *The Song of The Lord* (London: John Murray, 1931), p. 86.
44. Sri Aurobindo, *The Life Divine,* Vol. 19 (Pondicherry, India: Sri Aurobindo Birth Centenary Library, 1970), p. 911.

3

Early Phase: Time Signals

Priestley did not spring up as a Time-writer overnight. His lifelong obsession with Time has its roots in his early writings. There are three phases in the development of Priestley as a Time-writer. The early phase extends from 1912 to 1932, the middle phase from 1932 to 1953, and the final phase lasts from 1961 till his very old age. There is, however, a definite pattern to be noticed in this development. The early phase is one of fiction barring one poem; the middle phase is one of plays and fiction both; the final phase consists only of fiction.

Even in his childhood Priestley was aware of "the whispers and movements in the dark",[1] of the possibility of the existence of dimensions other than the one in passing time. Discussing his juvenile poem 'Atlantis' years later Priestley felt that the poem which deals with the destruction of a great civilization suggested that it might not be a thing of the past but one that was going to happen; coming as it did from the young Priestley's unconscious it suggested a glimpse of a future event, that is, the disastrous First World War. In fact, in 1912, there was no sign of the War, but the poet's unconscious, with its wider 'Now', had felt it.

Three of Priestley's essays of the 1920's contain the Time-element. *On Beginning* and *On Strangers* have the idea of circularity, the end returning to the beginning. This circular device involves a manipulation of the time-scale. Circularity may not itself be a profound philosophical idea of Time, but it is certainly a part of Priestley's broader view of Time which is noticed even in his later works like *The Good Companions, An Inspector Calls* and *Ever Since Paradise*. The essay *Dissolution in Haymarket,* included in the collection *Open House* (1927), contains the author's sense of 'otherness' felt at 'magical moments' which, he believed, gave a peep into the unknown lying infinitely outside passing time. The essay describes a strange experience that Priestley had, while going on a bus, an experience of a sudden change of mood in which he saw the whole cheerful pageant of the street immediately crumpled, and collapsed, and he was left 'shivering' in the midst of a tragedy. This metaphor of 'shiver' or 'cold' is indicative of a change in the time-dimension and it is found in a number of his Time-works in all the three phases of his development as a Time-writer.

This early phase produced four novels in which Time makes its first appearance as an idea which became a major haunting theme in the subsequent phases. They are *Adam in Moonshine, Benighted, The Good Companions,* and *Music at Night*. John Atkins recognises in these works "a series of rather shy signals"[2] of Time. Though they do not mainly deal with Time and its enigma, they certainly foreshadow that Priestley is going to make use of certain Time theories and concepts. For example, so far as the fantasy-creation is concerned *Adam in Moonshine* and *Benighted* are precursors of plays like *People at Sea, Desert Highway, They Came to a City* and *Summer Day's Dream* and novels like *Jenny Villiers, The Magicians* and *The Thirty First of June* and stories like *The Other Place* and *Night Sequence*. At this stage Priestley was mainly a fantasist. These four novels move in a double dimension of the real in passing time and the possible outside linear time. Besides containing the metaphor of 'shiver' as indicative of change of time-dimension as experienced by some of the characters, they mark the beginning of Priestley's treatment of consciousness functioning at different levels and along different dimensions of Time. Particularly *Music at Night* is his first attempt at turning the Dunnian Serial Time into art. These four novels clearly show how Priestley was, during this early period, in the process of becoming a serious and full-fledged Time-writer.

Adam in Moonshine (1927), Priestley's first novel, is deeply concerned with fantasy. Priestley aptly calls it "a little coloured balloon".[3] Fantasy is the very soul of the novel. Its essential quality lies in the atmosphere of noman's land. John Atkin's observation that Priestley "is fascinated by borderlands —between dream and wake, reality and fantasy..."[4] mirrors the spirit of the novel. The dream world of this work lifts the central character, Adam, out of passing time, albeit for a short period, into a timeless order of mind. The young man Steward embarks upon a long journey to the north in order to spend his week-end in the Yorkshire Dales. The novel begins as a realistic account of this young man's journey from St. Pancras, but soon turns out to be an explosion of magic. He is mistaken for the Stuart heir whom Baron Roland and his Companions of the Rose have planned to coronate in order to replace the outdated monarchy of the time by a real republic with a true royal head. The mistaken identity of Adam happens to be the cause of his high romantic adventures and misadventures; Adam conducts himself in the manner of a medieval hero. Adam's brave romantic adventures—his wanderings in the dales in the neighbourhood by day and at night—first with Nina, then with Peter and finally with Helen make him a hero of a mid-summer-night high romance. His midsummer wanderings, his moon-flights and sunny feats with these three enchanting girls take him to another plane of existence, to a new dimension of the spirit where clock time stops dead for a few hours and minutes.

On a number of occasions Adam is shown as experiencing 'magical moments' when clock time comes to a halt, and he is connected with something unknown in a timeless dimension; on such occasions the novelist uses the word 'shiver', an experience felt by Adam, and it is indicative of a sudden change of time-dimension. The lovely moonlight, described in the chapter 'The Kingdom of Moonshine', creates a waking dream for Adam which brings him awareness of an order of existence which is outside passing time.

Adam and Helen, having finished their little meal, were standing up. Helen came closer to Adam, and he looked through the night into the deeper night of her eyes, now brooding over her. See how Priestley catches Adam's peculiar experience: "You're shivering, Adam," She told him, "You are cold." He had been cold this long time, but had forgotten about it. "No, it is not cold. It's just excitement—or delight—or something—at being here with you."[5] This "something", not adequately put in words by Adam, is a peculiar experience of moving out of passing time into a timeless state of ecstasy which only the spirit can feel.

Observing through the window, the silent moonlit world, Adam's mind travelled back to the ancient Greek world. His feeling is recorded thus: "The life of the house, of the garden, of the shining world beyond, ebbed away into a silence that might have been that of the drowned courts of Atlantis."[6] Here the time past is eternally present. While recounting to Templake the fantastic adventures he had passed through, Adam thought of the memorable moments and his introspection is described in these words: "Everything, he told himself, was just beginning, but now he had a sudden premonition that everything was soon at end too, that these very moments now shredding away were those above all others that he would return to in wonder once they had grouped themselves, radiant in lost sunshine, in his remembrance."[7] Here Priestley speaks of the timelessness of certain significant moments, as does Proust in his novel *Remembrance of Things Past*. Baron Roland's words speak of the presentness of the past when he is admiringly speaking of Helen, one of the three girls in the story, comparing her to Homer's Helen: "Everytime I've looked across at you, I've heard these thousand ships crashing into the water."[8] Here echoes of the epic past come ringing through.

All these instances clearly show that Priestley attempts in his first novel itself to give an artistic expression to his awareness of 'something' in human life which is too elusive and mysterious to be grasped by our senses in passing time. He presents the spirit of man as being capable of intuitive perception of higher realities possible only in higher dimensions of Time. The novel does not attempt to create anything against the background of any Time theory: Priestley was not at the time acquainted with Dunne and Ouspensky though Time had begun to haunt him.

Benighted (1927) followed *Adam in Moonshine.* Both these novels move along the twin dimensions of fantasy and reality. The moonshine meanderings of Adam in the Yorkshire Dale country and the actions of the benighted travellers in the weird atmosphere of the old dark house belong to the same dim-lit world of fantasy. Susan Cooper calls *Benighted* an intriguing piece, a kind of philosophical thriller, and goes on to observe: "The fantasist is stirring: the Time-haunted man already seeing shapes in the dark."[9] As already noted in the discussion of *Adam in Moonshine* Priestley had not yet come under the influence of any Time theorist, but was certainly a man haunted by the mystery of Time.

Three people, a young architect called Philip Waverton and his wife Margaret, and Philip's friend Roger Penderel, driving at night through wild Wales found themselves caught in a titanic storm between landslide and flood and came to a lonely sinister house for shelter. The ominous house belonged to an ancient titled family called Femms who were now either mentally deranged or physically grotesque and odd. Horace Femm, a 'spectral creature' was the only sane man in the house. If Rebecca was a deaf, shrivelled figure breathing cynicism and frustration, Saul Femm was a terrible maniac shut up in a lonely cell, and Morgan, the servant, was a dumb brute of a man. Morgan, dead drunk, became uncontrollable, and then was overpowered and thrown down by Philip. A real danger came from Saul. A terrible fight took place between Saul and Penderel. The fight ended in the death of both of them. The melodrama of the night ended with the coming of a bright morning.

The clock time of the novel covers one night but so much of so many lives is glimpsed through a hindsight glance over their past. Time is either expanded or slowed down or suspended. True to his own principle of narrative fiction, which he discusses in the new preface to this novel, Priestley tries to combine the subjective world of the characters and the varying states of their minds with the objective narration of a story. He calls this method 'dramatic symbolisation' which sets the novel in two worlds at once: the world of fantasy and the world of reality. The fantasy stuff moves outside time, while the story of the benighted travellers follows in time. The novel presents its world in a double time-dimension, the dimension of time and that timelessness.

When a real man is put in the midst of people and things and events which he cannot understand and consequently he gets confused and bewildered, then that world of confusion and bewilderment becomes a fantasy. *Benighted* and *Adam in Moonshine* have this brand of fantasy. Recognising the quality of the double structure of the novel—the fantastic and the realistic—the critic Susan Cooper observes: "And though *Benighted* is not one of his major novels, it does contain a few striking moments in which the two-world structure brings out a sudden flash of truth."[10] What the travellers, trapped in the Ghoulish old house, say and do at the conscious level constitutes reality governed by clock time, while what goes on in their unconscious and sometimes subconscious constitutes a reality of a higher order in a different dimension of Time where there is no tyranny of clock time.

A number of occasions fully bring out the fact that during this period Priestley was trying to put his thinking about Time into creative form, though he was not yet preoccupied with what he calls the Time problem or the Time theme. Time's tyranny, the popular view of Time, was still a puzzle to Priestley and this notion is reflected in Rebecca's words. The old weird woman Rebecca touched Margaret's dress and then her soft white skin and sardonically mumbled, "That's fine stuff, but it'll rot. And that's finer still, but it'll rot too in time."[11] The futility and boredom of life in passing time is expressed by Gladys when she says to the whole circle busy at 'Play Truth': "...You've nothing to live for. You are just passing the time and it's rotten. Everything so far has been a washout, and now it's Monday morning all the week."[12]

Priestley points out the queer experience the characters pass through while passing from one dimension of Time into another. The author describes the effect of Rebecca's sudden appearance and shrill voice on the whole circle who were absorbed in talking about their lives: "That entrance had obviously put an end to their talk, during which they had seemed to be sitting on a bank, watching life go by like a river and pointing out to one another its eddies and ripples and gleams; but now, with the opening of the door and the sound of another voice, life seemed to be roaring around them again; they were in the river again."[13] This description of the situation is a clear proof that Priestley had begun thinking seriously and keenly about the different levels of consciousness and the dimensions of Time. Undoubtedly the image of the river is in consonance with the metaphor of river for time. Deeply absorbed in their inner world during the talk these people were unaware of passing time, their minds moving in a timeless dimension, but were suddenly flung back again into the cold reality, the realm of passing time. By then Priestley had surely felt that the conscious world functions in passing time and the unconscious operates in a different time-dimension. The change of time-dimension is indicated, as in *Adam in Moonshine,* by the metaphor of 'shiver' which Penderel feels while sharing certain intensely emotional moments with Gladys, the enchanting girl he loved. That Priestley was aware of the relative character of Time is clearly brought out by some of the events. For example, Time seemed very long to Margaret who had in reality spent only a few minutes in the bizarre room of the sinister house to change her dress. Rebecca filled her mind with the pathetic past of the Femms; the old ugly creature's touch created a sickening feeling in Margaret who rushed out to her husband and asked whether she had been a long time away from him. Philip replied that she was quicker than usual. Very much puzzled and confused, Margaret replied lamely, "I seemed to have been away a long time. It was rather frightening, this difference in the point of view, leaving you so lonely."[14] This illustrates the common experience that the shortness or lengthiness of time depends upon the state of the mind of the person concerned. A happy state of mind makes people feel that time is short, and unhappy situations, and moments of anxiety and boredom make them feel that the duration is long.

By 1927 Priestley had come to know the Bergsonian view of Time, but was yet to know Dunne. He treats certain events in terms of Bergsonian psychological time. This fact is noticeable in the description of Margaret's state of mind while meeting the bed-ridden Sir Roderick who enquired whether Philip and she were husband and wife. She forgot her present uneasy relation with Philip, and at once a hundred happy little things rushed to her mind:

> She thought of that (her marriage), and then innumerable little pictures flashed across her mind: the two of them dining together that night at the *Gare de Lyon*; then going through the dust and faerie of Province; the tiny flat in Doughty street, with Philip painting the fire-place; the Hampstead house and Betty in the garden.[15]

Thus in flashback her past begins to expand and impinge upon her present moment in the Bergsonian way. A host of memories of her past made her present happy and meaningful.

On one occasion in the novel Time seems to stop. Philip was locked in a fight with the drunken Morgan. Penderel, in the grip of anxiety for the safety of his friend, was waiting in the hall with bated breath at the peak of that dangerous fight. Then he felt totally withdrawn from the actuality of the moment, and the state of his mind is expressed by the novelist in this way: "Time stood still for Penderel, waiting there in the hall."[16]

The description of what went on in the mind of Penderel just a few moments before his death at the fatal fight with Saul, a maniac, is proof that Priestley had begun addressing himself to the understanding of the function of consciousness at different levels and in different dimensions of Time. How Penderel's unconscious follows its own time is vividly shown:

> And all the while his mind, escaping from this shameful nightmare of stench and blood and pain, went darting back to queer memories and flashing along the edge of

> vivid little dreams; and once more he was lying in the long cool grass near the playing-field wall, or listening to Jim and Tom Ranger, outside a tent, a glimmer of starlight there, or standing under the blossom at Gurthstead; and oddly mingling with these memories were thoughts that came and went like swallows, thoughts of dusk and glitter of town at early evening, quiet pipes in the nights, the loud Jolly orchestra and the brightening curtain, that little place up five flights of stairs, Gladys laughing at him, brave eyes meeting his through a door suddenly opened. They were so long, so long swaying there in the dark, there was a time for a whole shadow show of life.[17]

A whole life, a whole shadow show of life, flashes by and is caught by Penderel's consciousness, in a few moments; years were telescoped into minutes and seconds; the barriers of Time like past and present vanished; it was all a timeless experience in the depth of Penderel's consciousness.

This examination of the novel bears out that Priestley was already seized of the Time mystery and was in the process of developing into a Time-writer, and had begun trying to present his ideas and convictions about Time in creative writing. But between 1927 and 1929 he produced no work with the Time element as a recurring idea, perhaps, because he was fully occupied with *Farthing Hall* (in collaboration with Hugh Walpole) and some critical works. Then came *The Good Companions.*

The Good Companions (1929), a voluminous picaresque novel, was meant to be a long happy daydream which would give Priestley a holiday from the tragic circumstances of his life and the resultant stress and strain. The novel became a fantastic success overnight.

Though the novel is a kind of escapist romance, it is not spoilt by false emotion or sentimental stuff; it is an escape from the world of dull dry reality into an enchanted world of freedom and adventure. 'The Dinky Doo', a touring company of ten entertainers, which had become a stranded concert party, became *The Good Companions* when it was joined by three fugitives—Jess Oakroyd, Miss Elizabeth Trant and Inigo Jollifant.

The novel does not exhibit a marked interest in the mystery of Time but Time as a buzzing bee in Priestley's bonnet peeps at places. There are two scenes where emotionally charged moments lift the characters out of clock time, though for a short spell. One is the love scene in which Mr. Bert Dulver, a hotel manager, proposes to Miss Elsie Longstaff, a singer and dancer of the troupe, and enquires whether she would give up her stage career to get married. Elsie expresses her consent by kissing him in a rapture. Bert Dulver's mind passes through an ecstatic state. It throws off in that single moment all the sordid and miserable past, and envisions a delightful and a colourful future; passing time is dethroned for a while. Dulver's timeless experience is described thus:

> Into that kiss went a whole captured ecstatic vision of the future and a glorious farewell to cheap lodgings, bad meals, old clothes, cramped dressing-rooms, bored audiences, and long Sundays in the trains.[18]

The other occasion concerns Inigo, another lover, who also experienced a timeless state of mind. It is a short love scene in which Inigo wishes Susie, with all ardour, many happy returns of the day on the latter's twenty first birthday, and in turn, she puts her arms about his neck and kisses him warmly, all in a flash. The author describes Inigo's timeless experience:

> For a minute or two he held her there. No, not for a minute or two. These were not minutes, to be briskly ticked away by the marble clock on the mantelpiece and then lost for ever; the world of Time was below, wrecked, a darkening ruin, forgotten; he had burst through into that enchanted upper air where suns and moons rise, stand still, and fall at the least whisper of the spirit.[19]

This kind of ecstatic experience, a thing to be felt by the spirit outside passing time, which here Inigo passes through, foreshadows the moments of timeless experience that Gregory (*Bright Day*), Ravenstreet (*The Magicians*), Richard (*Lost Empires*) and others in Priestley's later novels experience.

During the two years between 1929 and 1931 when Priestley wrote *The Town of Mayor Miraucourt* and *Angel Payment* Time slipped back in his mind. Then came *Faraway.*

Faraway (1931) is a definite advance over the three novels already discussed so far as Priestley's contemplation about Time is concerned. This novel is in the tradition of the adventure story. The plot is simple. It concerns the chain of adventures on the part of William Dursley, a forty year old bachelor, Commander Ivybridge and his friend Ramsbottom, an American businessman, who together embark upon discovering Faraway, an unknown island in the South Seas, which William's uncle Baldwin has described as a place with large quantities of pitchblende, the ore from which can be drawn uranium, the source of radium. After months of suffering, privation and disappointment the adventurists discovered Faraway, an island with rocks and thorns. After a number of ups and downs William and his friends found, and lost and found again their El Dorado. Besides containing various Time references as the earlier three novels of this early period do, *Faraway* gives a proof of Priestley's first attempt at interpreting life and events in the light of Dunne's Serial theory expounded in *An Experiment with Time,* of which he was one of the early reviewers. The novel has certain situations which foreshadow the emergence of Priestley as a writer of multiple Time in the late 1930's. A few examples are examined here.

William, sitting with the Commander Ivybridge and Ramsbottom in the smoking Room of the Lugmouth Hotel, discussing with them the proposed trip to the South Seas, suddenly felt that he had known them before. He asked himself whether he had dreamt about them, had caught a glimpse of the future in a dream; he was puzzled. Then follows the passage describing his confused state of mind and then a mysterious feeling:

> Perhaps he had talked to the commander and listened to Ramsbottom many a time before. And the island itself, was that really new? ....Had they all three been there already? ....But then something occurred that turned his backbone into a fiddle-string and brought a huge

> spectral hand to pluck it. 'The three of them sitting on a rock, very hard, hot, jagged, talking earnestly'. It had happened somewhere, and now he remembered it.... The hand plucked the fiddle-string again; his bones melted; his flesh crept; and he stood for a moment in a world of ghosts, in which Time merely juggled with diaphanous curtains and dissolving views.[20]

Here Priestley is definitely turning the Dunnian serialism into fictional art. William had a prevision of what was going to happen. First, he had a dim vision of the future event, and then 'something' inexplicable happened: he ceased to be in the objective world of clock time; saw the future through the diaphanous curtains of Time; his mind transcended the conscious level, and the unconscious, which has its own time, started functioning. In Dunne's idiom, William's Observer Two in Time Two caught a glimpse of the future. He wandered into a new time, a new dimension. This is certainly a future part of the eternal 'Now' experienced by William's Time Two self. William's premonition, preceded by something creeping through his blood, comes true with the discovery of Faraway, a treasure trove. William's experience of Time, as grasped by his consciousness, anticipates Ravenstreet's (*The Magicians*) efforts to understand the conflict between his younger self in Time Two and the older self in Time One and also Tom's (*It's an Old Country*) puzzle over the Helga-time, the time he spent with Helga, a bewitching woman he was infatuated with for days.

Contrary to William's prevision of a future event caught by his Observer Two in Time Two, Observer Two of Ramsbottom travelled backward in time by two decades under the yogic influence of the Old Russian nature man. The account of the Russian man's magical powers and their effect on Ramsbottom who was transported out of passing time into his past, another dimension of Time, is a proof that by 1932 Priestley was thoroughly acquainted with mystical and magical powers practised by Oriental Yogis. The Russian nature man is a precursor of the three magicians of *The Magicians,* the Old Man on the blue mountain (*Saturn Over the Water*) and

Dr. Firmus (*It's an Old Country*). The Old Russian nature man asked Ramsbottom to think of any one he knew well so that he would make that person appear before him. Ramsbottom wished to talk to Maggie Armitage, his sweetheart, whom he had not seen for twenty years since his holidays at Blackpoal. The old man brought his nose close to Ramsbottom, stared and stared, and told him to wait there for a minute or two and went away; the American businessman fell into a trance. There came to him his Maggie as if just off Centre Pier, Blackpoal; she put her arms round his neck and her cheeks against his, just as she had done many times before; then led him to the pool to sit by; they enquired of each other's life. Ramsbottom ends the account of the Maggie affair with the following words:

> Then all of a sudden—and Ah remember it as plain as plain can be—Ah gave a sort O' shiver. No waking up or anything like that, just a sort O' little shiver....[21]

Here either Maggie was removed from the past to the present or Ramsbottom was shifted from the present to the past. The shifting of the time-dimension, again, is operated in a typical way: Ramsbottom feels a 'shiver'. The mysterious experience of a 'shiver', already pointed out in earlier novels, precedes the change of dimension. It is clearly seen that Priestley had begun thinking seriously about consciousness vis-a-vis Time: he felt that consciousness is continuous through dimension after dimension, and that the change of consciousness from one level to another involved a change of time-dimension. The change of consciousness from one level to another in case of Ramsbottom, effected under magical and yogic powers,—from the conscious to the unconscious or, in Dunne's language, from Time One to Time Two—is shown as being bound up with Time in different orders.

One more occasion highlights the multidimensionality of Time and the continuity of consciousness connecting the inner world and the outer world of man. William, a contemplative and introvert type, was sailing on the waters of the Pacific, musing over the objective world of nature and the inner world of his mind. The following passage traces the movement of his consciousness backwards and forwards in time:

> He would go back and back into the past, feel again the sting of a cold morning on his cheeks as he ran from Ivy Lodge to the Grammar school, catch the smell of the cut grass in the old cricket field down by the river, wander into a rich dark Christmas of thirty years ago, find himself drowsing by his mother's side in some cavernous railway carriage of the remotest ages, go running and prattling among huge smiling ghosts.... It seemed to him that he had always been hurrying through the present to dive into the glorious future....[22]

William's distant past as well as immediate past thronged back to his mind. Just as Priestley's later characters like Ravenstreet, Gregory and Richard Herncastle feel that their past comes curving back to them, William too passes through the same kind of experience showing that the past is never dead, that it is in its own time and brought back alive by consciousness. There is no triggering agent of memory like *madeleine* in Proust which brings to the fore the 'essences' lying deep in the well of memory. All this comes to William automatically; he begins to see life in a timeless order into which past, present and future have melted. While William's Time-One self is observing the present, his Time-Two self is reliving the past and leaping into the future.

William's thinking about what happens to the spirit of man after death is Priestley's own thinking. William does not agree with Ramsbottom's thinking that Uncle Baldwin's life had been snuffed out. He feels in his bones that nothing of the past is dead and gone and that his uncle is carrying on somewhere else. A later Priestleyan character would have said that the old uncle was out of passing time and carrying on in a different dimension, a different order of existence unknown to those living in passing time.

Besides containing the Dunnian theory of Time and some concepts and ideas like *ESP* concerning the relation between Time and consciousness which were further developed in the Time-plays and fictional works of the later phases, *Faraway* involves circularity, a Time-loop. The story begins on one evening in Ivy Lodge, William's house in Buntingham, where William and his friend Greenlaw are playing chess. It ends after two years, again with the same game of chess in the same room in the same house on an evening. This Time-loop is similar to the one in *The Good Companions* already discussed.

The foregoing discussion of Time references clearly establishes that Priestley was obsessed, even in this early period, with the mystery of Time. These Time references, and the Dunnian serialism which finds its first manifestation in *Faraway,* place Priestley on the threshold of a development into a non-Bergsonian Time-writer, a writer of multiple Time.

NOTES

1. J.B. Priestley, *Man and Time,* p. 284.
2. John Atkins, *J.B. Priestley,* p. 164.
3. J.B. Priestley, *Margin Released,* p. 177.
4. John Atkins, *J.B. Priestley,* p. 53.
5. *Adam in Moonshine* (London: William Heinemann Ltd., Popular edition 1952), pp. 188-89.
6. *Ibid.*, p. 102.
7. *Ibid.*, pp. 154-55.
8. *Ibid.*, p. 172.
9. Susan Cooper, *J.B. Priestley,* p. 42.
10. *Ibid.*, p. 47.
11. *Benighted* (London: Heinemann Ltd., 1951), p. 50.
12. *Ibid.*, p. 110.
13. *Ibid.*
14. *Ibid.*, p. 56.
15. *Ibid.*, p. 206.
16. *Ibid.*, p. 232.
17. *Ibid.*, pp. 240-41.
18. *The Good Companions* (London: William Heinemann Ltd., rpt. Nov. 1933), p. 488.
19. *Ibid.*, p. 553.
20. *Faraway* (London: William Heinemann Ltd., cheap edition 1950), pp. 109-10.
21. *Ibid.*, p. 289.
22. *Ibid.*, p. 441.

4

Middle Phase: Multi-vision of Time

If the early phase is Priestley's advent into the world of Time-literature, the middle phase is a plunge right into the heart of it with gusto, exuberance, and versatility. This phase was spread over twenty years, from 1932 to 1953, and saw the production of the major proportion of Priestley's Time-works. This was a period of intense preoccupation with Time for Priestley. The period can be divided into two parts: Part-I and Part-II. The work of the early thirties and the early forties can be grouped under Part-I and those of the late forties and one fictional work of the fifties under Part-II.

The Part-I period of this middle phase is marked by Priestley's passion for experimenting with ideas, form and technique; it is a period of fecund prolificacy and great originality. In his forties—Priestley approvingly quoted Jung's opinion regarding the forties of a writer as being the best period in his life—he emerged as a full-fledged Time-writer with the Time theories making up the panoply of his literary armour. During the thirties, there was a general fascination for Time in vogue among writers; all the major writers did say something or other about the subject in their works. Priestley could not have been an exception to this trend.

In fact, he was far ahead of his contemporaries in respect of using Time theories for creative purposes. Besides Dunne's serialism theory of Time and the Ouspenskian one of Eternal Recurrence, which have been critically examined in Chapter I, there were other theories and concepts of Time like the Jungian unconscious and *ESP* which influenced Priestley's writing. He was impressed by H.F. Saltmarsh's idea of precognition and consciousness discussed in the book *Foreknowledge* (1938) and also by Du Prel's theory of Extra-Sensory-Perception. He used these theories and concepts in his Time-works in one way or another, as they caught his creative imagination and lighted up the dim and dark areas of his understanding of time and reality. Except for *Let the People Sing,* a novel, the Time-works of this period are all plays. The contribution of these plays to the English stage is unique. They broke the rigid convention of the naturalistic drama. John Atkins's words give a measure of Priestley's contribution to the drama of this period when he speaks of him as one "who tried to rouse English drama during a very slack period, who experimented in both manner and content...."[1] They are not mere exercises in the art of entertaining but dramatic expressions of the writer's inner life as a man. Likewise, G.L. Evans observes, "These plays form one of the very few corporate bodies of dramatic writing, certainly in this country, in this century."[2]

The thirteen plays representing the first part of the middle phase of Priestley's development as a Time-writer are discussed here.

Dangerous Corner (1932) was Priestley's first independently written play. Though Priestley calls it "mere an ingenious box of tricks",[3] he took professional pride in it. The play proved his ability beyond doubt and established his place firmly in the English theatre. *Dangerous Corner* is a theatrical rendering of the idea of circularity of Time, the end returning to the beginning, by splitting linear time into two in order to show what might have happened, an idea which always fascinated Priestley.

John Agate was the first critic to express unreserved praise for the brilliant technique of the play. He wrote, "If this is not a brilliant device, I do not grasp the meaning of either word...."[4] A.V. Cookman writes, "it is perhaps the most ingenious play ever put together."[5] All critics are unanimous on the score of the play's originality of technique.

A group of 'nice easy-going people'—Robert and his wife Freda, Gordon and his wife Betty, Stanton and Miss Mockridge—are attending a party, one evening, in Robert's house. The title of the radio play "The Sleeping Dog" becomes a subject of discussion among them. They are convinced that truth is the 'sleeping dog' and that the husband in the play comes to grief because he insists on disturbing the sleeping dog, that is, truth. In the opinion of Stanton and Freda it is dangerous to know the truth and it is always safe to avoid it, but Robert, a staunch upholder of truth, who holds that truth must be revealed no matter what the consequences, opposes it.

The distinction of the play lies in the use of the split-time device. The chiming of Martin's musical cigarette box divides clock-time into two; the present is replaced by the past; the real makes room for the possible, a might-have-been. The action of the play on a double plane of time is handled in masterly fashion. Once the music of the cigarette box, a sinister *deux ex machina* triggers off a switch from the real to the might-have-been, excitement and tension go on building up almost to the end of the play. The might-have-been part of the play goes on exposing the evil motives and dark deeds of the characters. Freda and Olwen give different versions of when they saw Martin's box in his house; Robert grows suspicious that his wife and Olwen are concealing something from him. Robert's ruthless enquiry opens up a Pandora's box; each one of them is found to be guilty and hypocritical and unscrupulous. Robert too fails to come off unscathed. The dark world lying deep in them is brought into the day-light: Freda had loved Martin, the attractive but quixotic brother of her husband Robert, even before her marriage with the latter and her relation with him had ended only with his death; and the musical cigarette box was a gift she had made to Martin; Gordon, Freda's brother, had homosexual relations with the charming Martin; Betty, unloved by her husband Gordon, had illicit relations with Stanton; Olwen admires and loves Robert but the latter loves Betty, the pretty wife of his brother-in-law. Stanton is found to be a culprit; he stole the money and played the nasty game of putting up one brother against the other. It is revealed that

Olwen, in self-defence, had turned the revolver held by Martin towards him when he was attempting to outrage her modesty, being dead drunk and beastly, and the revolver had gone off and killed Martin. People thought, and even the police inquest concluded, that Martin had killed himself but now Robert's cross-examination brings out the truth.

Robert, the central character, finds his cozy world crack up and a hell break loose all around him; he stands deeply disillusioned at the reversal of everything. The revelation that the pretty girl Betty, whom he thought to be a paragon of virtue, but was 'a greedy little cat on the tiles', proves the most unkindest cut of all for him. Now the truth is too strong for Robert to face, and in despair he shoots himself dead.

Priestley adroitly employs the chiming of the musical cigarette box as a point where single track clock-time splits into the actual and the possible. The split-time device helps the playwright concentrate on the inner world of his characters. It is shown, as though in a magic scene, how clock-time begins to recede making room for inner time. The way the action is manipulated to move at the level of mind, in the dimension of psychological time, testifies to the fact that even in his first play Priestley had mastered the art of handling dramatic action in different time-dimensions. The movement of time back and forth adds to the depth of Priestley's dramatic revelation of the mystery in human relations and affairs.

The might-have-been with its magical atmosphere is conjured up in such masterly fashion that it is hard to distinguish the real and the possile. After the brilliant success of this play, with the novelty of 'split-time' device, Priestley embarked upon treating the Time theme against the backdrop of Time Theories. His first attempt in that direction was *Eden End*.

Eden End (1934) was Priestley's first play to take Time seriously. It is certainly a step farther than *Dangerous Corner* which merely uses the split-time technique in a novel way. The Dunnian Serial Time is at the background of this play which shows that though the outward pattern of human life is changed by passing time the essential quality of what men are within remains unaffected and unchanged in spite of 'temporal succession'.

Priestley regarded this play as his most favourite one, and said, "The illusory pursuit of happiness is its chief theme."[6] The theme is treated against the backdrop of Serial Time theory which holds that Time destroys nothing and only moves us from one peep-hole to another and that our ordinary self, Observer One, is observing and experiencing in passing time, while the inner self, Observer two, is moving in Time two, which is a timeless dimension.

Dr. Kirby, a medical practitioner at Marthinbro, a Yorkshire village, is a widower. Stella and Lilian are sisters and Wilfred is their brother. Stella, the elder sister, comes back home after eight years of her reckless pursuit of an ambition to become a famour actress which she could not realise. Because of her impulsive act of abruptly leaving home she caused the death of her mother and ruined the happiness of the Kirby family. Though she has married an Australian comic actor called Charles Appleby they have not got along together; they are living separately. Lilian, who has been keeping the house and looking after her father and brother since her mother's death, holds no good opinion of her 'reckless' and 'selfish' sister and is perturbed at the unexpected arrival of Stella. But Dr. Kirby received his prodigal daughter warmly. When Lilian comes to know that Stella has begun courting Farrant whose love she once turned down and whom now she (Lilian) loves and wants to marry, she secretly writes to Stella's husband to come down, and he arrives and Stella is left with no choice but to leave the place.

The play is remarkable for the haunting atmosphere of loss and melancholy due to flashbacks of the past. Though Time is not a major problem as in *Time and the Conways* and *I Have Been Here Before,* it is felt as an ever-present mystery. Sarah, the old maid-servant, also expresses her sense of the ever-present past, of the time when the children of the family were smiling kids. The lives of the characters are shown at a number of places outside the purview of chronological time. From the raised platform of the past there comes a light, as it were, and focuses on the present of the characters; a cumulative effect of their life fusing the past and the present into one strikes as a rare quality of this play. There is an arresting sad-sweet atmosphere of mutability but the fact of 'something' being there which is not bound and cribbed by linear time is triumphantly established. Although the play is mainly about what happens to Stella, it also effectively focuses on what changes in passing time and what it is that remains intact and changeless. The changeable and the changeless—the mutable and the immutable—are fused to create an awareness of the ambivalent nature of existence. The essential quality of life is shown in a timeless dimension and the rare timeless moments constitute the very soul of the play.

Stella, who regrets that the time gone cannot come back and that she will never see herself thirty again and her hair is turning grey, gets excited and feels young again when she sees the old china castle intact, while all other things including human relations are breaking up. The old little curio piece tolls her back to her happy childhood time.

To Sarah, a septuagenarian, nothing ever perishes, everything is simply there before her. The sight of the fancy costume Stella had put on when she acted years ago in the Town Hall at Martinbro makes this old soul see again the 'grand baby, a fine little lass' Stella was then. The fancy dress brings back to Stella the glorious moment when she had received a loud clapping from the audience, and a box of chocolates from fat old Burton. Stella never lets go an opportunity to relive the memorable moments of her past. Her intense emotional response to the past which is vibrantly felt within her finds expression in the following outburst:

> .... But Eden Moor and Eden End looked just the same. And, coming up, there was a lovely deep rich autumn smell—smoke and dead leaves and the moors all mixed up and I was absolutely drowned in it and I didn't seem to have been away at all. Millions of smells, mostly beastly, that I've smelt these last eight or nine years were completely washed out. Nothing had really happened. I might have only been in to Martinbro for the day. You

were still at school, Wilfred. You'd only just left, Lilian, and you'd still two long plaits....[7]

Nothing is obliterated by Time; all things and events exist in another time. Stella's words prove that the timeless quality of reality is grasped not by the ordinary conscious self in passing time but by the inner observer, Observer Two, in Time Two in Dunne's language. This is not different possibly from Eliot's own view of Time: "Only through time time is conquered."[8]

The past of the Kirby family is caught through flashbacks; the sisters and brother remember certain funny incidents and experiences of their childhood. In a romantic and poetic mood Stella reminisces about her past experiences with her old lover Farrant with whom she wants to have a free relation neither bound by Time nor shackled by custom. She and Farrant being alone in a cozy little room, lost in the moorland rain, she feels that time has stopped for them. She says to Farrant, "Just be quiet. Trying to make time stand still for us. It flies at a terrible speed really, Geoffrey."[9] Stella is aware of two kinds of Time, passing time which flies at a gallopping speed, and non-passing time which is a richer experience, belonging as it does to the inner domain of the spirit. She wants to have the maximum of a rich timeless experience out of intense and powerful moments when the human spirit is totally free from the shackless of clock time.

Dunne's serialism of Time is expressed in Dr. Kirby's view that the future is always there in its own time, just as the past is always there in its own time. Consider the following dialogue:

Dr. Kirby: .... There's a better world coming, Stella—cleaner, saner, happier.

We've only to turn a corner and it's there.

I don't suppose I shall turn it, but, you will....

Stella (sitting at his feet): It is a muddle, isn't it?

Dr. Kirby (sipping his drink): Yes, and it's mostly our own fault.

> Yet it isn't either. Have you noticed—or are you too young yet—how one part of us doesn't seem to be responsible for our own character and simply suffers because we have that character? You see yourself being yourself, behaving in the old familiar way, and though you may pay and suffer, the real you, the one that watches, does not seem to be responsible.[10]

Two things clearly emerge out of what is said here by Dr. Kirby. While the conscious self in each one of us is observing and experiencing in passing time, the unconscious self in us is observing the conscious self.

In Dunnian language, Observer One in Time One is being observed by Observer Two in Time Two, because the latter has a wider length of Time One. The second thing is that the higher unconscious self-Observer Two—is a detached observer. "Behind the personality which pays and suffers there is an uncommitted self which watches us. The inner observer in us is a sort of Stoic who remains unaffected by the sea of troubles to which our shadow personalities are heir."[11] Notwithstanding the factor of her career being a 'dismal failure' and her sufferings flowing from it, Stella endures everything with an unruffled philosophic fortitude as does her father, because like him she is aware of the dual order of living, life in passing time and life in a timeless dimension.

Thus it is clearly shown that *Eden End* has a deep concern with the nature of reality and Time and it is the first of Priestley's plays to have, at the background, the Dunnian Serial Time, though it does not fully exploit the theory as *Time and the Conways* and *Johnson Over Jordan* do. This play gave Priestley an impetus to move decidedly towards treating the Time theme in a variety of ways.

Time and the Conways (1937) is Priestley's first serious and brave attempt to put the Time problem in drama. Also it is his first bold experiment in breaking away from the naturalistic tradition of the English prose drama; here the action is put into a philosophical frame-work without discarding the naturalistic background. The Dunnian Serial Time helps Priestley dramatise here his firm belief that if men take a long view instead of a short view of Time, they will not fret and fume at their fate.

Act One presents the 'cozy and happy circle' of the Conways and their friends gathered in the Conway house to celebrate the twenty-first birthday of Kay Conway. Mrs. Conway is proud of her two sons and four daughters who promise to go far. They enjoy the happy get-together in a gay atmosphere. The charade in which most of them took part is over, all of them have had drinks and are ready for Mrs. Conway's German song. Kay is in her 'inspired' moods, 'bursting with all kinds of feelings and thoughts and impressions'; she leaves the hall, goes into the room, walks up to the window and opens the curtains. Sitting still on the window-seat, she begins to listen to her mother singing Schumann; staring not at but into something, she begins to sail forward in Time as the sound of music rises in pitch. Act II is all of a vision of the sad future of the Conways as seen through the eyes of Kay.

Kay's Observer Two leaps from 1919 to 1937, to the fortieth birthday of Kay. The act shows a sad change; the Conways have fallen into 'a vale of tears'. Time's sickle has played havoc with their lives. It is a terrible shift of scene, from pleasure to pain, from hope to despair, from light to darkness. Carol, the sweet-natured girl with a bubbling zest for life, has gone into her grave; Madge, the Fabian revolutionary, who wanted to establish a 'new Jerusalem in England', has soured into a mercenary schoolmistress; Hazel, a golden young creature, who had hoped to marry a tall and handsome man and wanted to travel all over the world with her husband, is sadly wedded to a short, unimpressive and aggressive businessman called Ernest Beevers; Kay, who wanted to become a famous novelist who would write to please herself but not silly people, has become a journalist writing worthless things for money; Robin, once a handsome young man who wanted to settle down, after demobilisation, as an industrialist, has made a mess of his life—he is estranged from his wife Joan and has taken too much to drinking. Alan is the only character in the play that is not changed by Time; he is going on, in all his wisdom of life and Time, working as a clerk in the town municipal office. Mrs. Conway, who has prodigally spent her husband's money, is facing a financial crisis. The meeting ends in a big fiasco. Kay is shocked at what Time has made of them all. Then she is consoled by Alan, who explains the true nature of Time.

Act III shifts back to the birthday celebration in Act I; Kay slowly comes out of her dreaming, prophetic vision, in which she saw what would happen nearly twenty years later. Act III is a continuation of Act I, but everything of it is seen in a different light, because of the irony born of illusion and reality. It is full of irony and pathos due to Kay's foreknowledge of the future through her vision.

The play moves in a double dimension of Time, at the naturalistic level of linear time in Act I and Act III and at the preternatural level of the future through Kay's eyes in Act II. Kay's vision is a leap twenty years forward into another reality and another time, and most of the action in Act II takes place beyond the present existence of the Conways and outside the action of the play in linear time. Kay sees the reality behind the illusory life of the Conways in passing time. She has before her a clear picture of the vast change the Conway family will undergo. But she herself does not stand altogether outside the world of change over twenty years as found in Act II. Though involved in the action projected by her prophetic dreaming self, as Observer Two, she yet stands outside that world of vision as well as beyond day-to-day existence. In Dunne's idiom, it is her Observer Two in Time Two that enables her to 'see into future', outside passing time.

Discussing how advantageously Priestley has exploited the Dunnian idea in this play Susan Cooper observes. "The peculiar vividness with which Priestley manages to convey this idea in *Time and the Conways* comes from the way in which, by switching his time-scheme from past to present and back to past again, he turns his audience during the third act into a kind of composite Observer Two."[12] Priestley succeeds in drawing the attention of the audience to the dramatic irony visible in all human activities; men build castles in the air, make plans and preparations for future but they may end up in dismal failure. The Conways in Act III are a gay lot projecting their dreams to the stars. As the audience have had a foreknowledge, through Kay's vision, of the reversal of fortune that is going to befall the Conways twenty years later, everything said and done by the characters in Act III is taken by them in the light of dramatic irony. The harsh reality of future in Act II showing the careworn and crest-fallen Conways, battered and broken in spirit, throws up a sharp contrast to the rosy world of colourful dreams and hopes in which the Conways are presented in Act III, which is a continuation of Act I, and the resultant dramatic irony creates a poignant pathos. The effective dramatic irony achieved by the play is due to the vantage ground of future time from where the lives of the characters are presented. How a strong pathetic effect is achieved by showing life outside passing time, in the Dunnian way, can be illustrated by citing some situations from the play. The strained relations between Robin and Joan which have reached breaking point, as shown in Act II, tinge the romantic courtship of the couple with poignant irony. The audience cannot have forgotten that Carol has remained just a sad memory when they hear Carol speak buoyantly: "The point is—to live. Never mind about money and positions and husbands with titles and rubbish—I'm going to live."[13] Madge, whose aim is to build a new and bright England, says in 1919 to Gerald warmly and happily, "This is the real me. Oh!—Gerald—in this New World we're going to build up now, men and women won't play a silly little game of cross-purposes any longer. They'll go forward together—sharing everything—."[14] The same person holds a diametrically opposite attitude in 1937; she is found to be an earth-bound, self-centered and money-minded neurotic spinster in her middle forties, declaring that this is her 'real life'. More shocking is the change Time has wrought in Mrs. Conway. Her rosy and cozy world of 1919, promising a marvellous time, 'one big happy family' of her children and lovely grand-children coming and meeting together on occasion as proud and happy Conways, has all gone sour. Nothing can give a more telling picture than the emotional "outburst of this 'Grannie'":

> .... All selfish—selfish. Because everything hasn't happened as you wanted it, turn on me—all my fault. You never really think about me. Don't try to see things for a moment from my point of view. When you were children, I was so proud of you all, so confident that you would grow up to be wonderful creatures. I used to see myself at the age I am now, surrounded by you and your own children, so proud of you, so happy with you all, this house happier and gayer even than it was in the best of the old days. And now my life's gone by, and what's happened?[15]

None of the Conways except Alan know how to take life because they are ignorant of the true nature of Time. Time is not a devil in the universe, as Kay thinks, ticking men away to extinction, but one eternal whole—as Alan alone knows—moving them from one scene of life to another in its endless landscape which has been there ever-fixed and laid out; one part may be dark and the next bright; it is an unchangeable pattern.

As a writer of multiple Time, Priestley shows life multi-dimensionally, in past, present and future. There are references to the power of prevision at several places in the play. In the first Act Carol and Kay mention the foreknowledge their father had of his drowning; Kay feels a 'shiver' as soon as her Observer Two begins moving 'before and after' in Time. Kay's Observer Two in Time Two has a much wider length of Observer one's time; when her Observer Two is in 1937 giving her Observer One to know what is going to happen to the Conways in twenty years, the action suddenly moves back to 1919; and this time-shuttle keeps her Observer Two outside clock-time which alone keeps ticking by. Staring into the past, seeing those old Christmases and birthday parties—all this takes place in the Second Act, the realm of her Observer Two—Kay says to Alan, "Yes, I remembered, I saw all of us then, Myself, too, Oh, silly girl of nineteen nineteen! Oh, lucky girl!"[16] The playwright wants to show that, in reality, there are no divisions of Time such as past, present and future; Time is multi-dimensional; it is a mode of seeing life which is multi-dimensional. Thus Dunne's serialism of Time is remarkably presented in terms of dramatic art.

Allan is the one character in the play that has fully understood life because he has grasped the true nature of Time. To Kay's complaint that Time is a great devil in the universe, devouring everything, his wise reply is that Time is only a kind of dream and it "does not destroy anything. It merely moves us on—in this life—from one peep-hole to the next."[17] To Kay's lament that the happy young Conways have gone and gone for ever, Alan's answer is that none are dead and gone, they are real and existing in their own time and the whole landscape is still there, and they (his sister and himself) are seeing another bit of the view, which may be a bad bit. Alan's voice is only Priestley's voice when he says that half the trouble men suffer is due to their wrong conception of Time that it is ticking away their lives, and that this short view of Time makes them snatch and grab and hurt one another. He advises his sister to take a long view of Time—this is a view of eternity and immortality —and that alone is the right and noble way of understanding life.

Alan is a sage-like character who stands like a rock of firmness of purpose, unruffled in his wisdom of life through the right understanding of Time which comes to him first from Dunne's book and then from his own experience. His explanation of the true nature of Time has a simple philosophy of living and makes a lasting impact not only on Kay but also on the audience with its quietness and illumination. In support of his Time-philosophy Alan quotes William Blake's lines:

> .... Joy and woe are woven fine,
> A clothing for the soul divine,
>
> ------------------------------------
>
> ------------------------------------
>
> Man was made for joy and woe;
> And when we this rightly know,
> Safely through the world we go.[18]

The play translates, in terms of art, the dramatist's conviction that nothing in life is lost to Time; the good as well as bad moments, the sunny and stormy days, are always present there in their own time. Priestley's reply to some critics who find pessimism in this play is: "It was my intention here to challenge and combat pessimism, that deep underlying despair about life which I believe to be one of the evils of our age."[19] Indeed, contrary to the charge, the play is full of optimism; it is a call for zest for living because life is wonderful and worthliving. This is pointed out by Irene Hentschel's statement: "Although *Time and the Conways* has a sad and sometimes a harsh quality there is never any feeling of defeatism in the play."[20] Priestley's moralism in terms of Time-philosophy never compromises on the aesthetic values of the work. The greatest triumph of Priestley's art in this work is "the fact that what it has to say about time is embodied in the structure."[21] Priestley does not agree with the view which some critics hold that the reversal of the second and the third Acts is a trick, and answers:

> It cannot be too strongly emphasised that this play is not merely working a trick, by reversing the last two acts, but that its whole point and quality are contained in the third act, when we know so much more about the characters than they know themselves. If this is not understood and appreciated, then the play fails.[22]

The unique quality of this play lies in the fact that it turns Dunne's serialism into art: it powerfully brings out how thin and illusory is human life in unidimensional clock time in contrast to the one accumulated and lived in the whole stretch of one's living time—the past, the present and the future. This remarkable quality is pointed out by G.L. Evans: "This play is meaningful in the sense that it shows the disparity between the thin conscious life that is lived from moment to moment, and the accruing reality of life when it is viewed from the vantage point of the future."[23] If this play dramatises a future possibility and drives home the need to take a whole and balanced view of Life, *People at Sea* uses the remembrance of a bright and happy past to make the gloomy present sunny.

People at Sea (1937) is primarily a play of social and political ideas. Time enters the work because a metaphysical concern for man's life is an important element in it. The Dunnian Serial Time helps Priestley demonstrate that life's reality is not bound and conditioned by linear time. The action of the play takes placc in the veranda Café of a ship called the S.S. Zillah, carrying passengers to Central America. The ship, greatly damaged by a fire, has only twelve men including the crew who have survived the accident, and has been stranded in the midst of a dangerous sea. The characters are not full-blooded people. The playwright himself calls them "rather a shop-soiled lot". They represent certain attitudes and speak mostly for the writer.

From the point of view of what happens to the author's handling of the material under the influence of the Time-philosophy, only three characters deserve close reading. They are Valentine Avon, a well-known English novelist, Diana Lismore, a famous English actress, and Prof. Pawlet, an English Professor of Philosophy. Once Valentine and Diana were lovers and then went separate ways. A chance meeting here aboard the ship brings them together again; they understand each other only now; the realisation of their folly, after a gap of eight years, leads to reconciliation. Valentine has earned both money and fame by writing fairy tales of a 'little dream world', by amusing people with that false stuff. Now he is thirty-eight and has no satisfaction and peace within himself; he deeply feels that his writing is not authentic and his life is phoney. To forget his disappointment he has taken to excessive drinking. No less miserable and meaningless is the life of Diana, the glamorous actress in her later thirties, whose life has been full of pretensions. Unable to face the hard realities of existence, she seeks to escape into a world of pleasant sensations by swallowing dope. Valentine and Diana meet twice in the play. If the first meeting shows the nostalgia of the lovers about their romantic past and a sense of loss, the second meeting enables them to see themselves 'really' in a timeless dimension. Consider their talk at the first meeting:

Diana: The ship all charred and deserted. My maid leaving me to drown. You here. I really am what you said you were, a stranger here...(Pause, looking at him intently, then suddenly) Oh—Val—you and I—a long wall somewhere—wistaria in the rain—great bunches of wet blossoms. They were so close, so vivid, I could have put out my hand and touched them. Where was that, Val? Can you remember?

Valentine (hesitating): No.... Let's see....

Diana: It doesn't matter. It's all dead and gone....
Youth.... All dead and gone.[24]

These very lovers who think that everything of their past is dead and gone realise at the second meeting that there is something in them which has not been changed by Time, and which is for ever enduring. The following dialogue between them clearly brings out this point:

Diana: We're a bright pair. We weren't like that—Before—were we?

Valentine: No, only half-way—or rather more than half-way—towards what we are now. But it was all waiting for us. You wanted more and more sensations. I was afraid of reality, afraid of my own sober thoughts.

Diana: It's terrible when you suddenly wake up and See how much you must have changed. And yet—Inside—you feel the same....[25]

At last the two lovers realise that their misconception of life was due to their wrong view of Time. Their life in passing time had made them blind to the reality of life which is timeless. Now they arrive at the truth that the illusion of change brought about by passing time in outward life can no longer deprive them of the enduring joy of existence in a timeless dimension, and their 'inside' is not at all affected by clock time. It is a discovery of their 'real self' outside passing time, and then they are reconciled and decide to marry.

It is hard to accept G.L. Evan's remark on the scene of reunion of the lovers: "In a totally unconvincing scene these two re-discover one another."[26] Why should it be taken as unconvincing when the two lovers put an end to their meaningless living in passing time by saying good-bye to brain-fuddling stuff—dope and alcohol—and decide to begin their life anew with a full conviction that their happy and meaningful past has not deserted them after all?

Prof. Pawlet's ideas are Priestley's own when he speaks of the futility in pursuing reason in quest of 'reality'. This philosopher's conversion, after the crisis by fire, from positivism to a kind of Oriental mysticism runs parallel to change of outlook on the part of Valentine and Diana. He refers to the Dunnian theory of life and Time. His explanation of the Dunnian serialism of Time reminds Priestley's readers of what Alan speaks of it in *Time and the Conways.* The Dunnian view of Time that life is multi-dimensional and that nothing is destroyed by Time finds a convincing artistic expression through dramatic action in the lives of Valentine and Diana. But serialism of Time is not dramatised in the case of Prof. Pawlet. It merely finds a symbolic expression when the professor gives up his writing of the proposed ambitious book on reasoning when the ship 'Orsata' arrives to rescue the stranded team because now he has evidence that life's mystery defies reasoning and he tears the manuscript of the work to pieces.

Though Priestley's overt intention here, as in *Time and the Conways,* is not to transmute Dunne's theory into art, the theory certainly remains as a guiding motif at the background of the work.

In the mid-thirties Priestley's imagination was hooked on Ouspensky's Eternal Recurrence which inspired him to write works like *I Have Been Here Before,* a notable departure from Dunne.

I Have Been Here Before (1937) is the only one of Priestley's Time plays which is actually concerned with Time as a subject of dramatic treatment. It is based on Ouspensky's theory of Recurrence and Intervention discussed in *A New*

Model of the Universe. The Ouspenskian theory has much in common with the Hindu reincarnation theory so far as it believes in the rising and sinking of individual lives in the scale of their existence according to their moral actions. The Reincarnation theory is closely connected with the Karma doctrine which allows, as does Ouspensky's, ample scope for changing one's destiny through good and noble actions. Although Priestley admits that the Reincarnation theory is more attractive and more plausible than the theory of Recurrence, he says that reincarnation has nothing to do with this play. In spite of Priestley's ruling out that there was anything to do with reincarnation, he came across people who enjoyed this play as "a play about reincarnation".[27]

Priestley shows a remarkable originality in turning the Ouspenskian Time theory, which is highly intellectual stuff, into a very fine play. The dramatic action is sustained not merely by its basic thought but by a deep rich vein of feeling and a haunting atmosphere in which the story is enveloped. Priestley explains why he wrote the play: "I wanted to make dramatic use of the familiar but always eerie feeling that we have been actors in a certain scene before, of the sense, known to most of us though not to all, of *deja vu*. But what I wanted more than that was to present dramatically a kind of everyman of my own generation."[28] This Everyman is Walter Ormund, the central character, who represents early on in the play the deep distrust of life felt by the Playwright's generation but eventually comes to believe at last that the universe is not hostile or indifferent to his deepest needs.

The play originates from an experiment with Time conducted by Gortler, a German professor, "a kind of experimentalist Yogi."[29] Gortler, whose ambitious studies of the universe and life include the human mind and consciousness, has taken up exploring into the mystery and meaning of Time, on the lines of the Ouspenskian theory of eternal Recurrence and Intervention, with a view to understanding the 'how and why' of human existence. He is a rare personality. This Jewish scholar, and refugee, has lost everything except his love of knowledge and faith in life. He is experimenting with his own experiences of dreams and consciousness in order to resolve the mystery of Time; he is visited by memories of the past cycles of his own life. He has recorded in a note-book the contents of the memories of past events in his own life and the lives of others. Believing as he does in Ouspensky's theory that what has happened before will happen again and again, that is, Time is eternal and recurrent, he is going to verify the theory experientially. He is convinced of the continuity of his consciousness in life after life, through eternal Time, which tells him that he has been an exile in past cycles of his life. He comes to a moorland inn in North Yorkshire called the Black Bull Inn, run by an old man named Sam Shipley and his daughter Mrs. Pratt, a widow, in order to verify the findings of his experiment. At first he thinks that he has come to the place in the wrong year, and goes away only to return to the inn with the conviction that it is the right and correct place. And now begins the real drama. Gortler first meets Oliver Farrant, the headmaster of a school at Lamberton, who is resting in this country inn as advised by his doctor, and then Ormund Walter, a business tycoon and his wife Janet, a young and attractive woman, who also come to the same place for a holiday. The Ormunds, a childless unhappy couple, are deeply disappointed in life; Walter, being much older than his young wife, knows that she is out of love with him; frequent quarrels between them have driven them desparate and gloomy. Both have come to this country 'rest house' in the hope that their overstrained relations will improve in the quiet and peaceful atmosphere of the moorland area; but here also they are restless souls.

Gortler recognises Oliver and Janet whom he has met in earlier lives; Walter is a stranger to him because he meets him only in this present life. Gortler alone knows the mutual attraction between Janet and Oliver whom he has seen in the same inn life after life. The lovers have a *deja vu* feeling that they have been here before but cannot know 'when and how'. Gortler knows that Walter, who feels haunted by the feeling that just round the corner there is going to be a sudden blotting out of everything, is fast moving towards an irresistable death-wish which is compounded all the more by the discovery of his wife's infatuation and flirting with Oliver, and that he has kept a revolver to kill himself with, as he has done in his earlier lives. When the relations of the lovers and the husband are getting tangled up and they are in a deep turmoil of anguish and perturbation as to how to find a way out, they wish to approach Gortler, a great Time-traveller, for guidance but he has already left the inn. Oliver and Janet get nervous because of the pricks of conscience but they are naturally moving back to what they were in their past lives. Janet is cocksure that their thickening tragic plot can be resolved only by Gortler who knows that all this affair has happened before. Torn between her duty to her husband and her love of Oliver, Janet is really in a tragic situation; her misery is no less painful than that of Walter. Janet's words addressed to Walter and others, when the situation is heading towards a 'no return point', speak of the mystery and complexity of life; "You know we're all equally bewildered. And there's something more—something that hasn't been accounted for yet—something that perhaps can never be explained—like so many things—."[30] Gortler is the only person who knows the 'truth', and luckily he comes back at that crucial moment to collect the note-book he has left behind in the room. Pressed by Sally and Walter he stays on and reveals the purpose of his visit to the inn: "I came to verify an experiment and, if possible, to make a further experiment."[31] He did know the love affair of Oliver and Janet and that it was going to happen in the inn again. This Time-traveller is fully satisfied that the 'Eternal Recurrence' of the love affair in this case has come true, and is now determined to try 'Intervention', the second aspect of Ouspensky's theory of Time. He recounts to Janet one of the memories of the past cycles of his life in which he found himself an exile living in London and the way he had to know of the self-destruction of a business magnate because of the elopement of his young and beautiful wife with a young man on Whitsuntide from a country inn where they were staying for a change—and this had led to the ruin of that businessman's business establishment and the lives of his employees. This makes Janet burst out emotionally, with an acute pain in her voice, "It was us he saw, Oliver, of course it was us."[32] Gortler's intervention saves the husband and the lovers. Though, much against her instinctive attraction towards her lover, Janet decides not to leave her husband, who, on listening to Gortler's words which give him the right awareness of life's reality, allows her to go away with her lover because he does not want to live on anybody's self-sacrifice. Walter decides not to destroy himself because he is thoroughly convinced, by the Professor's explanation of life's reality and Time's mystery, of the futility of finishing his earthly existence when he is bound to have endless existence as miserable as the present one, bound to the treadmill of Time over and over again. Thus Gortler succeeds in his experiment with regard to Ouspensky's theory of eternal recurrence and intervention. He saves not only the life of Walter and thereby the lives of those dependent upon his business, but he also saves Janet and Oliver from public condemnation and unhappy situation.

After the successful conclusion of his Time-experiment, Gortler is happy that Walter is "moving out on a new time-track, like a man who is suddenly born into a strange new World...."[33] Walter is spiritually a new-born man with none of the troubles and tensions, fears and suspicions, that had haunted his mind for twenty years. After the raging and tumult the sea is calm.

Walter Ormund, Everyman of the dramatist's generation, has something of Hamlet in him: a highly sensitive and contemplative introvert, troubled by doubts and fears and driven by a deep sense of betrayal to the brink of self-destruction. It is Gortler's Time-philosophy, put across to him convincingly, that saves Ormund. The long scene at the end of Act III ends with Gortler's converting 'this giant Atlas' of the big business world, who had become a despairing life-hater', into a believer in the purpose and worthwhileness of human existence. The play apparently undertakes to resolve Walter's despairing but fundamentally philosophical question: "Who or what are we? What are we supposed to be doing here?"[34] And the question finds a convincing answer in terms of an artistic rendering of Ouspensky's Spiral Time.

The play turns on the Ouspenskian proposition: Time is eternally circular and this Circular Time can be changed into Spiral Time through the intervention of good and virtuous deeds or some enlightening agents (like Gortler in the play). Time works in the play on two levels: temporal time, symbolised by a clock in the sitting room, and timeless time (here the Ouspenskian Recurrent Time), represented by Gortler, which adds a philosophical dimension to the work.

Time enters the play early on in the first Act itself; but at this juncture it is only clock time. The clock chimes four times in the play. The first chiming is on Gortler's entry into the room; later it chimes at the arrival of Janet. When Walter and Janet are alone, Oliver enters; Janet and Oliver look at each other and immediately the clock ticks and chimes at them. It once again chimes when Oliver remarks that he thinks he has met Gortler somewhere before. The chiming of the clock gives the audience not only a sense of passing time but also foreboding of some mystery or something supernatural going to happen. G.L. Evans succinctly observes: "A reading of the play suggests that the clock represents a kind of Tiresias who observes now, and has observed it all before."[35] This observation can be truer of Gortler, an able exponent of Ouspensky's theory. Gortler too is a kind of Tiresias but with this difference that he looks 'before' not 'after'; to him Time is eternal and circular; he never believes in seeing the future because it is a recurrence of the past. This view is clearly expressed when he says: "What has happened before—many times perhaps—will probably happen again. That is why some people can prophesy what is to happen. They do not see the future, as they think, but the past, what has happened before. But something new may happen."[36] This wise man's conviction—it is Priestley's too—in non-passing time, in the timelessness of life, finds pointed expression in the words with which he comforts Sally and Janet, two ill-starred women, who complain that Time is their greatest enemy and has taken a lot away from them: "No. All that is an illusion. Nothing has really gone, nothing is really lost."[37] As a great believer in multiple Time, he means to say that everything is in its own time. He puts his knowledge of Time into practice, and acts as a good Samaritan to lead people, groping in the dark, to light. His method of observation of events is one of adopting a new attitude to Time: "We have to change the focus of attention, which we have trained ourselves to concentrate on the present. My problem was to drift away from the present—as we do in dreams—and yet be attentive, noticing everything."[38] He has mastered the ability to be in passing time and out of it at the same time, owing to the fact that he has enriched and expanded his consciousness. He knows how to transcend world time, which is just one dimension of man's existence, and to enter the higher dimensions; Time is not single and universal; it is multi-dimensional as life is multi-dimensional; to go beyond time is to grasp the reality of life.

Gortler's right understanding of Time is the source of his optimism which kindles a light in the ever-darkening world of Walter. The crux of Ouspensky's theory is contained in these words of his: "Some people, steadily developing, will exhaust the possibilities of their circles of time and will finally swing out of them into new existences. Others—the criminals, madmen, and suicides—live their lives in ever-darkening circles of their time. Fatality begins to haunt them. More and more of their lives are passed in the shadow of death. They gradually sink—."[39] Gortler's superior knowledge helps Walter turn circular Time into Spiral Time and certainly it is a positive and notable development in the journey of his soul. The Time-philosophy governing the plot of the play lends Walter the freedom to choose and the will to act, and its practicability is effectively expressed in Gortler's words: "It is knowledge alone that gives us freedom. I believe that the very grooves in which our lives run are created by our feeling, imagination and will. If we know and then make the effort, we can change our lives. We are not going round and round in hell. And we can help each other."[40] In fact, this philosopher successfully translates his philosophy of life into practice and the result is exemplary: Walter becomes a new self, a re-generated personality determined to rehearse his part 'until the drama is perfect'.

It is interesting to note how the artist in Priestley breaks away from the theorist in him. He advocates that he has no belief in the theory of re-incarnation, but the impression the play leaves on the reader's mind is that it is about re-incarnation. One cannot think of the theory of circular time or spiral time without thinking of re-incarnation. Janet, Oliver and Gortler have memories of their earlier lives. They feel that they have visited the inn before. Consider the following little scene between the professor and Janet:

"Janet: Have you been up here before, Dr. Gortler?

Dr. Gortler (watching her): No. Have you?

Janet (Frowning a little): No—I haven't—really.

Dr. Gortler: You do not seem very certain.

Janet (slowly): I've been wondering—

Dr. Gortler (as she hesitates): Yes?

Janet: I was only wondering if I could have been Here when I was a very small child............................

Janet (hesitantly and with wonder): You see...suddenly I felt...I could have sworn....You'd said all that to me before.... You and I.... Sitting, talking like this...."[41]

Oliver too feels that he has been here in this place and has met Gortler before.

Where could this *deja vu* feeling be from unless it is from the dim memories of earlier lives? For purposes of comparison of two similar instances, one from D.G. Rossetti's peom *Sudden Light* and the other from the poetic drama *Shakuntalam* by Kalidasa, a fifth century Indian poet, are cited below:

The lover in Rossetti's poem perceives a sudden light coming to him, an intimation of an earlier existence, and grows pensively eloquent:

I have been here before,
But when or how I cannot tell;

I know the grass beyond the door,
The sweet keen smell,
The sighing sound, the lights around the shore,
You have been mine before—
How long ago I may not know:

Shall we not lie as we have lain
Thus for Love's sake
And sleep, and wake, yet never break the chain?[42]

This sweet agony of the lover in Rossetti's poem is matched by the haunting beauty of Dushyanta's words in Kalidasa's drama:

> If when in the midst of happiness the mind is perturbed at the sight of beautiful things or the hearing of sweet sounds, it must surely be due to a vague reminiscence of loves or friendships in a previous birth which have left an indelible impress on the soul.[43]

These quotations clearly show that the chain of consciousness is not broken because Time is recurrent, events go on happening on the same pattern over and over again. There is a lot of similarity between the import of these two quotations and Gortler's philosophy of life and Time, as illustrated by what happens in the play. The climactic moment of the play comes when Walter unloads the revolver, and puts it back into the pocket, making up his mind to play his part until the drama of his life becomes perfect. Walter's (everyman's) enlightened and fearless adventure in Time, which is a bid to be out of Time, is symbolic of the spiritual victory of man over Time's relentless sickle.

The Ouspenskian Circular Time turning into Spiral Time through Intervention has a lot of similarity with the doctrine of Karma which also holds that meritorious souls can, through noble deeds, break the bondage of Time. The basic difference is that the Hindu Karma doctrine has a godhead as the key factor, while Ouspensky's concept has no place for such godhead. But the intervention that can turn the circle of Time into a spiral, through which, in course of time, the soul will be able to shoot out and escape from Time altogether, can be a substitute, though a poor one, for the divine factor in the Hindu Re-incarnation theory which is bound up with the Karma doctrine and its consequences.

The critic, John Atkins, rightly opines that the play is also a strong statement of belief in the interconnectedness of human relations, and this belief was later developed into a major theme in plays like *An Inspector Calls*. The play uses Intervention to stress the need to preserve interconnectedness in human affairs. Gortler in *I Have Been Here Before* is used not simply as a commentator, but as an agent of meaningful change in the life of Walter. In fact, the German philosopher acts as a great moral force and a personification of intervention to break the recurring pattern of Walter's life of 'doubts and fears'. It is shown how the people in the play depend upon one another: Oliver owes his headmastership of the school to Walter who actually runs it, Sam and Sally are indebted to Oliver in whose school Sally's boy is studying, Ormund depends upon Janet, and Janet and Oliver are each other's breath, and hundreds of employees depend upon Walter Ormunds' business world. This point is aptly expressed by Gortler: "Yes, we are like threads in a pattern."[44] To preserve this essential pattern of humanity, Gortler enters as an intervention in the lives of these people, puts the Ouspenskian Time theory into practice, and his humane efforts are nobly rewarded.

A lesser artist would perhaps have turned the story into a thriller, a run-of-the-mill love triangle in which either the husband or the lover would have ended up tragically or the lovers would have eloped, leaving the poor husband in tears. Priestley's serious Time philosophy brings about an attitudinal change in Walter, the central character, who is then set free from the ever-darkening cycles of Time, and is also prompted to help the lovers go their natural way without a guilty conscience. The Time theory puts into an artistic mould an answer to the question 'what is the purpose of human life?', and holds aloft the greatness and purposefulness of man's life and his efforts to develop nobly. All this is shown by fleshing out the Time theory into a vibrant piece of dramatic art. John Atkins rightly says, "with it he reaches the peak as a playwright".[45] The 'Times' re-viewer (23rd Sept. 1937) made a just and correct assessment: "Everyone in it is interesting in himself, not the puppet of a theory...the stage becomes suddenly a place of spiritual adventure...."[46] Truly, the play is a masterpiece of spiritual adventure. The theory is not allowed to run away with the theme; Priestley never loses his hold on the essential human side of the characters. Certainly the play delights and enlightens, which is a rare thing on the stage.

Priestley is not bound by any theory. Rather, he makes theories subserve the demands of his art. This fact is clearly borne out by *Johnson Over Jordan* which almost dethrones clock time, and Serial time is employed in a way not found in his earlier plays.

Johnson Over Jordan (1939) is a remarkable advance over *Time and the Conways.* If *Time and the Conways* dramatises a future possibilitiy through the prophetic vision of Kay's Observer Two in Time Two, against the background of Serial Time, the present play dramatises, against the backdrop of the same theory, the life of Robert Johnson in his Time One existence as looked at by his Observer Two in Time Two, after his death. This ambitious drama, which created a lot of heated controversy in its time, was at once a bold experiment in content and technique, with theatrical means to assist like music, mask, dance, lighting, ballet and megaphones. Priestley wanted to take his characters outside passing time, as we are in our dreams. He insists, and rightly so, that the drama must not be regarded as one about 'life-after-death' and claims that "it is really a biographical morality play in which the chronological treatment is abandoned for a timeless-dream examination of a man's life."[47] The characters move freely in and out of time. Being 'sick of the triviality of the average biographical play' Priestley wanted to create, through an apparent fantasy, a work of deep and moving significance. And he succeeds in this objective, in a big way.

Linear time is annihilated in order to show the continuity of Johnson's consciousness even after his Time One existence and to show the immortality of life through consciousness on the Dunnian line. The consciousness of Johnson, who dies of pneumonia at fifty, moves into a mental state called 'Bardo' in the Tibetan language of The Book of the Dead—"a prolonged dream-like state, in what may be called the fourth dimension of space filled with hallucinatory visions directly resultant from the mental content of the percipient",[48] a bridge between the world men are familiar with and the promised land, called 'Jordan' in the play, which is the final destination of man after death. Johnson looks back over his shoulder at his past; the memorable moments of his Time One life are re-enacted; they are the moments of enduring illumination, peaks of joy, for him.

The play deals with the progress of Johnson's consciousness after death in different dimensions of life. Johnson's consciousness has left his body, but he still senses that the body has not ceased to be. The reader feels that he is following Johnson as if through a hazy dream-world. Susan Cooper considers this work "the most advanced of all Priestley's so-called Time plays, since it dethrones Time altogether and examines the life of Robert Johnson, businessman, Englishman, Everyman, through the fragmented fantasy of an afterlife dream."[49]

This drama has a definite pattern. The three stages in its three acts—the dream-like world of Johnson's mental state, the Jungle Hot Spot, and the Inn at the End of the World to be followed by his journey towards 'Paradise'—are comparable to the three stages of Dante's *Divine Comedy,* namely, Inferno, Purgatorio and Paradiso.

The first two acts show the ugly and ignoble side of Johnson; he is found to relive—all this goes on in his consciousness—the weaknesses of the flesh, the mistakes and lapses, the doubts and fears, the jealousies and hatreds he experienced in his Time One while he lived in flesh and blood. Johnson stands again a sulky school-boy commanded by his schoolmaster to attend to his work, stands a puzzled and dismayed young man, a junior office clerk, before Mrs. Gregg who is hesitant to accept him as a husband for her daughter; he is a much harassed man in the office of the Universal Insurance Company examined by two monstrous-looking Examiners. Charlie, his friend, for whose death in prison he was responsible, appears as a policeman, and his searching questions expose Johnson's sense of guilt: once he stole stamps out of the stamp book at the office; he evaded income tax; cheated a Singapore businessman and concealed the accounts ledger from the accountants.

The tall figure that appears thrice in the drama like Johnson's guardian angel can be interpreted as Time, though the Figure is depicted as one wearing a terrifying death's head. Johnson's lust for money is exhibited by his greedy act of stuffing his pockets with the bank notes which are being thrown into a burning furnace by the Figure. He does not mind being called a fool by the Figure when he expresses his burning desire for the pleasures of the night-club, the 'Jungle Hot Spot', which he wants to purchase with the money. From the moment of his entrance into the 'Jungle Hot Spot' in Act One to his departure towards the Inn at the End of the World, at the end of Act Two, Johnson is shown to be a beast of a man steeped in sensual pleasures. He drinks 'Hell Diver' and 'Dragon's Breath'; dances with a girl called Dot and then with Lottie Spragg, a stout middle-aged woman who was once his childhood playmate. This giggling and grinning middle-aged man, driven by an insatiable carnal hunger and thirst, sends Madame Vulture, a trader in flesh, for 'a pretty little brunette'. He plays the clown in a floor show; cruel jokes are played on this despicable drunken fool; he laughs and giggles at himself and depreciates himself in self-pity. He is struck with horror and remorse when he discovers that the girl in mask he pursued hotly is none else but his own daughter Freda, and the youth who tried to rescue the girl and was killed by him is his own son Richard. At this juncture again appears the Figure, and calls him a fool because he does not know enough about life. Johnson's doubts and fears are dispelled by the Figure, who makes him know that what he thinks to be real is all an illusion and his children are mere 'Masks and shadows and dreams'. Commanded by the Figure to go to the Inn at the end of the World where he does not have to pay money, which he has thrown away on the way, except remember the things and persons that have illumined his mind and touched his heart, he moves in the direction of the Inn, turning his back for ever upon his Inferno.

Act Three presents Johnson's 'Paradise'. This paradise should be taken, not in the orthodox sense of the term, but in the sense that Johnson here feels secure and free from fears and illusions; the happy moments which made his life in Time One worth-living and meaningful are re-enacted in this act. He has already passed not only through Inferno but also through Purgatorio, being purged as he is of all the 'hell within'; now he is eminently fit for his paradise. This act dramatises Jill's vision of her husband's happy state in the Inn which stands as a sharp contrast to the 'Jungle Hot Spot' in both character and atmosphere. Johnson is delighted to find that the Porter in the Inn is none else but the famous batsman, Jim Kirkland, one of the heroes of his childhood. He looks out through a window and sees a number of near and dear ones, who meant a great deal to him in his Time One life: Albert Goop, the older comedian with his magic cane in hand whom he tried to imitate in his childhood, who is a waiter here, whose presence now brings him a sense of security and whose reassuring voice fills him with hope that he can hear and see through the window anyone dear to him; he hears his mother's voice; he sees Pickwick and the fat Sam Weller driving the coach. He is thrilled with joy to see his brother Tom, who was killed in the War, come down to him in his teens; both brothers look out of the window and enjoy the landscape they used to see from their bedroom. The old schoolmaster Morrison greets the brothers; after a while Tom leaves, making Johnson desire still more of his company. Morrison's company helps Johnson relive the supreme moments of joy and beauty the literary masterpieces had brought to him in his school-days; he hears a number of voices from Shakespeare's world and those from 'Grimm's Fairy Tales' and 'The Arabian Nights'. Again he is extremely delighted to pass through those moments when he had received approabation and job promotion for his efficient work from his boss Clayton, when his wife Jill had given birth to a male child and, again, when he had had a very idyllic time in his early wedded life and enjoyed the company of his little kids. This scene presents all the persons Johnson has met and talked to in his life, and they march in parade as it were. At the suggestion of Richard, his son, Johnson jumps up to dance with Jill, calls her but she is not to be seen there; his mad shout after her is in vain. The dancers stand still and the music also stops. Now is heard the clergyman's voice at the funeral service, just as it was going on at the beginning of Act One.

Finally, there appears the Figure with his face covered with a hood and commands Johnson to go, as now it is time for his departure. When at Johnson's request the Figure pulls back the hood, the handsome face of a young man, like Apollo's, is revealed. Johnson with a deep emotion says farewell to everything he has seen, felt and experienced on earth, and is prepared to leave for Paradise. After a few words exchanged with the Figure, Johnson sees the latter disappear. At first Johnson appears a small, forlorn and solitary figure, then looks about shivering a little and turns up the collar of his. A solemn and peaceful scene appears: there is the blue sky and there is the glitter of stars on space and against them the curve of the world's rim, and at last Johnson, wearing his bowler hat and carrying his bag, slowly turns and walks towards that blue space and the shining constellations.

Here Priestley's objective is to give an account of a man's life in a new way and thereby to present a composite image of humanity. Time is the most important factor in the play. Priestley's grand poetic vision is writ large in the delineation of Johnson's biography outside chronological time. "The appeal, therefore, becomes intellectual, and it is in the brilliance of the play's ability to summarise a life-time, to compress many years into a couple of hours without losing the sense of their length and difficulty, that lie the value and fascination of the piece."[50] A long stretch of four decades is telescoped into a couple of hours. The time-shifts, as in *Time and the Conways* and *Music at Night,* "are presented as personal experiences, as projections of internal vision."[51] The timeless quality of life is vividly brought out. The Figure can be taken as one symbolising Time rather than death. There are several occasions in the play which tend to substantiate this interpretation. Johnson's discovery of the handsome, calm and wise-looking face behind the mask, a terrifying death's head, is a symbolism reflecting the true nature of Time. The 'appearance' of death disappears and the 'reality' of life dawns on Johnson's mind, and he finds a number of familiar faces in the face of the Figure. A deep sense of mystery about Time is expressed in Johnson's words addressed to the Figure in whom he recognises all the persons he has met:

> You are like—and yet not quite like—so many people I have known. It's as if they all looked at me together. My father...and our old family doctor, Macfarlane...and my first schoolmaster...even our old nurse...and a parson I once talked to, just one night, crossing to France... and....[52]

Johnson's discovery of the Figure's angelic smiling face is symbolic of his conquest of Time in the sense of freedom from the tyranny of Time through an understanding of what it truly is: it is not a dreaded monster, 'Kãlabhairav' (Time monster) as described in the Hindu Puranas, but a mode of perceiving life which, if rightly grasped, looks beautiful and noble.

The timelessness of life is again established by the work. The portrayal of Johnson outside the fourth dimension conveys the truth about his personality embodying all the emotional complexes deeply hidden in him; his whole personality stands fully revealed in a blaze of light. The shifting and juxtaposing of Time One and Time Two show life in a timeless order and successfully drive home the multidimensionality of life. The barrier between life on earth and life after the decease of the body—in Dunne's idiom Observer One and Observer Two—is totally demolished when Johnson hears, by the grace of the Figure, the conversation between Richard and Freda and the words of the clergyman at the funeral service and, again, the voices of Jill and Freda. Johnson's teacher, Morrison, says that there is no such thing as time at all; it is an illusion; life is one and multidimensional.

Johnson's realisation of life's reality comes through his proper perception of Time. This realisation brings him supreme quiet in the final scene, just before his final journey towards 'Paradise', when there is no longer heard the clanking of the machinery of existence; now the door to a timeless order of life has opened up.

In Act Three, it is shown how Johnson grasps the whole personality of Jill in a timeless dimension. All the highest peaks of joy of his Time One life, caught in a timeless dimension, throng to his mind at once as it were in a flash:

> You are Jill, my wife. And you are Jill, the mother of my children. And you are Jill, the girl I saw for the first time at a dance nearly thirty years ago.... You are all those, and something more as well, something even more than the Jill who went with me on that wedding journey to Switzerland, so young, so happy. You are the essential Jill, whom I was for ever finding, losing, then finding again....[53]

These words issue from a wholeness of vision, which is not a three-sectional one in passing time but a four-sectional view of life.

The unfamiliar theatrical devices, violation of the realistic conventions of time and space and allusiveness and telescoping of images have made some critics regard this play as an expressionist work. If R.S. Furness opines that it "seems a very dim reflection of Kaiser",[54] Ernest Short, considering Johnson as an 'English Everyman', places the play squarely in the tradition of expressionist drama. But this view is quite rightly disputed by G.L. Evans on the ground that two important characteristics of expressionism are absent in the play, namely, pessimism and the contemporary social picture. On the contrary this critic finds it a work embodying the spirit of great optimism and observes, "Society was making a headlong dash towards annihilation, while Johnson moved towards Nirvanah."[55] Alan Dent's charge that the play has "stark insensibility"[56] is unfounded and unjust, because the central character, Johnson, is nothing if not human in his relations with the people he loves or hates. The play is not an escapist attempt, as alleged by some. It is one of hope for mankind which will certainly find life wholesome and worth living, provided it takes a long view of Time.

In the late thirties, Priestley came under the influence of Carl Jung. The Jungian Unconscious could answer, Priestley felt, the mystery and enigma of personality. Hence he used the Jungian concept of self in *Music at Night* which depicts life outside linear time. If he uses Serial Time to create a four-dimensional drama in *Johnson Over Jordan,* he uses the Jungian Unconscious in *Music at Night* for the same purpose.

Music at Night (1938) also is a four dimensional-drama like *Johnson Over Jordan*. If *Johnson Over Jordan* is based on Serial Time dealing with human consciousness in a timeless dimension, this play is based mainly on the Jungian Unconscious which rejects unidimensional chronological time. It shows that the minds of men and women have common roots; individuals may seem to be separate solid 'lumps of ego' influencing one another but, in reality, they are partakers of one universal consciousness which operates in a timeless order. The play focuses on the oneness of the human condition and the unifying relationship between the conscious and the unconscious, not only of the individual mind but also of the minds of separate individuals.

This drama is largely made up of the mental adventures and varying moods of a group of men and women at a musical concert, whose minds move in a timeless order under 'the influence of music'. The music works like magic, throwing open the minds of the listeners to a new world of experience, and during one hour's traffic of the concert, clock time stands expunged. Priestley's own words point up the power and effect of music on the consciousness of the listeners: "The progress throughout the play is from the surface of the mind to deeper and deeper levels of consciousness. The strange happenings in Act Three arise from my belief that at these depths we are not the separate beings we imagine ourselves to be."[57]

There are sixteen characters, ten living and six dead. Mrs. Amesbury, an old snobbish busybody hosts a music party in her house. All the ten people gathered at the party are, in one way or another, liars to their conscience. A kaleidoscopic method of presenting the action, which is primarily mental, is employed. The quick-moving images of memory and desire and speculation give a composite view of the human condition, one single pattern of humanity. The montage technique employed, with time shifting back and forth, gives a vivid picture of the innermost drama of the characters. The effect of the concert goes on increasing from the first movement to the third. During each of the movements not only are the windows of the minds of the characters, so far shut, thrown open, but also the barriers they have carefully built up inside themselves crumble down; these people are stripped, layer after layer, down to what they have been inside all along, and made to speak without reservations; clock-time is annihilated during the self-exposing mental operations of these men and women.

The first movement in Act One ('Allegro Capriccioso') shows some of these people in a queer world of their own desires and imagination. Chilham, a hypocritical gossip journalist, a pleasure-loving bachelor, imagines a 'swell story' of Lady Sybil's murder when Katherine, the wife of the music maestro David, says angrily that she will kill Sybil if the latter does not check her naughty tongue; playing the super detective Morton Ferrett, he detects that Sybil is murdered not by Katherine but by Mrs. Amesbury who wanted to take revenge upon Sybil, because she had ruined the life of her son Rupert. Then Ann's vision is presented: she sees herself as the beautiful white queen of the South Sea Island in whose honour the natives hold a festival with processions and dances and songs. Dirnie, a business magnate and a womaniser, who is tired of the company of Sybil, a fashionable flirt, imagines that he has had Katherine for his wife. A might-have-been in which Katherine and her kids are waiting for Dirnie and the way he soon falls foul of married life and gets out of it vividly unfolds before us. A fruitless past is acted out: David courted Sybil twenty years ago and was spurned. Peter, the communist poet, appears as a Red Army General followed by Ann, not as his sweet young woman but as his military aide. Bendrex, a dyed-in-the-wool politician, a cabinet minister now, who carries with him till his last breath the heavy load of equivocations of thought, words and actions, refuses to come out of his golden Edwardian pre-1914 world and, after making a tired speech, slips into his chair.

Act Two presents the same characters but in a sad and pensive mood created by the second movement called 'adagio'. Most of the little scenes put them back into their past; a number of years are telescoped into a few seconds of psychic time. The action of the play moves in a timeless dimension: Time is not parcelled out into past, present and future. The more the music progresses, the deeper their minds go down to their unconscious which starts surging up, revealing what has been hidden within. The music exercises its hypnotic power not only on the listeners but also on the music-makers. Lengel is tolled back to those days when he was mad after Katherine; he says that not being loved by Katherine he had cursed love as a 'senseless cruel thing', but today the same Lengel declares that without love the world wears 'a vast weary face', and speaks angrily to all those around him: "You sit there like lumps of clay. By God, I'll fiddle the dead out of their graves—the dead men and women, the great hours that are dead but once were alive—and full of magic. Look out, you clods, the earth's stirring...."[58] Indeed under the influence of the great music earthly time is dead, the listeners being transported into a timeless existence. The little scenes that follow, in a string as it were, are all mental operations moving outside temporal time. It should be noted that throughout this act a highly emotion-charged prose, suitable for evocation of feelings and sentiments of long-lost happiness or missed opportunities, is used. There hovers an atmosphere of regret, melancholy and remorse throughout the act. To Bendrex with his 'boater' behind his back, all this slow and sweet music is the swan-song of a civilization; he regrets the loss of his vanished Edwardian world; his cosy warm world is glimpsed through his conversation with the dead servant Parks, who appears before him and bows to him. In a flashback Amesbury's sad past is acted out, showing Rupert, her young and attractive son, appearing and talking with her—Rupert whose death is caused by air-crash is effectively suggested. Peter, the communist poet, sings in praise of the classless society and revolutions and the proletariat; all this talk comes from his conscious thinking in passing time. But when his mind comes under the influence of music his consciousness is released from passing time, the poet in him taking wings floating through the history of mankind. The scene showing Chilham in conversation with his dead mother, who has appeared before him, focuses on his dark side —his greed of money and publicity, his weakness for wine and women. His unconscious part overpowers his conscious part, and he confesses to his mother what he has been in truth all along: "I'm like a man driving a racing car round and round a track. I daren't stop or make a turn—I'd crash. All I can is to go round faster-faster-faster. And I'm, sick of it. And I'm frightened."[59] Chilham's restless living in single-track passing time has blinded him to the enduring wealth of life which can be had only in a timeless dimension. Dirnie battles with his conscience when he is faced by Tom who committed suicide fifteen years ago because he was betrayed by Dirnie. Sybil goes back to her girlhood days, where she meets her dead elder sister Deborah. The scene of the happy sisters chatting away their time is followed by the scene showing the gloomy face of the present older Sybil. There is a lot of pathos in her narration to Deborah of how wretched and miserable her life has been since the end of childhood at Brankleford, since everything 'wobbled and slipped out'. David holds an intimate talk with his music maestro Dr. Ebinthal, who appears, in a vision, after thirty years since he saw him last. Thus there are scenes of past memories, fond hopes and happy reveries and dreams which are effectively presented in terms of dramatic action.

The third movement called 'Allegro' starts in a nice, brisk, cheerful style to wake up the listeners, then it becomes agitated about life and finally it all turns out to be grand and noble. The listeners are lifted out of their conscious world in clock time and placed into their timeless unconscious. David's observation, made at the height of the performance, that the listeners have been asleep for years and years, and that now they should wake up, means that their going into their unconscious is a real waking. The 'movement' makes the characters feel that nothing of their life is dead and gone, everything is in its own time. The magical corridors of their memory are opened and it is the opening of the door of a timeless existence. Mrs. Amesbury and Katherine relive the sunny days of their childhood and youth. The men spell out their brave plans and adventurous ideas; they sing in praise of the achievements of modern science. They laugh and relax, feel everything is fun and just divinely idiotic. Dirnie's exploding laughter is joined by others' till it works up to a crescendo of laughter. The big laughter is then suddenly shattered by a shrill cry of pain and fear from Bendrex. A universal fear grips their minds for some time, and then the fear is replaced by a growing sense of guilt and remorse. These feelings are commonly felt by all of them. They are compelled from within to confess their sins. Dirnie confesses that he was responsible for the death of his 'pal', Tom; Chilham feels that all the time his dead mother is watching his not having returned her money; Sybil admits to having betrayed her maid. The characters who have not been guilty of anything also feel the burden of guilt. Their speeches prove how one universal consciousness is found in all human beings. Mrs. Amesbury voices the conviction of them all when she declares: "We are all guilty creatures."[60] Their experiences are crossed like wires as it were.

The play deals with three higher levels of consciousness and its functioning in three orders of Time. The first Act presents the characters under the influence of the first movement of music which makes their consciousness move in a world of possibility, a might-have-been world, operating in non-passing time. The second movement tolls the characters back to their past where their consciousness goes on recapturing the 'lost time' in a timeless dimension. At these two levels consciousness is not altogether separated from the characters, and they are aware of what is happening to them, though in a different time-dimension. This can be illustrated from two scenes. One is—this has already been cited—where Dirnie imagines himself to be Katherine's husband, etc. The other scene is where Mrs. Amesbury goes back nostalgically to those days in every spring when her son Rupert, a lovely and cheerful boy of five, was running about and dancing among the apple trees in full blossom in a little village in Hereford. In both cases the action takes place outside passing time. But the third 'movement' in Act Three introduces a different and complex world. Here is the third level of consciousness, that is, the superconscious. The playwright further recognises three stages of the superconscious. At the first stage, individual consciousness joins their unconscious which feels the pulse of the world mind but still maintains its identity; then at the intermediary stage individual selves, their separate egos, knock down the walls between themselves and share the common stuff of consciousness; then there comes the last stage where these separate entities disappear and merge into one universal mind which speaks through them, and earthly time stands totally expunged here. This truth is expressed by David:

> What is David Shiel? Nothing.... In the real and greater world, David Shiel is a mere appearance, a part, a mask, a shadow. So I tell you—sink deeper, deeper. Forget and then remember. Go down and down and discover what you are.[61]

David's idea of "forget and then remember" clearly shows that the individual consciousness, though merged into the universal consciousness, does not melt away into 'nothingness'. The Priestleyan reader may recall Priestley's thinking about the individual self: "I suspect that you save your soul by losing it as a trickle of water loses itself in a river".[62] This is the true way of discovering oneself. The play suggests both 'dualism' and 'non-dualism'. Both artistically and philosophically the play is complex.

The final majestic theme of the music makes the entire ten living characters group together, and the dead also join them. The scene shows a composite picture of humanity outside passing time. The living begin speaking from out of mankind's collective unconscious which is not bounded by Time and Space. Timelessness rules supreme, wiping out the apparent difference between the living and the dead. The march of human history, right from the Stone Age to the beginning of Agriculture and Weapon-making, is briefly recapitulated through the lips of all these characters. Thus it is shown how man's civilisation, covering thousands of years, and crystallized in the collective unconscious, finds a telling expression in the words of these men and women.

At last these characters salute the 'one heart' beating through all their hearts and the 'one mind' which is infinitely greater than theirs. In one voice they pray to the universal consciousness, the Supreme Mind, that binds them together, to keep them for ever and ever.

Thus dawns on them the wisdom of life. Unequivocally the play establishes that 'reality' can be grasped, in a timeless dimension, by those whose consciousness transcends the material existence bound by Time. Once again the difference between the dead and the living is wiped out in the scene where Bendrex slowly opens his eyes, comes back to life and the smiling old man is led through an entrance by his Edwardian attender Parks who rolls up through the same entrance. Scene after scene the oneness of life is established through the unbroken progress of consciousness through the different dimensions of Time.

In the main, there are two charges against the play. One is: "...instead of characters we are given types, and when this happens no other consideration can save the drama."[63] Before answering this charge, Priestley's main intention in writing this drama should be considered. He mainly concentrates on expanding and developing individual consciousness into the corporate consciousness of humanity so that it could reach universal consciousness, and this he achieves artistically with the help of music. In doing so naturally the characters are subordinated to that universal binding force which works in a timeless order, and so they tend to become types. Priestley found it a challenging and even a hopeless task trying to dramatise the philosophical idea that Jones is Brown or Tom or Harry. G.L. Evans justly observes: "The characters are metaphors which are intended to create a total image."[64] The second charge is that the verse used, particularly in the third Act, is not equal to the job of expressing the poetic vision the playwright is dramatising. True, Priestley's verse is not good poetry; he himself admits this fact. He used the verse only as 'heightened dramatic speech' to suggest the promptings of the deepest level of consciousness. The *Times* reviewer (11 October 1939) pointed out the distinction of the drama: "There is refreshment of spirit in watching a good craftsman struggling with courage and honesty to loosen stage conventions that for him and many others have grown oppressively rigid."[65] G. Wilson Knight reads Nietzsche's philosophy of the Dionysian music into the theme of the drama. But undoubtedly Priestley is attempting here an interpretation of human personality in the light of the Jungian Unconscious. Indeed, the world depicted in the drama lies outside linear time, and it is a work embodying lofty philosophical thinking.

Jung continued to be as strong and lasting an influence as Dunne on Priestley's art. If *Music at Night* uses the Jungian Collective Unconscious for interpreting human personality, *Let the People Sing,* a novel, gives an artistic expression to Jung's concept of dreams and reality.

Let the People Sing (1939) is the only novel of this early part of the middle phase which contains the Time element. The novel deals with the smiles and tears of the old English music-hall artists as do *The Good Companions* and *Lost Empires.* It artistically exploits two theories: Dunne's Serial Time and Jung's Collective Unconscious.

Timmy Tiverton, once a popular comedian, but now an out-of-work artist, is charged with the toppling of the statue of Sir Benjamin in the public park of Birchester. He manages to escape from the 'police hunt'; makes friends with Prof. Kronak, a Gzech who is frantically hiding his identity lest he may be caught by the British police for want of a valid permit to stay in England. Timmy and the professor halt for the night in the mansion of Sir George, and in the morning their journey begins and they join on the way a travelling auction-shop-cum-musical party; then the musical circle at Dunbury comes into existence. The novel has, naturally, something of English picaresque novel. A tussle ensues between two groups: those that want the Market Hall for the activities of the Dunbury music party and those that want it to be converted into a museum for the United Plastics. The case is left by Judge Frederick to the arbitration of Sir George who declares *Let the People Sing*. Thus this novel ends on a happy and hilarious note.

The novel has parts which concentrate on certain timeless moments both in the Dunnian way and in the Jungian light.

Timmy, sitting near the statue, closed his eyes and found his past come back to him alive; saw the huge Empires crowded to the roof, heard the bands raffling out his old opening numbers; he was seeing again all the boys and girls on Sunday at Crewe or Doncaster stations; saw his sweet Betty, who had brought him Paradise and died three years after marriage, appear again smiling and dancing before him. He felt that Time had not passed. The timeless experience of Timmy and his friends singing together Timmy's popular song "You cann't give Father any Cockles' is described as follows:

> They seemed to sing themselves back into another and happier world...the years that stood between him (Timmy) and his youth and success now seemed only like the flying soundless years of a dream.... As for George and Ketley, no doubt they too returned in spirit to an earlier and happier time.[66]

Another occasion is when Timmy finds Daisy Barley, a star comedienne of the old days, one who was known for fire and fun. Her very sight rushed him back to the golden past, his Edwardian age. Both artists relived those exciting and glorious days and felt that nothing of their past was dead, that it was all in its own time.

Priestley describes an occasion when Daisy felt Time to be a dream:

> ...and she put her arms round him and talked to him for a minute as if he (Timmy) were a tired child and the

> hour too long and the world too big and strange. During that minute there was no show, no 'Dog and Bell', no years that were gone for ever, and Betty and some others they had both known and loved were neither alive nor dead, and time was a dream.[67]

The events and and situations cited above illustrate the Dunnian Serialism of Time: when Observer One of these characters in Time One is in the present, taking cognisance of things and happenings in passing time, their dreaming self, that is, their Observer Two in Time Two, sails back to their past which has always been there but in a different time.

The old Candover, a strange dreamer and a puzzlesome personality, with glittering light grey eyes suggesting something supernatural about them is capable of precognitive and postcognitive dreams. His dreams can be interpreted in the light of Dunne's 'serialism' as well as Jung's collective unconscious. He can have dreams not only every night but any time if he just shuts his eyes for a minute or two; they are picturesque. Here is one such dream which the old man himself describes:

> I see armies taking cities and setting them on fire, all kinds of soldiers and cities...and big ships fighting on the sea and even up in the air—not like our aeroplanes at all, much bigger—and storms, and awful storms, and earthquakes and huge waves coming in from the sea and fire coming out of the ground, and thousands and thousands of people, all kinds of people running and screaming.[68]

This may be foreknowledge of a nuclear disaster. It may be interpreted on the Dunnian line that it is a vision of this old man's Observer Two in Time Two who has a wider length of Observer One's time; here Observer One's future becomes Observer Two's present. This queer man's dreams illustrate Dunne's statement that dreams contain "a displacement of time". Prof. Kronak recognises the Jungian Collective Unconscious at work in these dreams. For example, the dream in which Candover sees a city in a desert, with towers and domes, the thousands and thousands of small brown men with hairy caps, is interpreted by this professor as one connected with the great sack of Bagdad under Hulagu, brother of Kublai Khan. The professor rightly observes, "By some accident, which we cannot understand, the unconscious dreaming mind of this man reflects the universal mind or world memory. Thus he witnesses great events separated by thousands of miles and, what is more strange, thousands of years perhaps from his waking self."[69] Priestley depicts Candover not just as an individual human being but as one in whom all men are seen; in him is reflected something greater than humanity, that is, consciousness which is not only outside Space but time as well. Candover differs from priestley's Time-travellers, like the Russian Nature man (*Faraway*) the magicians (*The Magicians*) and the Old Man on the blue mountain (*Saturn Over the Water*) in the nature of his vision: through a kind of yogic power they have acquired, while his power comes to him by birth. The novel presents Candover as an involuntary vehicle of World Mind or Collective Unconscious. Similarly the dream he describes before the Judge Sir Frederick, which is a precognitive dream of the outbreak of the Second World War, can be interpreted according to Dunne's Serial Time theory as well as the Jungian Collective Unconscious. This queer old man confuses and bewilders the learned judge when he replies that he has been in this court before, because he has passed through this trial once in a dream. It can be said that his dreaming self, his Observer Two, has experienced all this by its capacity to leap into the future which is ever present in the eternal 'Now'.

This novel gains an additional depth owing to the Time element in it. It can be said that this novel is definitively an advancement over *Faraway* and a positive anticipation of a further development that was to appear in novels like *Bright Day, The Magicians, Saturn Over the Water* and *It's an Old Country,* which deal with multiple Time in a variety of ways.

Priestley's belief in taking a long view of Time is at the core of this novel and all the earlier plays discussed so far. This 'long view of Time' leading to an optimistic view of immortality forms the central idea of *The Long Mirror*.

The Long Mirror (1940) is a minor play. It illustrates that the 'reality' of life is covered by Time. The right knowledge of Time will 'discover' and reveal that reality. Michael Camber and Branwen Elder meet for the first time in a remote hotel, and feel—Branwen's feeling is more acute—that they have met somewhere before, not in the flesh but in some *deja vu* way. They know many things about each other. Branwen calls this mysterious experience of another time or another existence just 'seeing' which includes the past and the future. Branwen recognises 'some link' between 'world reality' and that which lies outside the fourth dimension, which connects men and all the facts relating to them individually.

Further Branwen illustrates the 'real' and the 'unreal' with a long mirror kept in the room of the hotel. First Branwen and Michael both stand before the mirror and their images are reflected in it. Then Branwen steps aside, and now only the image of Michael is found. Branwen explains to Michael what is real and what is an illusion:

> I think the outward world in time, where you and I are going to say goodbye and then vanish from one another's sight, is only like a long, long mirror, full of twists and cracks and corners, stretching from the cradle to the grave. All you see in it are images. What is real and true—and—'alive'—is here, not there.[70]

The mirror metaphor reminds one of Plato's famous cave-image and Shankara's Maya-concept (the world as an illusion). The *deja vu* feelings of Branwen and Michael remain only at the level of feelings, just to serve the dramatist to explain his belief that Time is an illusion; the feelings are not turned into dramatic action as in *I Have Been Here Before*. Priestley's Time-philosophy here subordinates his dramatic art, and the result is that the Time theme fails to find an aesthetically appealing version.

Priestley's advocacy of viewing life out of the purview of chronological time is successfully put forth in *Desert Highway* in terms of art, whereas the theme of *The Long Mirror* is not presented in an effective way.

Desert Highway (1943), a two-act play, originally meant as a gift to the British Army to be produced by the Army Bureau of current affairs, saw civilian productions after the Second World War in London and elsewhere. The action of the play centres round six British soldiers, during the War, stranded near an old highway in the Syrian Desert. With their tank broken down, their wireless set being dumb, these men have no way out of this dismal desert. Wick, the Baby of the party, wounded in a burst of machine-gun fire by the enemy, is fetched by his colleagues and placed in the tent.

The Interlude jumps twenty-six centuries back to a similar situation in which the same six characters are found but in different garbs and different ages. The happenings of a misty distant Biblical world are re-enacted. If Joseph is shown as an Israelite shepherd, Donnington has become an Egyptian scribe in the scene, and Elvin, Shaw, Hughes and Wick are caravanners of Near Eastern nationalities. Joseph, the Israelite shepherd, acts as a guide to these people through Samaria and Judaea; recites the prophecies of Amos. Act Two brings the action of the play to the present war time again; though it is a continuation of Act One, it is, in fact, a continuation of the cruelties of the ancient world, shown in the Interlude, but now witnessed in the Second World War.

The play's primary concern is human life as seen from outside linear time; it focuses on the sad core of man's life, of human history, which has remained substantially unchanged all through the centuries. The device of jumping twenty-six centuries to a distant past with a view to showing how mankind has paid and is still paying for its craving for fighting and blood has been successfully employed; the immensity of the time-range widens the scope of the dramatist's message and deepens the effect of his art. The stone monument buried in the earth, which was an idol worshipped in the ancient past by different races as shown in the Interlude, is a symbol of Time, of the continuity of the story of man's civilization on this earth. Joseph, disturbed by the death of Wick, picking up the Bible from among the dead youth's possessions, says the following words which give a timeless view of human happenings:

> About twenty six hundred years ago, which was a time rather like this, with huge armies on the move and cities burning, from the desert not a long way from here there came a prophet called Micah the Morasthite. And he had listened to the voice from the heart of the silence, and had seen visions in the darkness of the night....[71]

This allusion to the event, already shown in the Interlude, points to the timelessness of events. It is not correct to hold, as some critics do, that the Interlude is an interruption in the continuity of the action between the two acts. On the contrary, it adds a new dimension, that is, one of timeless quality to life's reality. This intervening scene stretching centuries back in time creates a solemn and sublime effect. Just as Act Two in *Time and the Conways,* giving a peep into the future of the Conway family, deepens the effect of Act Three of the drama, the Interlude in *Desert Highway* makes the audience see the action of Act Two of this play in a different light. David Hughes observes that the movement of the plot back in time "proves an effective way of suggesting the immensity of time which stretches with an even more arid cruelly than the desert itself...."[72] But it may be said that Time's immensity in this case rather heightens man's dauntless spirit in the face of cruelty and death, and it is worth noting that an immense philosophic and spiritual calm descends on the characters at the end of the drama because of the vast timeless view of life.

There are references in the drama to the gift of prevision which some of the characters possess. It opens with Hughes's words that his grandfather and uncle had the power of seeing the future. Joseph speaks of Micah's prophecy in the Interlude that there would appear "vast magical contrivances that would do with ease in a day the labour of ten thousand men. And yet, said Micah, these visions too were filled with fire and blood, anger and suffering...."[73] Act Two shows how these visions have come true. Similarly, the Egyptian scribe (Donnington) speaks of how his old master, a worshipper of Thoth, the moon-god, could put himself into trance, free himself from time and gaze into the far future. All these references to previsionary powers speak of the potentialities of life which are outside the sphere of Time.

The drama makes use of both Serial Time and Eternal Recurrence. So far as the previsionary powers and prophetic visions of some of the characters are concerned, it dramatises Dunne's view that life lies in various dimensions and Observer Two in Time Two has a wider length of Time One and thus either the past or future can be caught by the former. Ouspensky's view that Time goes on repeating itself in the same way again and again is illustrated by the fact that Joseph and other characters appear again in modern times, in the twentieth century, as soldiers performing the same duties and speaking the same language. The playwright emphasises the continuity of consciousness from one dimension of Time to another. But the play fails to provide a suitable and effective aesthetic form for Priestley's Time philosophy. That the characters are ignorant of their earlier existence, as shown in the Interlude, prevents them from having a profound living experience of the kind Janet and Oliver in *I Have Been Here Before* are capable of. Likewise, the Interlude does not have a direct influence on the characters in Act Two in the manner in which Act Two does make a profound influence on the actions and words of the characters in Act Three of *Time and the Conways*. But still Priestley's vision of man's history outside chronological time is quite poetic. If the novel *Let the People Sing* merely speaks of the wars of the past and the one that will break out in future, through the dreams of Candover, *Desert Highway* points to the unchanging pattern of man's history including the bloody wars of the past and the present. A possible solution to modern man's problems is suggested through the creation of a fantasy world in *They Came to a City*.

They Came to a City (1934) is a symbolistic play in two acts. One of Priestley's most popular plays, it had a long run in the Globe Theatre. It was interpreted in several widely different ways: as a study of personality in the Jungian light, a drama of life after death, a slab of Left Wing Propaganda, etc. Priestley created this play out of the very different attitudes of mind that people had to post-war changes. Though it is a kind of fantasy dealing with a Utopia, it is far from being a mere work of debate; its action—though dramatically thin—is richly symbolic.

There are nine characters who carry with them their class distinctions. They are confused and bewildered to find themselves outside the long and high wall of a mysterious city; they know nothing about why and how they have landed there. Each one of them has his or her own way of looking at things. Their common situation in an unknown and mysterious place brings them together to discuss life from various points of view; their debate is so presented that the attention of the audience is directed to the ideal order of human life to be aspired for.

At first there comes up from the wall a dim and hazy light of dawn. Joe and Alice, the lovers, climb up the steps to look over the wall to see what lies there below. They see nothing, come down and look for a door or a way through the formidable wall; they chance upon a tower with a door, a gigantic door shut fast. All of them try in vain to open the door. Philippa catches a glimpse of a city lying beyond the wall. No one knows how to enter the city. Though the golden gleam of dawn is drawing them towards the city, filling them with a passion for a colourful and creative life, they are a helpless lot. At last the door opens of its own accord. Struck with wonder and transported with joy all these people rush through the door. Some like the city and others do not, and all of them except Philippa come out of the door at dusk, and the door shuts again.

Nearly all critics are agreed that the play is a symbolistic work; they point out its dream quality and the Utopian stuff. G.L. Evans calls the play "a piece of sincere propaganda for Priestley's belief in the perfectibility of man."[74] It is admittedly propaganda but not for any belief or doctrine; it is, however, an artistic expression of the dramatist's view of life outside clock time. It is really surprising that not many critics have seen this play's symbolic expression of life in a timeless order. Allardyce Nicoll is the only critic that recognises Time as a powerful element of the play. He says, "...in diverse ways the same 'time continuum' concept provides the mainspring...."[75] Certainly Time is the mainspring here. No doubt the playwright attempts to establish the theory of the perfectibility of man but he does so outside chronological time, unlike most Utopian writers. The philosophical idea of Time widens the thematic scope and deepens the dramatic effect of the play. The strange city with its dream stuff gains an enchanting colour and tone in contrast to the cold realistic world outside the wall. It is a world of harmony and order, beauty and gaiety, innocence and honesty, friendliness and happiness, and these values are contrasted with the mechanical and meaningless existence in passing time.

The frantic search for a way through the wall, the discovery of a door in it later, then its mysterious opening—all symbolize the problem of Time and a way out of it. The metaphor of the wall for Time appears at a number of places in Priestley's works, and this point has been discussed in the second chapter. Quite a number of speeches and scenes here symbolically express the nature and enigma of Time. The following conversation suggests that the door in the wall stands for an intuitive grasp of the nature of Time that can be had in rare moments:

Joe: Nobody's going to break down this door in a hurry.

Alice: What's it made of?

Joe: Don't know. Looks like a kind of plastic to me.

New Stuff.

Alice: There's nothing to open it with—no handle or anything.

Joe: No, it's not that kind of door. This door's either tight shut, as it is now, or it is wide open. That's the sort of door it is.[76]

The women characters of the play, like Mrs. Batley and Alice, are depicted as being capable of grasping the true nature of Time. Philippa, who is fascinated by the life of the city—symbolically, it is her intuitive understanding of a timeless existence—expresses to her mother her deep disgust with life in clock-time:

> But I can't go back with you. I'd rather die. Going back there would be only a kind of slow death. Those people in Bournequay aren't 'real'. They don't want to do anything. They only want to keep on existing from one meal to the next, from one bit of gossip to the next, from one bedtime to the next....[77]

Alice, too, who loathes leaving the city which she regards as her dream come true, speaks eloquently about it, that is, about the winsome and wholesome life outside passing time: "Here, they don't work to keep themselves out of the gutter. They work because they've got something big and exciting to do. They can see their life growing. They're building it up. And they're enjoying it all. They're not passing the time waiting for the undertaker."[78] The high point of the play is the way Priestley dramatises in human terms the quality of life in a timeless dimension. Even Joe's world which exists outside clock-time is nonetheless tempered by realism. He too believes that men will be really happy only when they come out of the shadow of the long and high wall of Time and stand in the broad sunlight of life in a timeless dimension.

The play reaffirms Priestley's belief in the perfectibility of man and the worthwhileness of human life. It bristles with rich symbolism. It is, therefore, hard to agree with John Atkins, who says that Priestley "is so conscious of the symbolism that the necessary underlay of reality gets lost".[79] If the play is rightly interpreted in the light of Priestley's Time-philosophy, its symbolic message is certain to come through. This is an artistic expression of Priestley's highly imaginative and creative vision, a dream of a noble life that is free from Time's tyranny.

Time moves at a preternatural level in *They Came to a City* owing to the free play given to fantasy. Fantasy of a different sort is presented in *An Inspector Calls* which dramatises a future possibility by twisting time's tail.

An Inspector Calls (1945), a three-act play, has been staged all over the world. Its technique is a throw-back to that of *Dangerous Corner*. It is a thriller with a serious moral. The theme is interconnectedness in human society: all men are accountable to and responsible for one another. If the idea that all individuals are knit together and interdependent has been dealt with at different levels of consciousness in *Music at Night,* the same theme is treated in this play against a naturalistic background, using the split-time device to dramatise a future possibility. The realism of action is tempered by the right proportion of mystery which is mainly due to twisting of time's tail. There is a magical atmosphere, a sort of fantasy, but it is under the control of the real and possible in human affairs. John Atkins rightly remarks that it is hard to find fault with the play in any way and adds: "Probably the best example in his work of superb construction allied with just the right degree of mixed reality and magic is to be found *An Inspector Calls.*"[80]

The plot is relatively simple. The entire family of the Birlings is responsible for the suicide of the girl Eva Smith. The happy atmosphere in the Birlings' house, where Mr. and Mrs. Birling, their daughter Sheila and her fiancé Gerald Croft are gathered to celebrate the engagement, is upset by the sudden appearance of Inspector Goole, who goes on asking them, one after another, searching questions concerning the death of Eva Smith. The Inspector points his accusing finger at all of them, telling sternly that they are all responsible for the poor girl's death. After the departure of the Inspector the hospital authorities are contacted on phone and it is learnt that no girl has died there. Now begins a moral fight between Mr. Birling, Mrs. Birling and Gerald on one side and Sheila and Eric on the other. The first group is complacent and satisfied with the conclusion that the Inspector and his business was all a big hoax; they do not hold themselves guilty; they choose to tell a lie each to their conscience. But Eric and Sheila do not absolve themselves of their moral responsibility; their argument is that whether the Inspector was genuine one or an imposter, their moral responsibility for the girl's death cannot be shrugged off. When Mr. Birling is beaming with satisfaction, teasing his children for their inability even to 'take a joke' and the curtain is about to fall, there comes a telephone message from the Brumley Police Station to tell that a girl has just now died on her way to the infirmary after swallowing some disinfectant and that a police inspector is on his way to their house to ask some questions. All of them stare at each other guiltily and are dumbfounded.

The mysterious Inspector is the central character. He is, in the words of G.L. Evans, "an embodiment of a collective conscience."[81] He represents our corporate guilt complex. The moral victory of the play comes through in a telling manner at the end where a deliberate twist is given to time by transposing the present and the future. First comes the police enquiry and then the girl's death which needs an enquiry. The Inspector's inquisition transpires to be an illusion, a sort of fantasy, and then turns out to be a prophecy of the event that happens later. David Hughes calls the end of the play "an unexpected twist of time's tail."[82] In fact it is a deliberate twist of time's tail, a significant rejection of chronological time at the end of the work. This twisting of time prevents the play from becoming a mere thriller. G.L. Evans recognises how this 'time's twist' firmly establishes the thematic purport of the play. He remarks, "The neat twist becomes a kind of judgement on the majority; the unexpected has been shown first to be a nasty illusion and then to be a prophecy."[83] This play also begins where it ends just as *Dangerous Corner* does. John Atkins recognises the strength of a poem in this play, and, referring to the device of 'time's twist' he regards the play as "one of the best examples we have of his (Priestley's) fascination with circularity."[84] *An Inspector Calls* illustrates Priestley's art of achieving not only dramatic effect but also his thematic point of view by experimenting with the technique of time, by advancing the future event to the present.

The first part of this middle phase ends with *Ever Since Paradise* which is remarkable for its use of cinematic flashbacks, and the informality of the stage which is not found in the earlier plays.

Ever Since Paradise (1946), originally written in 1939 and much revised at odd intervals, had a long and successful provincial tour in 1946. The play is about love and marriage in a subtle psychological sense. The play is remarkable for its bold use of the split-time technique in order to dramatise the complexity of man-woman relationship at varying stages and in different moods.

Paul and Rosemary, a couple in their thirties, are the example used to illustrate the man-woman relationship at different stages; Philip and Joyce are the musicians, and William and Helen are the commentators. With its novel and bold technique this play "looks forward to the Brechtian theatre that became popular in England after the second war."[85] The action of the play takes place in different places and at different times, and cinematic flash-backs are used to show the happenings between the two wars. The informality of the stage is so managed that the characters move in and out of action, scene after scene, bridging the distance between art and life, and this informality is achieved by splitting time and looping it again. William and Helen, the mature couple and commentators, direct the action which revolves round Paul and Rosemary. William and Helen put on different garbs for different roles required by typical scenes in which Paul and Rosemary appear in varying moods, and accordingly time goes on shuttling back and forth. The originality of the play lies in 'chronological looping' which enables the stage to accommodate the "free expression of personality at large within a broad subject."[86]

Paul and Rosemary are shown in three stages of their wedded life—romantic courtship, a short period of conjugal bliss, followed by one of boredom, misunderstanding, suspicions, quarrels, and estrangement. First comes the third stage and then follow the remaining stages of their relationship and, naturally, the play takes the audience back in time to the first phase of the couple's relationship. As in *Johnson Over Jordan* and *Music at Night* here also scenes roll by one after another at a preternatural level, back and forth in time. What happened to the couple during the first and second stages is bracketed between the Time-split in Act One and the Time-loop in Act Three: the scene left behind comes back exactly with the same details presenting Paul and Rosemary again in the same situation as found in Act One. The whole event repeats itself as before in action and words.

The technique of circularity is used in this play as a necessary means of presenting on the stage the theme and the point of view, as in *An Inspector Calls,* and not as a mere trick as in *Dangerous Corner.* For example, when Paul gets bored with Mrs. De Folyat, a fashionable flirt, he recalls the romantic moments he had had just three days before his marriage with Rosemary; the little rosy scene showing the lovers in Act One is repeated in Act Three. The circularity device brings into bold relief the vicissitudes in man-woman relations which all men and women have been experiencing since Paradise, the time of Adam and Eve.

Apart from the 'chronological looping' embedded in the structure of the play there are references to the enigma that Time is and the eternal 'Now' and different kinds of Time. The critic, John Atkins, finds the play a failure because he thinks that there is an uneasy contrast between the novelty of its form and the nature of its content which is no more than a woman's mag platitudes about life, love and marriage. But a close study of the work reveals that the technical innovation goes well with Priestley's serious purpose of presenting in drama the unhindered happenings of the mind and heart of man and woman in their mutual relationship at different times in different moods. Therefore, the play is a dramatic success, one could say.

The Second part of the middle phase is represented by five works, three fictional works and two plays. This period marks more of flexibility in the treatment of various ideas of Time. Priestley had closely watched the causes and effects of the Second World War. He was convinced that the muddle, the chaos and destruction all around originated from man's wrong attitude to life, which had, in turn, its roots in his misconception of Time. The characters in the works under review here see life at last in the right perspective and, as a result, hope dawns on them. This is a period of hope and faith. *Bright Day* marks the beginning of the period.

Priestley's art too undergoes a change: he no longer works within the strait jacket of Time-theories, moves on a wider landscape with greater freedom. He operates different timescales with ease. For the first time he chose fiction seriously as a medium to treat his ideas of Time. He might have felt that fiction was the most suitable form in which to embody some of his ideas and his increased knowledge about the subject. The works of this period clearly show how Time exercises an impact on human mind and behaviour. Here Time is markedly more dominant than space and consequently most of the characters in these works grow in stature because of their accumulated personality. Priestley's pre-1914 Edwardian world, his seed-world of youth, illumines *Bright Day, The Linden Tree* and *Summer Day's Dream* with a hope for a better, brighter world. An integrated and wholesome view of Time brings optimism and a fresh and noble outlook on life. The holocaust of the Second World War is looked at with the fearless eyes which see light beyond the meagre dimension of passing time. A timeless vision of life brings freshness, beauty and liveliness into the lives of the characters who people these works.

The five works, which represent the second part of the middle phase of Priestley's development as a Time-writer, are examined in the following pages.

Bright Day (1946) is one of Priestley's major novels. Priestley regarded it as his favourite novel. In *Benighted* and *Faraway* he had already used not only psychological time but also the Dunnian Serial Time at places. *Let the People Sing* also develops against Serial Time and the Jungian Unconscious. But it was *Bright Day* that came as the first of such fictional works of Priestley's as deal with multiple Time by attempting to depict life in a variety of Time-dimensions and give proof of the author's much wider vision of life and his understanding of its reality as grasped by consciousness at different levels.

Priestley shows himself as being capable of a rare detachment in spite of the fact that he shares the ideas, feelings and convictions of the central character, Gregory Dawson. Both Priestley and Gregory belong to the same golden Edwardian age, and are too close to be separated, but Priestley maintains a dispassionate attitude to the life he portrays mainly because he sees it outside passing Time. Gregory's perception of his own life in a timeless dimension adds a strange charm and depth to the novel. Priestley expresses his satisfaction about the novel in these words: ".... I did succeed in weaving into one fabric many different fibres; Dawson's personal history and that of the Alington family, the changing social scene, the ironies that passing time leaves behind it."[87]

Time, rather than space, dominates the scene. The novel, written in first person technique like *Saturn Over the Water* and *Lost Empires,* is mostly an act of retrospection on the part of the central character Gregory Dawson. The individual inner pattern recognised by Gregory in his own life and in the lives of those connected with him, which he sees outside passing time when a detached view of the past is taken from the vantage ground of the present, is more important than the collective social scene, and this inner pattern is created by a free movement of time, back and forth. The constant time-shift, a sort of cinematic 'flashback presentation' of things, is superbly handled by the novelist.

Gregory Dawson, a veteran film-script writer, commissioned by a Hollywood producer to write the script of a story for the screen, was staying in the Royal Ocean Hotel in Conrwall. The Schubert Trio in the hotel lounge takes him backwards in time, far back into a lost world and a lost time, the magic days of his youth in 1913 at Bruddersford; the time past and the time present become one timeless experience for him. The distant past—now he is in the post-Second World War England of 1946—when he was a clerk in Hawes and Co., a wool trading firm, under the manager John Alington, comes back all alive. He begins reliving in the magic circle of the Alington family of the two boys Oliver and David, the three attractive girls Joan, Eva and Bridget and their friends and parties, charades and picnics and pastimes. It is then that he suddenly remembers that the Harndeans, whom he failed to recognise when he saw them first in this place, are none other than Malcolm Nixey and his wife Eleanor he had seen in 1913 one evening when a similar performance of Schubert Trio was given in the Alington's house. From this moment onwards Gregory's past and present begin to move together weaving a regular pattern of narration. The narrative method is Proustian, that is, flashbacks form the substance of the plot. But throughout there remains the Dunnian Serial Time in the background, producing, in scene after scene, the details of Gregory's past and the past of the Alingtons. Dawson's Observer Two in Time Two is freely moving back and forth in time, while his Observer One in Time One exists in the present in 1946.

It is shown, through the flashbacks, that Gregory was fascinated by the magic circle of the Alington family, the laughter and hilarity and jokes and music in the family; Joan loved Jock Barniston, an enigmatic bachelor of forty, but he did not agree to marry her; Eva loved and adored Ben Kerry, a handsome young journalist, but he was ensnared by the exciting young Eleanor Nixey; Bridget loved Gregory and proposed to him but he remained cold and indifferent even though he did love her, and in fact loved a little all the three girls; Eva fell down to her death from a high cliff of Pickeley Scar on a picnic day. He enjoyed Christmas in those days with his uncle and aunt and with the Blackshaws, another intimate family, and the Alingtons. We also learn how he was greatly impressed by Jock's sister Dorothy, a mysterious personality, and Stanley Mervin, a talented water colour-painter; then came the war of 1914 and took away most of the brilliant and promising youths of Bruddersford; among the victims of the war were Jock, the Alington boy Oliver and Ben Kerry; Gregory survived the war and after his demobilisation joined the Hollywood Celluloid World. Gregory tells the success story of Malcolm Nixey, recounting how unscrupulously he rose to grab power from Johnson Alington and how the Alington family fell on bad days and eventually Alington died of a stroke. The story of the Alingtons was one of tears, tears, all the way.

The series of flashbacks restore Dawson's vanished world. John Atkins rightly observes, "It is the story of a Lost Paradise but not lost irrevocably."[88] This lost world is revoked and restored because Dawson takes a long view of Time, an integral view of life, in which there is no place for a narrow idea of linear time. David Hughes rightly regards the novel as a wise, moving and optimistic book, which is Priestley's most mature contribution to the experimental science of living, and observes that "...a step has been taken in...illustration of the way that in a man's life reference to the past can cure the present and provide the future with energy simply because only the present can give a lucid and dispassionate view of the past...."[89] The remembrance of the golden world makes Dawson's present meaningful and his future hopeful. The gulf between *Bright Day*—pre-1914 England—and Gloomy Night—the demoralised and culturally decadent England of 1946 after the Second World War—does not turn Dawson an embittered and disillusioned man because he observes the course of his life in the Dunnian way, taking a long, not a short, view of Time. He regains and relives his paradisal past through memory; feels confirmed that nothing of his life is lost; every moment of the present he is experiencing pulsates with the whole of his life. He can hear, in the Proustian phrase, 'the music of experience' because he is totally free from the soul-killing tyranny of clock-time.

The Priestleyan view of life and Time as reflected in some of the events and situations is discussed in the following pages.

As Proust describes his return to his childhood on hearing the bell in the Combray garden, Dawson too floats back to his youth in 1913 on hearing the Schubert Trio in 1946, which the following passage describes:

> The Alingtons' house...the office and warehouse in Canal Street...and the cottages on the moors...and all the Alingtons—Oliver, Eva, Bridget, and the rest—and their friends...uncle Miles and Aunt Hilda and the whist—players...and Ackworth and Old Sam and the others in Canal Street—and the wool samples in their blue paper seemed close to my fingers...and somehow I could smell lilac and the bitter scent, so long forgotten, of summer dust pitted with raindrops...and over the ling on Broadstone Moor—the larks were rising again.[90]

He felt that a great stir and challenge of life had come flashing out of the Schubert slow movement. Even while he is reliving the magical world of his youth he bounces back to the present post-Second World War period on receiving a telephone call from London. A constant weaving of past and present becomes a recurrent and natural pattern in the novel and this pattern goes on forming the fabric of Dawson's personality and revealing the true character of the other people in the novel.

The Bruddersford days go on haunting Dawson day and night at the hotel. His inner consciousness begins operating in a unique fashion. He feels a timeless existence of two selves in him, the young Gregory of 1912 and the present middle-aged man in 1946. He speaks of how he felt then:

> ...and yet within a few minutes of lighting my first pipe I was back in Bruddersford again, back in the sleet and dark of that far-off December. I was a middle-aged man lolling on a sunlight Cornish Cliff; I was also a youth in a West Riding town in 1912 once again, and I had a feeling too that I was neither of them, that both were character parts in their appropriate sets....[91]

This is how he sees his own life outside passing time, and understands his real 'being' in a timeless dimension.

The Trio brought back Dawson's youth so sharply that he was again with the Alingtons and their friends at that far-off concert in 1913, when there arrived Malcolm Nixey and his wife Eleanor. With that event standing out in his mind he was busy holding the image of Eleanor, a dark swan queen, and was startled by the appearance of the elderly Lady Harndean. He speaks of his thoughts then:

> It was Lady Harndean; it was Eleanor Nixey with thirty-odd more years on her back. And as she came nearer, looked at me with those same eyes, recognised me and smiled, I experienced a sensation so profoundly disturbing that it seemed as if my spine contracted and shivered. What I perceived then, in a blinding flash of revelation, was that the real Eleanor Nixey was neither the handsome young woman I had been remembering nor the elderly woman I saw before me, both of whom were nothing but distorted fleeting reflections in time,

> that the real Eleanor Nixey was somewhere behind all these appearances and fragmentary distortions existing outside change and time; and that what was true of her was of course true of us all.[92]

This is the Dunnian view of seeing life freed from the illusion of time. This is an excellent example of taking a four dimensional view, the whole view of life, which alone reveals the reality of our being untainted and unfettered by the wrong conception born of the usual three-sectional view of our four-dimensional existence. Change of time-dimension, change from Gregory's present to his past, is signalled as it were by the word 'shiver'.

Even when Dawson is sitting in the hotel lounge chatting with Elizabeth and producer Brent, he experience an unexpected over-lapping of two worlds, past and present, with Time playing tricks with both of them. Dawson again returns to the Bruddersford days. The Blackshaws stand before him for a comparison with the Alingtons; Malcom Nixey stands a dinner at the Market Grill and a show at the Imperial Musical; Oliver, an undergraduate at Cambridge, full of zest for life and wonderful plan of becoming a publisher and editor, who was killed in the war, appears before his mind, cancelling all the years in between, with his excited young face raised to the starlight and crying "Shlumpumpitter". The past is not dead; it is in its own time. Even across thirty three years, he hears the loud laughter of Eleanor and Ben Kerry at the party given by Nixey.

Dawson's meeting with Jock's sister Dorothy in 1913 was memorable. She was a Time-traveller. He found her a terrifying woman with strange deep violet eyes and a mind capable of retrocognitive and precognitive visions. She seemed to have come from Somewhere Else, slipped through a crack in ordinary reality. Dawson was struck with awe and wonder when she said that his mother had been dead and she had seen her. He could not understand where, when and how she could have known his mother. He was simply thrilled by Dorothy's words of wisdom and prophecy; he saw something of a seer in her. She spoke enigmatically that some people we think alive are really dead and others we think are dead are really alive. She meant that those that are living only in passing time at the material level do not really live and those that are bodily dead and are out of passing time-out of Time One—are not, in reality, dead but have entered a higher dimension. This was Dorothy's true understanding of life, of human existence, which she had gathered from a right understanding of Time. She muttered, playing Patience (a game of cards) something concerning the future; "...change and an ending...everything changing...ending and beginning again...with rivers of blood flowing towards us...great rivers of blood...."[93] This was a prevision of the war. She foresaw the early death of her brother Jock and foretold what was going to happen to Dawson: he would leave Bruddersford in less than a year and for ever; there was going to be the end of everything, his love and trust. He was astonished to hear her say that she would tell his mother about him and they would never meet again. Indeed all her words came true. As one with an apocalyptic vision of life she belongs to Priestley's creations like the yogic 'indomitable trio' in *The Magicians,* the Russian Nature Man in *Faraway* and the Old Man of the Mountain in *Saturn Over the Water*.

Jock too is capable of seeing things ahead of time; he does not attach much importance to clock time. His real understanding of Time is revealed in his reaction to Dawson's disgust with passing time represented by the ticking of the 'beastly' clock in the corner. He echoes Alan of *Time and the Conways* when he says that time cannot tick us away. He feels that all of us inherit something of the world mind, universal consciousness. He foretells that a disaster will descend on them all when a war breaks out. He says, "We'll all be in it. That's Dorothy was meaning, I don't know if she gets it from my mind, or I get it from hers, or both get it from somewhere else. But there it is. Perhaps in a year or so."[94]

Once Joan also felt the future in the present. Dawson and Joan were going hand in hand on a dark windy wet night towards Wably Wood. They were discussing a number of things. Dawson hinted at the sinister design of Malcolm Nixey and Croxton to malign and harm John Alington. Joan felt the ominous future in that very instant. She had slipped a hand under Dawson's arm, and he felt that she was shivering. The following conversation brings out Joan's intuitive grasp of the future events:

> "We can go now, if you like," she said in a toneless voice.
>
> "The rain's almost stopped." "No, we'd better wait a bit,"
>
> I told her, "Unless you're feeling cold."
>
> "I wasn't shivering because I was cold, Oh, Gregory—" and her voice trailed off.
>
> "What, Joan?" "I don't know," she whispered. "I don't know."[95]

Like Kay in *Time and the Conways* Joan gets a vision of the sad future for the Alingtons, and her 'shiver' is due to her experiencing the change from one time dimension to another—a typical experience in the Priestleyan works.

Dawson says that Ben Kerry's unconscious had a longer view of time; he foresaw his early death. Dawson's assessment of his behaviour, made years later, is expressed:

> And perhaps he was greedy for experience, with his conscious mind in a turmoil from bewildering and conflicting urges, just because in the dark of his unconscious, there was already a whisper that time was running out fast.[96]

Perhaps, because of his premonition of imminent death he wanted to have the maximum out of passing time, being torn between the beautiful and adoring girl Eva and the bewitching young married woman Eleanor.

At one point in the course of recounting some important moments in his life, Dawson speaks to Elizabeth Earl, the actress:

> One mistake we're apt to make, though, is to assume that we are just ourselves as we are now, whereas that's only the thin top slice of us. And whatever has happened to us in the past is still there, perhaps still working away at us.[97]

This is Priestley's own voice echoing Dunne's theory of continuity of Time in a series. Dawson's narration of his story either to the reader or to Elizabeth, the actress, is a sort of self-discovery; he goes on digging out a lot of himself buried deep within. He learns from Eleanor (now Lady Harndean) that she had really loved Ben Kerry; hers was not, he was convinced, a flippant flirting with him just for fun or amusement.

A meeting with Bridget arranged by Elizabeth had a shock in store for him—he was shocked to see that the girl whom he had loved and might have accepted as a life-partner was incredibly changed. He felt, Bridget, his real Bridget, was as far away now as Eva and Oliver. But he was thrilled to find in this woman something that was not broken by Time and change, and that something was the reality of life that would flow on forever.

He narrates how his meeting with Laura, now one Mrs. Childs, changed his very attitude to life. At the suggestion of Lord Harndean, Dawson met Mrs. Childs; he had no knowledge that he had before him the same Laura, the Blackshaw girl, now a middle-aged woman under the name of Mrs. Childs, and she was surrounded by shouting and enthusiastic young film-world people who wanted to make 'real pictures' not the commercial ones of 'mischievous nonsense'. She showed him a water-colour picture painted by Stanley Mervin; this was the sketch that Mervin had shown Jock and himself in the pub at Bulsden in 1913 on the Sunday of the first arrival of the Nixeys.

Seeing it, Dawson said that he felt as if he was staring through a little window at another world and another time—the great gold Maytime—now all gone, lost and forgotten. Laura said:

> And it's the same world. Even the little bridge is still there. I saw it last summer. But you must stop going back like that—it's the wrong way. I felt like you when I lost my husband ten years ago. We'd been very happy together, and it was for such a little time—and I said, 'Lost, lost, lost—everything gone, everything lost' until I made myself stop, made myself realise that life goes on—

> and the worst thing is to turn your face away and hold yourself rigid and not let life go flowing through you....[98]

Dawson's misconception of life simply melted away at the touch of these words of practical wisdom of life. This right understanding of men and things has come to Laura through her right understanding of Time's work. Her message—in fact, it is Priestley's own—breathes optimism. Laura's words and the effect they exercise on Dawson's mind have prompted John Atkins to pronounce this novel as "a powerful declaration of faith."[99]

Dawson had, for long, built a wall around himself; by nature an introvert, he had not bothered to see the world outside the wall.

In fact, he was not aware of the self-built wall until he saw the Nixeys. The meeting with Laura showed him a peephole through the wall which went on widening till he could find that there was world outside, and learnt to reconcile himself with it.

As David Huges—whose remark has been noted earlier—has observed, a reference to the past can cure the present and fortify the future with energy. Occupying as Dawson does the vantage ground of the present, he can have a dispassionate and detached view of his past. His self-centred and narrow interests and concerns yield place for a much wider and really sympathetic understanding of life; he becomes a really purposeful and useful individual to march on with life around him; this is how his present is cured by the remembrance of his past. When he was a youth at Bruddersford he could not see men and things in their true light; they were either exaggerated by his youthful romantic eye or muddled and distorted by his prejudiced mind. But today, standing as he does, far from that time, he takes a lucid and dispassionate view of the period of his youth; there is now no magic, no aura around personalities and happenings. It is from Laura that he learns that Eva did not commit suicide by jumping off the ledge as falsely reported by Joan but was pushed down to death by Joan herself in a quarrel with her. Laura, who was actually present at the time Joan pushed Eva down, had kept the truth corked up within herself, and the unspoken secret had been hanging like lead on her mind. The revelation of it took the load off her mind, and brought about a catharsis in her; tears rolled down her cheeks in anguish and relief. Dawson comforted Laura saying that she had got rid of all that and they should forget it and march on. What he says to her is also a self-addressed reminder of his own duty to others. He resolves to join the young and buoyant team to make 'real pictures'.

The novel established a reconciliation between living in passing time and a timeless quality of life. Dawson realises that it is no use mourning the ironic wreck Time leaves behind, and that wisdom lies in marching on in spite of time. Susan Cooper remarks succinctly, "The time-haunted Gregory Dawson can make a future for himself only if he takes the past with him, for it is pointless to mourn Time, and impossible to make it stand still."[100] But there is no question of attempting to make Time stand still because one cannot wish it away. The only thing one has to realise is not to mourn the loss of Time or the change Time brings because one cannot wish it away. Happily Dawson realises this truth at the end of the novel; he gives up his nostalgia about the past and wisely begins his forward journey with a hopeful heart towards the future.

The novel is a proof of Priestley's distinctive ability as a writer of multiple Time. His is not the Bergsonian way of treating Time only psychologically. Past, present and future are a series of the eternal 'Now', and Time is a mode of looking at life which is multidimensional. This Dunnian theory of Time is remarkably exploited here to show the true quality of life. Priestley displays a much greater skill in manipulating the different dimensions of Time in the next Time-novel, that is, *Jenny Villiers.*

Jenny Villiers (1947) is the only novel of Priestley's which is primarily concerned with Time just as *I Have Been Here Before* is the only play of his which primarily treats of Time. The consciousness of Martin Cheveril, a fifty-year-old playwright of the Theatre Royal at Barton Spa, is presented as a focal point of universal consciousness functioning in a timeless order. Cheveril, the central character, gloomy about the dwindling position of the Theatre in the 1940's regains his faith in the future of the Theatre through the life-giving encounters he has had with two young and talented actresses, one called *Jenny Villiers,* who had lived a century ago, in the 1840's, whom he meets in a sort of dream, and the other called Ann Seward of his own time whom he meets in the flesh. The novel appears on the surface of it to be a kind of thriller, a ghost-story but, in actuality, it is a profound artistic rendering of Priestley's multiple vision of Time. The poltergeist phenomenon is used as a means to a metaphysical end. The novel establishes how the mystery and greatness of human personality which is a part of the world mind, of universal consciousness, cannot be contained in the strait jacket of passing time.

Like Marlowe's *Dr. Faustus*, who meets Helen of Troy in a vision, Cheveril also meets Jenny in a kind of dream. But Cheveril is not a necromancer; he does not conjure up the face of Jenny by means of any black magic but encounters her through the mysterious working of his consciousness, which is an integral part of the universal consciousness operating, in a timeless order, in all human beings. Therefore, Cheveril's is a deep spiritual experience which expands and enriches his consciousness, and sets his mind free from doubts and fears and gloom, as a result of which he emerges full of optimism for the future of the Theatre.

The old-fashioned Gauntlet glove floating out of the portrait case of *Jenny Villiers* and its rushing past Ann before it fell on the floor is indicative of the continuity of the same personality—the same consciousness—from the former to the latter, demolishing barriers of Time. The impression of the portrait of Jenny and the details about her and her colleagues of the 1840's which Cheveril gathered from a booklet set the imaginative part of Cheveril's half-dreaming and half-waking mind soaring; then begins the drama of the past of Jenny in this artist's consciousness. The artist is mystified, when he wakes up, at the mysterious way his dreaming self worked. Could it be a dreaming wake or a waking dream? he wondered. Much puzzled, he floated into sleep again. He saw and heard Jenny and Walter Kettle, the stage manager of the theatre, discuss the true quality of acting, and found himself talking to them across the invisible gulf of years. He felt a kindred relationship between Kettle and himself. Cheveril's impassioned cry "Jenny!" and the actress turning back in bewilderment on hearing it suggests a mysterious communication from the consciousness of the living to that of the dead. Jenny heard Cheveril's cry across a hundred years, from a distant future, a part of the eternal 'Now', This was the first miracle, Cheveril felt. The second miracle was when Jenny was rehearsing Viola's Willow Cabin Speech from *Twelfth Night* and made a mistake which she immediately corrected on Cheveril's spontaneous dissatisfaction with it. The third miracle took place at the romantic scene in which Napier, Jenny's lover, received red roses from her. The novelist says that the moment had been suddenly arrested, its time jerked to a stand-still but Jenny alone of them was free of that moment and that time, and could communicate in some other and mysterious dimension. Cheveril in his earthly time is intended to throw light on the mystery of personality and consciousness which defies the bounds of linear time:

> "You see, I had to throw him the rose...And I wanted him to be happy too. You understand, don't you?"
>
> "Are you talking to me?" said Cheveril.
>
> "I'm talking to somebody who's here now, who wants to understand me, but who wasn't there when it all first happened.
>
> "When it first happened?"
>
> "It all goes on happening. You can get back to it, if you think hard about it, although it's never just the same—"[101]

That epitomises Priestley's conviction that nothing that has happened ever vanishes at all; it is in its own time. This is the Dunnian Serial Time put in the form of fiction. Priestley uses the Ouspenskian concept of imagination as a reality in depicting Cheveril's will and power to create, in his mind, the celebrated actress and her age. Priestley also puts the Jungian world mind, otherwise called the Collective Unconscious, operating, in a timeless order, through individuals.

Cheveril's consciousness has something of the consciousness of Kettle. Therefore he speaks, "I wish I could talk to you properly, Walter Kettle. There's something of me in you. I know exactly what you're feeling."[102] Priestley shows that when Cheveril was face to face with Jenny, the barriers of Time crumbled away and vanished. Whether Jenny darted out of her time into Cheveril's time, or Cheveril strayed into her time, they were partakers of the universal consciousness working outside passing time; both were in the eternal 'Now'. When Cheveril was in the midst of this 'spiritual' experience he was disturbed by the ringing of his telephone; he was back again in his passing time.

The tragic death of Jenny caused by the sudden leaving of Julian Napier, her lover, and the mourning by her colleagues was caught by Cheveril's mind. The sudden appearance of Jenny in the form of light is tantamount to a manifestation of the immortality of consciousness. Priestley exploits Serial Time in a unique fashion: Jenny's Time Two after her death, the living time of her colleagues in their Time One existence, and Cheveril's Time One are merged into one universal consciousness. While Jenny's voice is not heard by her colleagues, Cheveril hears her and her colleagues. This kind of experiment in any creative literature is rarely to be met with. The interlocking of different time-scales has been purposefully tried out in order to drive home the idea of the mystery and magic of human personality. Priestley shows a remarkable artistic skill in presenting almost the whole of the complex plot of this novella in a dream-like world, at a preternatural level of Time, as he does in his plays *Johnson Over Jordan* and *Music at Night*. His matchless skill is to be seen in the interlocking of different time-scales and blending of diverse theories like the Dunnian serialism, the Ouspenskian Eternal Recurrence theory and the Jungian theory of the Collective unconscious. Everything happens in the fay-like world of Cheveril's half-dreaming mind. Priestley's conviction that death cannot put an end to life, to consciousness, comes from the lips of Jenny, when she pities her colleagues, whom she has left behind in her Time One existence, and who, in their ignorance, mourn her death. She says to Cheveril, "You tell them it doesn't matter about me or about anybody, so long as the flame burns clear. You know."[103] When she begins to fade out after saying these words, Cheveril, crying to see her again, tries to catch hold of her but fails and crashes into a dead cold mirror, shouting "The Glass Door! only the Glass Door." This image of the glass door is significant in that it is symbolic of life's illusion, its shadow show, only Time's illusion. To understand reality one has to go beyond the illusive mirror of Time which stands between reality and our earthly existence. This illusion-working mirror reminds Priestley's readers of the symbolic long mirror in the play *The Long Mirror*.

Cheveril recognises that Jenny's personality has entered Ann and Julian Napier is present in Ann's lover Robert, just as something of Kettle is in himself. The continuance of consciousness from the previous lives into the present lives of individuals is proved by the reactions of Cheveril and Ann to each other's presence at their first meeting. Everytime Cheveril met Jenny in his dream he had felt a 'shiver', a word often used in Priestley to denote change of Time-dimension. When Cheveril sees Ann, he experiences the same feeling of a 'shiver'. She looks straight at him, sitting face to face, and Cheveril feels a cold pricking along his spine. They regard each other steadily for one queer second; Cheveril feels as if the room waited for something strange to happen. Priestley points to the *deja vu* experience they go through; they smile at each other as if they were old friends. Both had a vague, annoying feeling that they had met before, but where? Immediately he recognised that she was *Jenny Villiers* and her lover Robert was Julian Napier; he had met them in the dream. Ann too felt that somewhere she had worked with Cheveril. Cheveril had some part of Kettle which attracted Ann to the former. All the three characters felt some inexplicable and deep kinship between them. When asked by Cheveril whether Robert was in love with her, Ann replied significantly, "And I am with him too. It's been going on for ages."[104] Two more instances further confirm Cheveril's feeling of association and friendship with Ann and Robert. When asked to deliver Viola's Willow Cabin Speech Ann readly agreed and began reciting. Priestley says, "Then she stopped and looked at him apologetically, and he could feel the cold pricking again, for she had made the same mistake that Jenny made and had stopped where Jenny had stopped."[105] Again there is a reference to the feeling of cold as indicative of a change of the time-dimension which, in this case, was from the present to the past. Ann spoke the same language as spoken by Jenny about a theatrical career. The other occasion was when Cheveril met Robert. The novelist speaks of what Cheveril felt when Robert, the young handsome Air Commander entered his room: "...(he) gasped, and once again felt an icy hand touching his spine. For Julian Napier had entered the room."[106] Cheveril's intuitive feelings about Ann become solid facts when he learnt that hers was a family of stage actors, her grand mother, mother's mother, had been an actress, and that Walter Kettle was the grandfather of her grandmother.

Jenny Villiers calls for comparison with *I Have Been Here Before* in some respects. This novella is largely based on Ouspensky's theory of Eternal Recurrence. Dr. Gortler and Cheveril have similar conclusions, but their ways of arriving at them are different. Dr. Gortler conducts experiments with the lives of certain people in different times, whereas Cheveril makes no such conscious philosophical and intellectual endeavours to arrive at the truth. Cheveril relies more on what he gains from his dreaming, imaginative and creative self than on reasoning and logic. The novel shows that the past is not totally changed but partially it is. Unlike Kettle—partially Cheveril's self—Cheveril did not remain a bitter and unhappy artist. Ann is not left by Robert as Jenny was by Napier. A big change comes into the life of Cheveril, as he resolves to devote himself fully to reviving the Theatre. The sight of the glove, Jenny's gauntlet glove, brought him all the hope of brilliant future for the Theatre. All his bewilderment, doubt, and self-contempt dropped away and he became a robust optimist. If a reference to the past of Dawson's life in *Bright Day* cures his present and fills him with a hope for the future, the reference to the past of Jenny's life through a dream cures Cheveril of his pessimism and makes him hopeful of a future for the Theatre. The Ouspenskian theory is artistically used here. We notice, as well, that Priestley wants to show the oneness of humanity which Cheveril speaks of, while talking to Pauline about the change his encounter with Jenny has brought about in his attitude and understanding: "Oh, well, communication and understanding outside our time, somewhere on the other side of things, where people aren't so separate as they think."[107] The same idea gets dramatised in *Music at Night*.

Priestley makes use of different scales of Time in the novel. Cheveril and his colleagues of the Theatre Royal are in Time One. Cheveril's dreaming self takes him into Time Two, which is Time One of Jenny and her group. Cheveril enteres Time Three, which is the dimension of the spirit and of the imagination in an artist—and this is the sphere where he meets Jenny who is out of her Time One life—life in passing time—and is in her Time Two existence. There is a communication between Cheveril's living time and Jenny's Time Two life, which is not at all seen or heard or felt by her colleagues who are in their passing time, which is time past from our standpoint. So far as time-scales or different dimensions of Time are concerned the novelist follows Dunne's serialism. The plot moves in very complicated time-scales employed by the novelist with a view to presenting life outside time. The work establishes artistically the permanence of life, the endurance of humanity and its consciousness beyond and above Time's reach.

The second part of this phase comprises two plays, namely, *The Linden Tree* and *Summer Day's Dream,* which mainly use Serial Time to suggest a way out of the muddle and chaos caused by the World Wars.

The Linden Tree (1947) suggests a solution to the problem of the generation-gap through a right understanding of life in a timeless dimension. *Eden End* had already pointed out the true quality of life in the Dunnian way and also shown the wise path of living through the character of Dr. Kirby. Also, Gregory Dawson in *Bright Day* was presented as one who could make the best of both life in passing time and life outside its purview. *The Linden Tree* goes one step further: it suggests a way of resolving the conflict of opposite values by means of taking an overall view of life in a timeless dimension. A wise view of living is presented through the eyes of Robert Linden, a professor of History in the University of Burmanley. The sixty-one year old professor, who believes that now he is, as a teacher, better equipped because of ripeness of age and experience, feels hurt and humiliated at the decision of the authorities of the University to divest him of the Chair of History. He determines to fight against the injustice. On the other hand, his wife, two elder daughters and son feel relieved at this development, because they want him to leave Burmanley for a more comfortable life in Hampshire. The professor does not want to leave the place; Dinah, his youngest daughter, alone stands on the side of her father. He protests against his roots being cut off from a place where he has lived for thirty-seven years, while his wife feels fed up with her life in the place and is all eagerness to go and live with their only son Rex in Hampshire where he has a mansion to live in and all comforts to enjoy.

Except Dinah they are all out to snatch the maximum material comfort from their life in passing time. Professor Robert knows that the old with their wisdom and the young with their enthusiasm should go together to make life noble and beautiful. But he is not prepared to give up the values and principles he has cherished all through his life. As he has begun seeing life free from the illusion of passing time, he does not lose his equanimity; bears no bitterness towards his wife and children who do not see his point of view; takes a philosophic view of their attitude and feels reconciled to the parting of ways and resolves to move on, with Dinah on his side, along the 'mucky old high road' which is unaffected by the passage of time.

On a closer look, the play is found to be complex in its vision of life; it has in its texture three main strands: the domestic picture of the Lindens, the contemporary social scene, and the true character of human life which is outside the uni-dimensional chronological time. To call it a 'domestic play' is to miss a lot of its poetic vision of life. Susan Cooper rightly disapproves of Trewin's description of it as the best domestic play of our time. Its scope is much wider; it goes not only beyond giving a realistic picture of the contemporary social scene of 1947 but also beyond depicting the magic circle of a family with the relationships between the individuals in it; the playwright calls our attention to the irksome problem of every society, the problem of the generation gap leading to misunderstanding, tension and bitterness between the older and younger generations. The play shows a solution to the conflicts it deals with—conflict in family, conflict between generations and conflict between periods of history—by making one see man's life and civilization outside time, outside chronological historical time. Professor Robert recognises the true quality of human life, the essential thread which runs unbroken and unaffected by the vicissitudes of civilization because it is not bound by Time. The professor recognises that there are two patterns of man's life recorded in history. One is of man as a physical creature and the other is of him as a spiritual creature. These two patterns are endlessly being superimposed on each other. The first is easy to understand and the second needs to be interpreted. The first pattern is man's existence in passing time, and the second is of his spiritual life which exists in a timeless dimension. One is incomplete and meaningless without the other.

The play has a melancholy beauty, a haunting charm, because it creates a double world, the world of the past and the world of the present held in a timeless dimension—a theme which we have seen treated in earlier plays like *Time and the Conways* and *Eden End*. In fact, Professor Robert reminds one of Dr. Kirby, and Dinah strikes us as a better and more subtly developed version of Carol. There are two divergent points of view. One is the down-to-earth materialism represented by Rex, and the other is that of noble values such as peace, sympathy and beauty which Professor Robert found in his generation, the Edwardian age. Rex is a modern young man very much living in passing time; his philosophy is to have the most out of this life before time runs out; he is a typical man in a hurry and to him money is God; he bothers little about the moral aspects of things; his aim is material gain.

Rex's attitude is clearly seen in the following conversation between him and Edith, his father's student, who is worried about preparing an essay on Charles the Fifth:

Rex: Well, Edith, that's my advice to you. Start
Living. There isn't much time.

Edith: Isn't much time for what?

Rex: For anything. And none for Charles the Fifth.
He had his share. We'd better take ours while we can.[108]

Talking with his father he puts forth his standpoint that life is to be enjoyed before it is too late, because it may be snuffed out at any moment:

Rex: As to what I'm upto—that's quite simple too—
I am enjoying myself—while there is time.

Professor: You don't see it lasting, you mean.

Rex: I don't see anything lasting...we can't last. And anyhow when the atom bombs and rockets really start falling, whichever side sends them, it's about ten to one we'll be on the receiving end here. I've Sometimes thought of clearing out—South America, for instance, or East Africa—but somehow I feel that wouldn't do. So I'll take what's coming. But before then I propose to enjoy Myself."[109]

To him the present time alone is life. While leaving her husband, Mrs. Linden is emotionally disturbed, and delays a bit in joining Rex, and this young man calls out impatiently but gaily; "Come on, mother, We're all set—the road's a-calling."[110] Indeed he feels the road of life, life in passing time, is calling him.

Dinah is the one person in whom the old professor finds his real ally. She is sensitive and sensible; has a sympathetic understanding of her father's ideas and feelings. She is not corrupted by the passage of Time. That is why Mr. Cotton, the housekeeper, observes that the girl is always in the land of childhood. Dinah is not happy on the birthday of her father, because she feels that it is not a happy family reunion but more like business. She suddenly bursts into laughter, remembering the really happy days of their childhood when they had so much fun. The following conversation brings out how her past has been a living experience and a part of her present life.

Jean: Now what is it?

Dinah: I suddenly remembered that time, oh years ago I was quite little—when we were staying in North Wales—and you two had a row about toothpaste or something.

Marion: It was cold cream stuff for sunburn—and we (smiling) fought—do you remember, Jean?

Jean: Yes—and the stuff came out and went over everything.

Dinah: That was a heavenly place—it smelt of white-wash and cows, and had gigantic fluffy brown hens, and I was just part of it—magic. That's what I don't like about growing up. You stop being part of places like that. You just look at them as if they were in a shop window. You're not swallowed up by them any more. And what do you get in exchange—by growing up?[111]

Thus she derives great joy from the remembrance of things past, which have been with her as a part and parcel of her existence. We are, thus, made aware of the play moving at places, in a double-world, of past and present. Dinah stands as a foil not so much to her sisters as to her brother. In her we come across the two patterns of life, recognised in human history by Professor Robert, going together in harmony; she lives in a significant world where the past is ever alive and the present is full of meaning and colour, while Rex lives only in the present tense, in passing time, which has no depth or additional dimension.

Another occasion too focuses on the double-world of time. The Linden children are playing the family game of 'Black

Sam'; all of a sudden Rex remembers how he cheated a farmer named Joe Sykes in Cumberland years ago at this game and how that rustic's collar 'popped', and he bursts into laughter and all of them join him in laughing and enjoying the fun. The professor's face lights up at their laughter which is reminiscent of the jolly young days of his children. But Mrs. Linden becomes gloomy and unhappy. The reason for the sudden onrush of gloom as given by her is: "I suddenly felt awful—hearing you all laughing again—and remembering what fun we used to have. Oh—I went back long before that holiday in Cumberland—to other holidays and time—to when you were all very little—and before that—when everything was beginning for us...."[112]

Remembering the happy and peaceful days of the Edwardian age—the pre-1914 world—the professor feels nostalgic, but does not despair at the present generation of sheer materialism and callousness because he takes a whole view of life in all its changeful hues. His wife is incapable of his point of view or perception of life, because she takes a short view of things. The Dunnian serialism recommends a long view of Time. Accordingly, life needs to be seen in a series of scenes moving successively. The professor's view is a serial view, taking happy and unhappy periods of scenes of life with equanimity. Therefore, he is capable of reconciling his attitude with that of his son, because there is a realisation in him that, in reality, there is no generation gap, but a gap in proper understanding; in fact his son and the two daughters do love and respect him; but they are different from Dinah. Dinah is capable of understanding life as grasped by her father; their (i.e. Dinah's and her father's) understanding results from a four-dimensional view of life. The professor gives expression to his whole view of life, which is not bound by clock time or passing time, when he says to his wife and son: "Some things are worse, some things are better. And the sun will shine for Dinah tomorrow, my love, as it once shone for you, forty years ago—the same sun. And while there's time to lose the world, Rex, there's also time to save it—if we really want to save it... Give us our counters, Rex—that is your job—while the old man, with his patience, shuffles the cards. Patience...patience ...and shuffle the cards...."[113] This is the wisdom of a man who has seen life patiently and seen it whole; this wholesome and integral view is put across for the benefit of Rex, a typical modern man, who is a victim of the illusion of Time.

Priestley introduces music in this play to transport the characters—especially the central character Professor Linden—to a timeless world. The professor and his family experience the rich melancholy music of the second subject of the first movement of the Elgar Concerto being played on the 'Cello by Dinah in the adjacent room. The professor is tolled back to the warm and peaceful pre-1914 Edwardian world with its smiling afternoons—Maclaren and Ranji batting at Lords and Richter or Nikisch at the Queen's Hall. But the bitterness and regret due to the loss of Edwardian values expressed by him in the earlier part of the play and his sense of incompatibility with the modern generation of Rex and his kind are no longer felt by him; he finds reconciliation to the changing times. Now his mellowed outlook of sympathy and understanding finds its expression in what he says about Dinah's music: ".... Young Dinah Linden, all youth, all eagerness, saying hello and not farewell to anything, who knows and cares nothing about Bavaria in the nineties or the secure and golden Edwardian Afternoons, here in Burmanley, this very afternoon, the moment we stop shouting at each other, unseals for us the precious distillation, uncovers the tenderness and regret which are ours now as well as his, and our lives and Elgar's, Burmanley today and the Malvern Hills in a lost sun-light, are all magically intertwined."[114] This wise man's vision, travelling back and finding the present in the wholesome light of the past, wipes out the yawning gulf of years between the generations. David Hughes recognises this change of outlook in the professor when he observes that "the professor gains the rare philosophic heights that take a person beyond time's reach.... He fights to give a pattern to disorder...."[115] It is his ability to see life outside the illusion of Time that enables him to find an order in the midst of disorder. G.L. Evans rightly observes that the play "gives an impression of existing in a timeless condition overall...."[116]

If *The Linden Tree* presents a timeless view of life in order to solve the problem of generation gap, *Summer Day's Dream* depicts an innocent dream world.

Summer Day's Dream (1949) is described by Priestley as 'a fantastic comedy' and he dismisses out of hand the view that it is 'a political economic manifesto'. The play is a futuristic work written in 1949 but with its action set in 1975; it takes an adventurous leap into the future. Though certain values come up for discussion, it is not a discussion drama or a piece of committed writing. In fact, it portrays a true human life of beauty, wisdom and peace, an ideal to be realised. G.L. Evans observes, "It is perhaps the most avowedly idealistic play that Priestley has written."[117] The play depicts a world outside the cribbing compass of passing time, a timeless order where the past is not forgotten, the present is not hurrying and the future is not a thing to be born, but one that has been there always for the inhabitants of that world where life is ever young and beautiful and tranquil.

The play is remarkable, not for its action but for its atmosphere. England has survived the holocaust of the Third World War, a terrible atomic war; now she has become an agricultural state, has no pretensions to world power and industrial supremacy; the survivors have returned to pastoral life, a life of farming, bartering, rearing domestic animals and birds, baking the food they grow and creating their own pleasures like writing poetry, playing music, and acting plays. Away from the soul-killing power struggle and commercial competition it is a quiet life of magic and beauty and wisdom.

The simple, beautiful and wise world, which is a throw-back to the Great Golden Age of the fabled past, is represented by Stephen Dawlish, an octogenerian, the head of the Dawlish family living in the English backwater, his widowed daughter-in-law Margaret, Christopher and Rosalie, his grandson and granddaughter and Fred, an old farm bailiff, while the modern materialistic world is represented by an international team of three experts, viz. Heimer, an American breakneck industrialist, Irina, a young Russian officer and Dr. Bahru, an Indian research chemist, who are on their official mission of investigating the global resources for synthetic products, and are forced, under odd circumstances, to stay in the old house of the Dawlish family.

The simple ways of the English backwater bring about a big change in the perception and feelings of these foreigners. They are forced to smell fragrant English flowers, listen to the birds, and enjoy bright sunshine and soothing silvery moonlight. They find the unhurried ways of this life in the midst of nature's plenty really wiser and healthier in contrast to the speedy ways of living which have only given them—especially Heimer—tensions and worries, ulcers, and nervous breakdowns. They are enchanted and enthralled by the rhythmic and deeply satisfying life of the island. We notice an incredibly great change in Irina, the cold and tough-looking young Russian woman. She falls in love with Christopher who adores her with all his heart. Irina and Christopher are Priestley's Miranda and Ferdinand, with the difference that their love does not consummate in marriage in the play itself. Irina loves to live there. But she has to return. Likewise, Heimer and Bahru have to care for their respective duties. All the three decide not to disturb the happy island and its contented inhabitants; they give up making a report for the starting of synthetic factories and return.

Irina, who at first finds England sunk in decadent romanticism, is fascinated by the life of the land and falls in love with Christopher. The playwright's point of view is that a slow and quiet life has in it real beauty and wisdom, though it appears dull and decadent at first to those that are used to the high-speed competitive life of modern mighty commercial nations. This is a dream play which shows a brave new world, a world of magical atmosphere with natural civilised men and women living in harmony with it. Each of the English characters contributes to the atmosphere of the play. The old Dawlish has come out of the fire and heat of three World Wars and cherishes the sweet memories of his childhood and youth; Fred, the farmer, is a son of the English soil and lives in the lap of nature; Margaret, a middle-aged widow, an intuitive, mystically inclined kind of woman with a gift for foreknowledge of events, has the wisdom of the old world and a deep concern for the new world which is taking shape out of the ruins; the youngsters, Christopher and Rosalie, are the natural inheritors of this brave new world.

In *Summer Day's Dream* Time is an important element. Stephen has walked hand in hand with Time. He sees his past alive before him; he remembers his soldiering days in the First World War. Talking with Fred he says that he could see before his eyes the rotten sandbags even after sixty years. As already noted, Margaret is possessed of the wisdom of right living because she lives outside the tyranny of passing time. This fact is brought out at several places in the play. When Irina arrives at the house, Margaret glimpses, in a sudden flash, the change that is going to happen in the latter. Margaret's remark that Irina is going to be really happy bewilders and somewhat annoys this young Russian lady who is still a stiff and cold communist. Stephen explains Margaret's intuitive words: "There are some people, Madame Shestova, who don't seem to be so firmly clamped on to time and space as the rest of us are. They wander on the border between the known and the unknown. They see round corners. They can taste tomorrow night this afternoon. And Margaret's one of these people."[118] Margaret foresees Irina's infatuation with Christopher. We can consider another occasion also as a proof of her prevision. The three foreigners are hospitably received and treated in the Dawlish house. But none except Margaret has any knowledge of the purpose of their visit to that part of their land; she knows their motive and knows it intuitively. Margaret surveys the foreigners sombrely and then there ensues a conversation between her and Heimer.

"Margaret (gravely):	I should like to say something to you.
Heimer (heartily):	Why, sure! Go ahead, Mrs. Dawlish.
Margaret (slowly):	You left us nothing but the bare thorn and our bleeding hands; but now our hands are healed and the thorn is beginning to flower. Remember that.

Heimer (embarassed): Say, wait a minute, Mrs. Dawlish. Why are you telling us this?

Margaret (slowly): I don't know yet."[119]

This shows how her waking self is ignorant of the future but her Time Two Observer sees the future and warns. Later in the evening she reminds Heimer of this apprehension she voiced at their first meeting. Also another occasion reveals her power of prevision. The T.V. set has beamed some blurred message, and Heimer is much puzzled because they do not know yet when they can get away from there. Margaret says calmly that they will know quite soon. Hardly is Heimer's surprise at these words over when Fred brings the message from the Post Office that an atomicar is coming from Shrewsbury between eleven and twelve that night to pick them up for the air flight from there early in the morning. Similarly this mystical woman foresees the reunion of the lovers, Irina and Christopher. Heimer expresses concern for the fate of the lovers, saying that it might be quite some time before they can meet again. Margaret says calmly and impressively that they will not meet again for thousands of years. Rosalie is shocked at these words of her aunt. Stephen correctly interprets this intuitive perception when he says that their period of separation will seem like thousands of years; here the relative nature of Time is hinted at. What Margaret says to Bahru about the nature of her fancies reveals her awareness of the multi-dimensionality of life. Bahru's science can never understand her vision and perception. Rosalie too experiences the timeless order of life under the power of violin music played by her brother. She describes that experience in these words: "There was a moment tonight, when Christopher was playing, when it was as if we had all broken through into a larger and different sort of time, like that of a clear happy dream...Everybody there was so completely and wonderfully themselves."[120] What she is giving expression to is the inexplicable joy of timeless moments when past, present and future merge into one overwhelming spiritual experience. What Margaret, Rosalie and even the Irina of the later part of the play experience is a peep over the wall of passing time into 'a larger and different sort of time', which the characters in *They Came to a City* experience while in the city and lose suddenly the moment they come out and fall on the 'cold hill side' of reality.

Priestley depicts female characters as being capable of a higher vision and enduring love and affection. Irina is at first cold and stiff, and belittles the warm English life as 'decadent romanticism'. But the same character undergoes a sea-change in feeling and outlook. Her intense and deep love for Christopher converts her to new ideas and a new attitude which are clearly expressed at a number of places in the work. She tells Stephen that when she was in the garden that night she was reminded of the holidays she had spent with her mother's brother—her uncle—as a child and suddenly felt that life had gone past her; that she had never known such a feeling. Stephen says, "...my dear, when you tell yourself that life has gone past, the very opposite is true. Some great blazing lump of life is just arriving, and you're only clearing a space for it."[121] The old man's explanation of this young woman's feeling is Priestley's own view of the past—in terms of the Dunnian theory the past is never dead but, on the contrary, it is in its own time. Irina grows contemplative about what it is that brought her here face to face with Christopher. She feels convinced that there is something in life which lies outside the dimension of clock-time. The dream-atmosphere is carefully maintained throughout the play. That Irina feels as if she is wandering in a dream and has been a child again speaks of her living outside the tyranny of clock time. The work gives us the feeling that we are hovering over the borderland of reality and fantasy, of time and a timeless order. At several places Shakespeare's *The Tempest* and *A Midsummer Night's Dream* are quoted by Rosalie, Christopher, Margaret and even Irina. These echoes from the Shakespearian ideal romantic world not only lend a special colour and tone to what goes on in the Dawlish house and around but also help keep up the timeless dream atmosphere of the play. Irina's love brings her timeless moments just as the violin music played by Christopher transports Rosalie out of passing time into a much larger and different time—the fifth dimension. She puts this experience which she has never known before into these words: "...Now I understand. It is life in another world. There is no past—no future. There are moments when I wish to die—of shame, of happiness...."[122] Her love of Christopher lands her into a world of unalloyed joy, freed from the tyranny of Time. This Russian lady, who is prepared to give up her job for the sake of her love, grows sad at her imminent departure from there and begins to cry at the end of scene I, Act II. Heimer consoles her by saying that everything is going to be fine. She too says, through her tears, that everything is going to be fine. This is a clear indication of Irina's vision of the future time when she will come back to join her lover in this charming land. Margaret foresees the return of Irina and Heimer to this English back-water. Talking with Fred she speaks slowly and dreamily that he would see them there again.

The futile and restless lifestyle of modern civilization, enslaved by Time as it is, is represented by Heimer who finds "Right bang in the middle of things—a hollow place—just where there ought to be something lasting and good."[123] Margaret voices the playwright's own view of life when she says, "We are nourished by this planet's clay and the flame that comes from behind the stars."[124] This is a wise and integral view which holds in balance the life of the body governed by passing time and the life of the timeless spirit, which receives its flame from the all-pervasive eternal 'white flame' experienced by Priestley in his dream of birds. The ending of the play surely establishes, once again, the character of true life, which is life liberated from the clutches of Time. Margaret, the mystic soul, moves forward a pace or two, staring intently out, as if at the audience, and recites the following lines:

> A thousand eyes narrowing to watch us here, Eyes that may never reach this time we show, but see us as so many shadows on the wall....[125]

These lines suggest that those that live only in clock time cannot have a vision of the future, which is being dramatised here. In fact, what they perhaps think to be 'shadows on the wall' are really a part of the eternal 'Now'. The play creates a fantasy as noted already. The *Times* reviewer (9 Sept. 1949) wrote that the special achievement of the play had been "to create the atmosphere of a beguiling day-dream for his vision of an England which has come through atomic disaster to quiet wisdom".[126] In fact, it is a vision of humanity itself which after the fret and fever of wars, has settled down to live in quiet wisdom. David Hughes observes that the play's atmosphere "is that of a dream, a magic of present and past times established in a nightmare of the future".[127] A similar opinion is cryptically expressed by G.L. Evans; "The play is set in 1975, but its atmosphere is timeless."[128] The dream quality which is akin to that of *A Midsummer Night's Dream* and *The Tempest*—suggesting the beauty of life in nature uncorrupted by man's meddling intellect—places the idyllic action of the play in a timeless atmosphere.

The Other Place (1953) is a collection of short stories most of which concern Time. The Time theories in this collection are based on the concept of precognition discussed by H.T. Saltmarsh in his book *Foreknowledge* and the 'Extra-sense' theory—later termed *ESP* by psychoanalysts—attributed to Du Prel, "according to which there is a stratum in the subliminal mind which is capable of obtaining sensory knowledge of events outside the range of normal consciousness".[129] To go outside the range of normal consciousness is to go outside clock time. Priestley did know 'spontaneous cases' of 'psi' faculty, the faculty responsible for various forms of *ESP*. It has already been shown how the Nature Man in *Faraway* exercises this faculty to release the consciousness of Ramsbottom from the ordinary level of clock time and also how Dorothy in *Bright Day* is capable of extraordinary powers of perception. In *ESP* cases, those that are capable of lifting themselves or others out of passing time release their consciousness, or that of their subjects from the present moment by means of needling attention to things like cards, crystal balls, palms, shining black stones, etc. The Time stories discussed in the following pages contain scenes and situations that belong to a timeless order.

The Other Place is a story which is based on the *ESP* theory. It does not mean any particular place but a timeless order of existence. The *deja vu* experience Harvey Lindfield passes through in the old library of Dr. Alaric while in the town of Blackley and which is recounted by him to the author is one which he experiences in the inner world of consciousness. When Lindfield opened the door set in the shelves of the library room after he finished his counting of a hundred while he was simultaneously staring into a shining black piece of stone at the instance of Alaric, he landed into a narrow dark passage, lit bright at the other end by gold-like streaks of sunlight coming through a broken sort of door on the right. Going out of the door this electrical engineer entered *The Other Place*. He had a strange kind of experience which was not a dream, but something else, something certainly other than the kind of reality he was familiar with. The garden he roamed in and everything he saw and felt appeared to be perfect, pleasing and beautiful and seemed to have an extra solidity about it. He felt that time had stopped. "The old 'tick-tock-tick-tock-hurry-up-must-go' had gone. Nothing was wasting away, running down, draining out."[130] Everything was more distinct, sharper, more itself and waiting to be noticed. He saw Movis, a woman he had befriended during his stay in Blackley, enjoying her romantic time with her lover Rodney whom she had loved and lost and been frantically searching for. This 'Other Place' was totally free from Time's relentless effect; there was no glass wall between the people. Harvey was surprised to see there the people whom he had made friends with in the town.

Lindfield was terribly disappointed when he did not find Paula, the enchanting young woman of *The Other Place* whom he was mad after, in the little sitting-room where she had told him to meet not before half-past ten, but he, being impatient, had gone into the room ten minutes earlier and landed back into the library. Though he had the whole day there, he was astonished to find from the grandfather clock that he had spent only three minutes! His infatuation for Paula drove him in all directions to find her again but he drew a blank. Alaric granted him a second chance, making him pass through the same ritual of concentrating on the black stone and all that, and this time he had a dry and dull and shocking experience.

The heart of the story lies in the narration of Lindfield's experience when, waiting at the London Airport to fly to Toronto, he felt that Paula was there, and he rushed to her only to find that she was not Paula—his heart told him it was none else—but one Mrs. Enderslay who was going with her husband. He speaks of that queer experience:

> I don't know what I had stammered at them, because what I'd suddenly seen in her eyes, like a sort of signal from miles away in their grey depths, had turned me upside down and inside out. And what it had seemed to say was something like this: Yes, I was Paula when I was there, and now I remember you too, Harvey Lindfield, but where we were and what we can do about it, God Knows![131]

Lindfield's conclusion is that all people do experience their 'other place', and are puzzled when they cannot make out how it is that they meet the people of *The Other Place* in actual life sometimes.

Lindfield's experience is one of his journeys deep down inside his consciousness passing through the composite consciousness of humanity wherein clock time stops. The first door Lindfield opens is symbolic of crossing the boundary of outer consciousness in passing time and an entry into inner consciousness—in Priestley it is always the 'unconscious', the second level of consciousness. The intermediate stage is one of blurred sensation. The second door is an opening of the unconscious which works in a timeless dimension and it further leads to the innermost world of universal consciousness. Lindfield is enabled to turn inside his self far below his ordinary consciousness in passing time when Alaric makes him concentrate intensely and deeply on the black piece of stone, which is a Hindu spiritualist method of concentrating one's attention on a holy piece of black stone called 'Lingam' practised in India by some yogic men which Alaric might have learnt while in India. The story symbolically presents that kind of reality which is free from the tyranny of Time, and the atmosphere of timelessness in the story recalls that of the play *They Came to a City*.

This story resembles, in some respects, the play *I Have Been Here Before*. If Oliver Farrant and Janet are mutually attracted due to the relationship in their earlier lives, Harvey and Paula are drawn to each other because of their having loved each other deeply in their 'other place', a domain of their inner consciousness in a different order of Time. The story has no Ouspenskian idea of Recurrent Time but the one of *ESP* which throws light on the inward world of man which is not cribbed and cabined by Time. A really beautiful and happy life that can be experienced by man by enriching and expanding his consciousness in different orders of Time is artistically portrayed here in contrast to the soul-killing narrow existence lived in unidimensional clock time. The story deals with two kinds of timelessness: positive and negative. Lindfield's first entrance into the 'other place' lends him a positive experience of timeless existence because it is prompted by a genuine desire to be free from Time's tyranny, while the second time he has a negative experience of 'empty time', 'sinister time', akin to the 'temporal vacuum' found in Kafka's works, because Lindfield's act this time was one of desperation.

Guest of Honour presents how a disturbed and frightened mind harbours hallucinations which move in psychological time. Sir Bernard, a business tycoon, is the guest of honour at a dinner party hosted by the Imperial Industrialists' Association where he is going to speak. His fast-moving car suddenly stops because a strange-looking oldish man suddenly comes in the way. The old man's sinister words of warning go on ringing in Bernard's mind, and a drama of strange happenings begins to take place in his consciousness. Bernard is at the centre of all the happenings in his mind: he is addressing the 'spectral creatures' his business friends are turned into; all around there are skeletons and coffins, etc. Again his speedy car suddenly halts because an oldish shabby-looking fellow, possibly a foreigner, with dull drowsy eyes, is standing in the way. Bernard's mental scene comes to a grinding halt, and then again his car proceeds. The story cleverly splits time twice and joins it again. A remarkable skill is seen in blending passing time and psychological time. The story shows the leaping of Bernard's mind out of clock time. All the happenings described, page after page, take place in the inner consciousness in the space of a few seconds or minutes. A sharp contrast is shown by the split-time device between the time of the mind in speculation and imagination and the single-track clock time.

Look After the Strange Girl is a complex story which interlocks different time-dimensions and blends different orders of consciousness. Mark Denbow, a social historian and teacher in a school housed in an old mansion owned, years ago, by a family called Broxwoods, received one old Lady Purzley, niece of the late Lord Broxwood, who had spent her childhood days in this mansion, accompanied by her granddaughter Ann now. Denbow had known the history of the old family. The old woman remained in the library, and Mark took out Ann to show her round the place. Mark for a minute went away saying that he would return after taking aspirin and Ann decided to wait for him in the old summer house. It was an evening in 1952. Ann, a dreamy type, floated into the past of the place as it was in 1902; found herself among the Broxwoods and the Bullers. His consciousness being released from him, Mark too jumped back in time to 1902, and landed in another time. Mark and Ann both had made a time-jump; their consciousness mingled with that of those living in their own time and in their own world. Lady Purzley slept for a while and had a dream, and her dreaming self too jumped back to 1902. Though Mark was observing the activities of the Broxwoods and the Bullers and their friends, gathered in the dancing hall and participating in music and dance and dinner, he was all the while aware of the mysterious mingling of his present with their past. He met Dorothy, Mrs. Buller's daughter. Seeing deep into the eyes of this pretty girl in pink, he felt sure, as the hair on his neck felt queer, that this shining smiling girl and Lady Purzley, the lone grim old survivor of that cozy colourful time, were one and the same person. While he was following Dorothy in the conservatory his thoughts ran thus:

> Yet somewhere along time's Scenic Railway, just before it dipped into the darkness, she would be Lady Purzley, gnarled in tweed, staring at him mistrustfully, opening thin and bitter lips to put insulting questions to him....[132]

Mark told Dorothy her future, that she would marry Mr. Geoffrey Purzley and live to a ripe old age, etc. Even while talking to Dorothy in his dream-like existence he did know that he was not part of Lady Purzley's youth. Mark felt that he had lost himself in a maze of Time-dimensions. Attracted by 'the strange girl' he ran after her, and she too started running, and then he caught up with her inside the old summer house. Time completes its full circle at this point. Ann too had the same experience in that world where she had met the Broxwoods and the Bullers and Mark. Lady Purzley also had, in her dream, met Mark who had predicted her future. All the three had emerged wiser and richer in their experience. Mark, Ann and the old woman are depicted as being capable of postcognition; they could sail into the past time of the old mansion. The realities shown through the dream or reverie of these characters establish the mystery and complexity of human personality which is presented in different dimensions of Time and at different levels of consciousness. The wandering of these characters—particularly that of Mark—reminds the Priestleyan reader of Cheveril's encounters with *Jenny Villiers* and her colleagues in the novel *Jenny Villiers.*

The Statues illustrates the concept of precognition which is part of the *ESP* theory. Walter Voley gets the vision of the city of London as it will be some five centuries later; he sees some gigantic statues of the city which is still in the womb of Time, a future possibility. The future which Walter envisions is the result of a mystic moment which shows things in a timeless order; what he sees is part of the eternal 'Now'.

Mr. Strenberry's Tale is a piece of science-fiction writing and is not a deeply earnest story connected with consciousness and the mystery of Time. If Well's *The Time Machine* takes a jump into the future, this story takes a leap into the past of our human ancestors. Time is treated as a line and hence has neither depth of mystery nor magic.

Night Sequence is woven round the thesis that the imagination creates a world in a different time-order. Luke and Betty, a couple stranded on a rainy night in an old country house, have their consciousness released from them and they consequently experience the company of two past personalities of the old mansion. Betty enjoys the company of the heroic personality of Sir Edward, and Luke that of the bewitching girl Julia, Sir Edward's niece, in their separate rooms. Morning comes and the reality or illusion vanishes. The suppressed romantic desires might have created the strange world.

NOTES

1. John Atkins, *J.B. Priestley—The Last of the Sages* (London: John Calder Ltd., 1981), p. 20.
2. G.L. Evans, *J.B. Priestley—The Dramatist* (London: Heinemann Ltd., 1964), p. 146.
3. *The Plays of J.B. Priestley* (London: Heinemann Ltd., rpt. 1973), Vol. I, Introduction, p. viii.
4. Quoted by Susan Cooper, *J.B. Priestley*, p. 88.
5. *Ibid.*
6. Quoted by John Atkins, *J.B. Priestley*, p. 64.
7. *The Plays of J.B. Priestley*, Vol. I, p. 71.
8. T.S. Eliot, *Four Quartets* (London: Faber and Faber, 4th Impression, 1946), p. 10.
9. *The Plays of J.B. Priestley*, Vol. I, pp. 97-98.
10. *Ibid.*, p. 116.
11. C.R. Yaravintelimath, *Adventures in Time—A Study of J.B. Priestley's Time Plays* (Dharwad (India): Chaitra Prakashan, 1988), p. 111.
12. Susan Cooper, *J.B. Priestley—Portrait of an Author* (London: Heinemann Ltd., rpt. 1970), p. 118.
13. *The Plays of J.B. Priestley*, Vol. I, p. 195.
14. *Ibid.*, p. 189.
15. *Ibid.*, p. 174.
16. *Ibid.*, p. 176.
17. *Ibid.*

18. *Ibid*., p. 177.
19. John Atkins, *J.B. Priestley,* p. 73.
20. Irene Hentschel, from Introduction to *Time and the Conways* (London: Heinemann Ltd., 1950), p. xii.
21. Neil Taylor, "J.B. Priestley—Time and the Conways", *The Times Literary Supplement*, 21-27 December, 1990.
22. J.B. Priestley, *The Plays of J.B. Priestley*, Vol. I, Introduction, p. ix.
23. G.L. Evans, *J.B. Priestley—The Dramatist*, p. 103.
24. *The Plays of J.B. Priestley*, Vol. III, p. 93.
25. *Ibid*., pp. 134-35.
26. G.L. Evans, *J.B. Priestley,* p. 192.
27. J.B. Priestley, *Rain Upon Godshill,* p. 50.
28. *Ibid*., p. 50.
29. Susan Cooper, *J.B. Priestley,* p. 111.
30. *The Plays of J.B. Priestley*, Vol. I, p. 254.
31. *Ibid*., p. 256.
32. *Ibid*., p. 258.
33. *Ibid*., p. 267.
34. *Ibid*., p. 226.
35. G.L. Evans, *J.B. Priestley,* p. 109.
36. *The Plays of J.B. Priestley*, Vol. I, p. 264.
37. *Ibid*., p. 238.
38. *Ibid*., p. 258.
39. *Ibid*., p. 242.
40. *Ibid*., p. 260.
41. *Ibid*., pp. 219-20.
42. D.G. Rossetti, "Sudden Light", *The Oxford Book of Nineteenth Century Verse*, Chosen by John Hayward (Oxford: Clarendon Press, 1964), p. 681.
43. Quoted by Sir P.S. Sivaswamy Aiyer, *Evolutions of Hindu Moral Ideas* (Calcutta: The Calcutta Univ., 1935), p. 148.
44. *The Plays of J.B. Priestley*, Vol. I, p. 222.
45. John Atkins, *J.B. Priestley*, p. 74.
46. *Ibid*., pp. 74-75.
47. *The Plays of J.B. Priestley*, Vol. I, Introduction, p. x.
48. Davind Hughes, *J.B. Priestley*, p. 153.
49. Susan Cooper, *J.B. Priestley*, p. 126.

50. David Hughes, *J.B. Priestley,* p. 155.
51. Holger Klein, *J.B. Priestley's Plays* (London: Macmillan Ltd., 1988), p. 54.
52. *The Plays of J.B. Priestley*, Vol. I, pp. 297-98.
53. *Ibid.*, p. 330.
54. R.S. Furness, *Expressionism, The Critical Idiom Series.* No. 29 (London: Methuen & Co. Ltd., 1973), p. 94.
55. G.L. Evans, *J.B. Priestley—The Dramatist*, p. 124.
56. *Ibid.*, p. 44.
57. *Ibid.*, p. 137.
58. *The Plays of J.B. Priestley*, Vol. I, p. 365.
59. *Ibid.*, p. 378.
60. *Ibid.*, p. 393.
61. *Ibid.*, p. 394.
62. J.B. Priestley, *Rain Upon Godshill*, p. 286.
63. John Atkins, *J.B. Priestley—The Last of the Sages*, p. 67.
64. G.L. Evans, *J.B. Priestley—The Dramatist*, p. 140.
65. Quoted by John Atkins, *J.B. Priestley*, p. 67.
66. *Let the People Sing* (London: The Book Club, 1940), p. 58.
67. *Ibid.*, pp. 258-59.
68. *Ibid.*, p. 95.
69. *Ibid.*, p. 111.
70. Quoted from the play by John Atkins, *J.B. Priestley—The Last of the Sages,* p. 70.
71. *The Plays of J.B. Priestley*, Vol. III, p. 260.
72. David Hughes, *J.B. Priestley—An Informal Study of his Work*, p. 174.
73. *The Plays of J.B. Priestley*, Vol. III, p. 240.
74. G.L. Evans, *J.B. Priestley,* p. 193.
75. Allardyce Nicoll, *World Drama* (London: George G. Harrap & Co. Ltd., 1968), p. 786.
76. *The Plays of J.B. Priestley*, Vol. III, p. 155.
77. *Ibid.*, p. 194.
78. *Ibid.*, p. 197.
79. John Atkins, *J.B. Priestley—The Last of the Sages*, p. 98.
80. *Ibid.*, p. 230.
81. G.L. Evans, *J.B. Priestley—The Dramatist*, p. 208.

82. David Hughes, *J.B. Priestley,* p. 198.
83. G.L. Evans, *J.B. Priestley,* p. 207.
84. John Atkins, *J.B. Priestley,* p. 217.
85. *Ibid*., p. 232.
86. David Hughes, *J.B. Priestley,* p. 198.
87. J.B. Priestley, *Margin Released,* p. 192.
88. John Atkins, *J.B. Priestley,* p. 187.
89. David Hughes, *J.B. Priestley,* p. 181.
90. *Bright Day* (London: William Heinemann Ltd., rpt. June 1949), p. 8.
91. *Ibid*., p. 74.
92. *Ibid*., pp. 127-28.
93. *Ibid*., p. 184.
94. *Ibid*., pp. 186-87.
95. *Ibid*., p. 193.
96. *Ibid*., pp. 206-07.
97. *Ibid*., p. 215.
98. *Ibid*., pp. 361-62.
99. John Atkins, *J.B. Priestley,* p. 187.
100. Susan Cooper, *J.B. Priestley,* p. 29.
101. *Jenny Villiers* (London: William Heinemann Ltd., 1947), p. 99.
102. *Ibid*., p. 77.
103. *Ibid*., pp. 148-49.
104. *Ibid*., p. 168.
105. *Ibid*., p. 169.
106. *Ibid*., p. 175.
107. *Ibid*., p. 188.
108. *The Plays of J.B. Priestley,* Vo. I (London: Heinemann, rpt., 1973), p. 416.
109. *Ibid*., p. 429.
110. *Ibid*., p. 462.
111. *Ibid*., p. 424.
112. *Ibid*., p. 443.
113. *Ibid*., p. 444.
114. *Ibid*., p. 450.

115. David Hughes, *J.B. Priestley—An Informal Study of his Work* (London: Rupert Hart-Davis, 1958), p. 204.
116. Gareth Lloyd Evans, *J.B. Priestley—The Dramatist* (London: Heinemann, 1964), p. 209.
117. *Ibid.*, pp. 204-05.
118. *The Plays of J.B. Priestley*, Vol. III (London: Heinemann, rpt., 1962), p. 418.
119. *Ibid.*, p. 425.
120. *Ibid.*, p. 471.
121. *Ibid.*, p. 440.
122. *Ibid.*, p. 454.
123. *Ibid.*, p. 470.
124. *Ibid.*, p. 475.
125. *Ibid.*, p. 476.
126. John Atkins, *J.B. Priestley*, p. 222.
127. David Hughes, *J.B. Priestley*, p. 212.
128. G.L. Evans, *J.B. Priestley*, p. 203.
129. John Atkins, *J.B. Priestley*, p. 81.
130. J.B. Priestley, *The Other Place* and *The Stories of the Same Sort* (London: William Heinemann Ltd., 1953), p. 15.
131. *Ibid.*, pp. 39-40.
132. *Ibid.*, p. 135.

5

Final Phase: Wisdom's Realm

Rightly speaking, the final phase begins in the sixties, though an earlier novel *The Magicians* (1954) was a forerunner. From 1954 to 1961, Time had taken a back-seat in Priestley's mind. The sixties found him again obsessed with it. *Man and Time,* a remarkable product of Priestley's probing and profound study of Time and its influence on man, appeared in 1964. The novels of the sixties, therefore, intensify the Time-association. *The Magicians* is treated here along with the four novels of this mellowed phase because it foreshadows the mystic and spiritual stuff that distinctly marks this phase. Each one of these five novels has at least one wise man, a seer type. These novels march farther than the earlier works in the direction of Priestley's efforts to show the progress of consciousness. They artistically emphasise that man has to expand and enrich his consciousness to become a worthy and noble human species on this planet. They show that the wisdom of life dawns only from the right understanding of Time. The five novels which show Priestley at his best as a time novelist of wisdom are thoroughly discussed in this chapter.

The Magicians (1954) presents Priestley's apocalyptic view of life which "is given full expression for the first time in a novel".[1] This novel is a serious explanation of consciousness and the reality of life. It contrasts the significant, soul-expanding experience of life in non-passing time with the soul-killing and mind-thwarting experience of mere existence in passing time. These two types of life are represented by two sets of characters. Life 'as it really is', which is not governed by linear time, is represented by three magicians who are of the Oriental yogic stuff, while the other type is represented by a mischievous coterie of businessmen, money-maniacs, and a self-spoilt scientist—a lackey of these merchants of death. The 'indomitable trio of magicians'—Wayland, Marot and Perperek—were unique Time-travellers. These magicians were old men but they had mysteriously maintained a vitality of mind and body. They were gifted with the power of precognition and postcognition; they could freely travel in Time, backward and forward, and read the minds of men. To them nothing was accidental, everything was preplanned in the universe. They contended—and this is Priestley's own view also—that people suffer because they think of nothing but making the maximum material gains out of passing time before it runs out; they held men's suicidal belief in 'tick-tock' time as being responsible for 'the cyanide philosophy' of the Nazi leaders who knocked the hell out of everything around. These Time-travellers met once every few years and discussed how to help mankind and save the individuality of men so that they remained human and did not tend to become zombies.

Mervil and his men and the scientist Sepman were enemies of mankind. These money-mongers whose aim was to make a fast buck in this age of 'admass' possessed a drug named 'Sepman Eighteen', an invention by Sepman; the drug was capable of stopping anxiety, worry and feelings of guilt; it could pave a smooth road from the cradle to the grave. This business gang wanted to use Ravenstreet, the central character of the novel, in pushing this drug in the market on a large scale and would allow the latter a share in the sale proceeds. The magicians smelt the sinister design of the coterie, and decided to save Ravenstreet and the world from the impending danger.

Ravenstreet, the central character, undergoes a sea-change in his whole attitude to life when he comes under the power of the three 'magicians'. An electrical engineer by profession, Ravenstreet had come out of a business house on a point of honour, was restless and gloomy, bored and disappointed and tried to calm down his mind in several ways: he went to movies and hotels and had the gay company of a widow called Mavis, read books, etc. But it was all a futile game. It was by chance that he met the three magicians on the way to his country house at Broxley; the magicians were not hurt even though the hotel where they were staying was hit by a plane because, being aware of the future happening, they had already shifted from there to a nearby field. Ravenstreet, impressed by their appearance and words, took them to his Broxley house. The three old men felt thankful to Ravenstreet for the warm hospitality they received from him and thought of making him happy and cheerful.

The three Time-travellers set at nought the evil designs of Mervil and his gang by means of their superior knowledge of Time and the mysterious powers they had: Sepman and his wife met with tragic death in a car accident, Mervil and Karney were humiliated and vanquished. They twice enabled Ravenstreet to enter 'time alive' and brought about his reunion with Philippa just a few hours before her death. During his re-entry into past events, re-living that time and that world owing to the mystical powers of the old men, Ravenstreet was conscious of his consciousness. On both occasions his younger self was experiencing and his older self was observing; his experience could emerge as something new and creative because the perception of the younger self was enriched by the knowledge of the older self. This novel resolves the conflict between the selves in a novel way: the experiences of the two selves of Ravenstreet in two different time-dimensions—the past and the present—are presented as one single reality of consciousness and this is the main theme of the novel. The novel mainly deals with the significant change Ravenstreet undergoes under the influence of the magicians. It is based not on one particular Time theory but on a synthesis of Dunne, Ouspensky, Jung, the *ESP* concept and something of the Indian Karma Doctrine. Apart from going through the 'time-alive' experience twice, Ravenstreet had different kinds of experience at the hands of these three seers who put him in different time-dimensions. The important occasions and events connected with Time have been highlighted here.

Marrot, Wayland and Perperek, desirous of setting Ravenstreet free from the wrong view of Time, which is the wrong view of life itself, started exercising their mystical powers on his mind. Priestley describes how Ravenstreet felt when he stared at Marot as instructed by the latter:

> Ravenstreet did not look away but met the challenge of these eyes, a luminous grey in that light. Ravenstreet had the feeling that his mind was being stripped, down to a level beyond his consciousness. He didn't move, didn't speak. It seemed as if the world waited in silence, as if time had stopped.[2]

Ravenstreet's experience is similar to the one that Paul Brunton, an American writer, had when he met Raman Maharshee, which he describes as follows:

> These luminous orbs (the eyes) seem to be peering into the inmost recesses of my soul.... I become aware that he is definitely linking my mind with his, that he is provoking my heart into that state of starry calm which he seems perpetually to enjoy.... Time seems to stand still....[3]

These wise men could make the past live again in human consciousness or place consciousness in a timeless state by virtue of some yogic powers they had acquired. For example, Wayland told Ravenstreet to look at the snow outside. 'Snow in July' could not be believed by Ravenstreet at first but the next moment he was astonished to see a heavy snowfall, with white flakes everywhere. "And what was really more remarkable was that he found at once in the scene all the enchantment he remembered from his childhood, as if the fairy tale world had returned."[4] He turned to look at Wayland who was sitting there smiling meaningfully at him. When he had a glance again at the window, there was no trace of snow; he found himself an ageing man back in his world and in his time. Such miracles as this were operations on consciousness which men like Wayland, a Time-traveller, could perform.

Perperek was a more seasoned mystic soul. His favourite words 'Tick-tock' were used to describe the popular belief that passing time destroys everything, hurrying people down a steep track to oblivion. His contempt for the wrong view of Time finds a sharp and biting expression, though in broken English, in the following words:

> A day is here, is gone. A minute is here, is gone. A second is here, is gone. Past is nothing. Future is nothing. All is thin slice—a tick, a tock—between nothing. You hypnotise yourself believe these things—all follows very very bad. A life for sheeps....[5]

Wayland's view of Time and life combines the crux of Dunne's Serial Time and Ouspensky's Spiral Time:

> There is no escape, no oblivion round the corner. Time is not destroying you, but neither can you destroy it. Life must be lived, but of course you can decide on what level you will live it. That is, if you know enough and are prepared to make the proper effort. Our chief trouble now is that we don't know enough and only make wrong efforts....[6]

This view is very much akin to the Hindu Karma view which makes allowances for free will that can be exercised within certain limits.

The 'time-alive' experience which Ravenstreet passes through twice under the spell of these wise men's powers is not like memory at all. His first entry into 'time-alive' placed him with Philippa Storer, the girl he had loved and lived with years ago, and wanted to marry, but had suddenly deserted her in a cottage at Pelrock Bay under very testing circumstances when he was torn between his love for Philippa and the lure of a fortune he would get if he married the only daughter of the manager of his firm. During this 'time-alive' he was witnessing himself to be a battlefield of two selves: the naive young Charlie, out to enjoy life, and the cool calculating young man Charles with his eyes on his manager Frank's fortune; at last the businessman Charles won out. Then he told a lie not only to Philippa but also to his conscience, and deserted her. Now he saw again his beloved girl standing at the door of the cottage, and her misery and despair rose like a dark tide to drown him. The following description speaks of the timeless quality of his experience during those 'time-alive' moments:

> ...he had more or less re-entered a past that was in some inexplicable fashion still going on,.... It was almost every kind of feeling at once; bitterness and horror and pain were there, reaching out to him from Pelrock Bay and 1926 but so were wonder and a strange hopefulness, even a sort of confused joy, coming from a sense of indefinable possibilities, perhaps time alive, perhaps life as it is.[7]

Ravenstreet was convinced that it was not memory, or simply traces in the brain, of what was over and done with. His suspicion that he had been hypnotised into an illusion of the past was set at rest by Marot who said that, instead, he had been hypnotised from the wrong belief that the past was dead and gone and Time was ticking away everything into oblivion. These wise men speak but Priestley's ideas and views about Time: man should develop fully as a conscious spiritual being, capable of being himself, of making free choices. Wayland's views stem from Ouspensky, Gurdjieff and the Karma doctrine. He observes, "...You are your life. And nothing has gone and nothing has stopped. Your time is your life. You can change it but you can't get out of it."[8] These words have something of Gurdjieff too. This truth about time and life dawned on Ravenstreet, when the spell of the magicians worked on him.

The end of Sepmanism and Mervilism—two complementary diabolical cults of modern civilization—dispelled all doubts and temptations from Ravenstreet. Wayland's words of wisdom made him see life in a different way: "Every age probably has its own riddle of the Sphinx that it must solve...our riddle is the riddle of Time. Our secret despair, hurrying us into deeper slavery, may come from our inability to solve the riddle."[9] The magicians, after setting Ravenstreet free from the inner crisis, decided to enable him to evolve a noble and wholesome course of life, and placed him again into 'time-alive'. Ravenstreet's second 'time-alive' experience is much more meaningful, wider in scope and deeper in effect. He found himself a boy of twelve again in 1910 in the attic bedroom of his house in Atworth Terrace;

entered the Kitchen, spent happy hours with his parents at the dining table; the sights and sounds and smells in the house and the neighbourhood delighted his senses; Edith Metson, a pale girl who had performed a Skirt Dance at a social gathering and then vanished in some region of beauty and mystery appeared again; enjoyed the bustling Christmas parties again; the magic girl Edith, her golden face shaded by a wide straw hat, smiled at Charlie! Ravenstreet was in the great golden morning of the world; he moved freely in that far-off pre-First-World-War world of Eden-like innocence; everything was bursting with promise, infinitely inviting, crammed with beautiful and mysterious possibilities, more than enough for a hundred long lives. The speciality of this 'time-alive' world was that it was a real and solid world, not one of memories triggered off by some external agent as in the case of Proust.

The account of the second 'time-alive' event is followed by Priestley's authorial reflections calling the reader's attention to his positive faith in human life and personality. Priestley's integral view of life, as emerging out of his 'whole view' of Time, finds a remarkable expression in the following words:

> We had in fact to think of ourselves linked forward and backward along these circular or spiral tracks, still in communication, through our deepest feelings, with every part of our lives; and this, Wayland argued, was the great responsibility we shirked by pretending that we moved forward in time with everything destroyed behind us, living a mere sketchy charade of life.[10]

This view of non-passing time keeps men aware that they are responsible for their actions of the past and the future, not simply for those which they do in the present; this view makes their living really meaningful inasmuch as they find every moment pulsating with the whole of their existence. Dwelling at length upon the mysterious working of Ravenstreet's consciousness during his second entry into 'time-alive' Priestley shows how life is multidimensional; Ravenstreet was not merely recovering a childhood memory but becoming aware of a wisdom, of a profounder insight into the nature of human life and being. He was neither the adult self of fifty-five called

Charles Ravenstreet nor the young Charlie of twelve; he was removed from place and Time. Priestley describes how Ravenstreet felt at that moment in the following comment:

> He seemed to have broken through into eternity, not everlastingness but the level of being not governed by passing time; and he felt like a man sitting high up and alone in some vast and solemn theatre, catching a glimpse on some multidimensional screen far below of a whirling panorama of his lives.[11]

Thus, the reader's attention is called to the multidimensionality of life in multidimensional Time vis-a-vis consciousness. Ravenstreet's experience brings out the contrast between the depth, colour and grandeur of life in non-passing time and the petty, sketchy charade that our life is in passing time.

There are certain similarities between *The Magicians* and the play *I Have Been Here Before*. Just as Walter Ormund decides to groom himself toward perfection through the intervention of Gortler, Ravenstreet undergoes a change in his outlook owing to the influence of the magicians. The basic difference between Walter and Ravenstreet is that the former feels assured of a noble change in his next life, while the latter is enabled to evolve a noble course of living in this life only. Because, unlike Walter, Ravenstreet finds light out of darkness in this life, he stands closer to us. Also this novel calls for comparison with *Bright Day*. *The Magicians* came eight years after *Bright Day*. Gregory and Ravenstreet undergo total change in their view of life owing to their right understanding of Time. But the basic difference is that while Gregory's past comes alive through his memory, Ravenstreet's past comes back to him as a gift by the three wise men who put him in 'time-alive'. As a novel with its action taking place in multiple Time dimensions, *The Magicians* moves farther than *Bright Day*.

As a Time novel, *The Magicians* goes a step further in illustrating not only the yogic, apocalyptic powers some people possess, but also in dwelling upon such Time-travellers as change the lives of other people who otherwise would run in dull and meaningless tracks. Because the wise men knew that Philippa was in her death-bed in the hospital they so arranged it through a letter left at the Broxley house that Ravenstreet could be present by her side in her last moments. Ravenstreet had a thrilling experience in the hospital; Perperek had linked himself telepathically with Philippa to whom he spoke across hundreds of miles. Also Perperek's words, that they (the magicians) would change life for Ravenstreet's grandchildren, came true in a big way when Ravenstreet joined his son and grandchildren.

As noted before, Time slipped back in Priestley's mind after *The Magicians* (1954). The Time theme occupied his mind again in the sixties: from *Saturn Over the Water* onwards it became the most haunting theme in all his major fictional works.

Saturn Over the Water (1961) is an intellectual thriller like *The Doomsday Men* and *Blackout at Gretley,* which were written under the gathering clouds of the Second World War. But the basic difference between the present novel and the two earlier ones is that this novel gains in depth because of Priestley's Time-philosophy guiding the course of the novel. The novel deals with the deeds of some wise humanitarians who save the world civilisation from the hands of some sinister misanthropes.

Like *Bright Day* and *Lost Empires* this novel also is an autobiographical work. This is a story of adventure and love, an account of what happened to Tim Bedford, the central character, who narrates everything. Tim's epic search for Joseph Farne, a scientist, the husband of his cousin Isabel lying in her deathbed in a Cambridge Hospital, is almost global in extension—from England to New York, from South America to Australia. The search-theme is combined with the love-theme, the love of Tim and Rosalia. The secret organisation called *Saturn Over the Water,* which was also called 'Wavy Eight', employed scientists. The 'Wavy Eight' was symbolic of its functioning: 'Eight' stood for Saturn whose number is eight, and the wavy line is water, a symbol of the unconscious. *Saturn Over the Water* meant that, Saturn being a symbol of authority and cold exercise of power, the members of the organisation could control men's conscious as well as unconscious minds. The Old Man on the Mountain explained the clandestine activities of these Saturnians. These evil-minded people wanted a total war and were bent on using all means to destroy the present civilisation. They held some key people under their control, used mass techniques, transmitted subliminal messages through films, drugs and medicines and all the usual propaganda channels.

The old man of the Blue Mountain was a kind of seer, a true Time-traveller. It was mainly because of his humanitarian efforts and great yogic powers that the Saturnians like Van Emmorick, Giddings, Dr. Steglitz and Lord Randlong were defeated, their powers crushed, and their institute at Charoke destroyed; it was again the powers of this yogic man and Mrs. Baro that saved the lovers, Tim and Rosalia—the granddaughter of the old Peruvian multi-millionaire Arnaldos —from the hands of the Saturnians and also restored Joe, the scientist, to Tim. This old man's extraordinary previsionary powers brought about the union of Tim and Rosalia—who inherited, after her grandfather's death, a big share of his wealth and power. Two characters need to be examined in some detail in order to know how Time works, through them, in this novel. They are the Old Man on the mountain and Mrs. Baro. The Old Man's appearance was deceptive: under the exterior of a shabby-looking boozer was concealed a real yogi who had conquered Time. He has in him the best of the earlier Priestleyan characters like the Nature Man (*Faraway*), Jock and Dorothy (*Bright Day*) and the magicians (*The Magicians*) who are Time-travellers possessing an apocalyptic vision of life. He is a much greater mystic and humanitarian than the trio of magicians. If the magicians aim at saving mankind from the soul-killing 'admass', this man's mission is to save the present civilization from total ruin at the hands of the Saturnians. Likewise, Mrs. Baro, a tiny Polish woman with bright eyes, is described as an unusual personality. She did possess 'Second Sight'; she was a prophetess; she foretold what was going to happen to the Steglitz place at Charoke. She told what had happened to Nadia, assured Tim of Rosalia's safety, and sent Tim and Rosalia away post-haste at dead of night as she had foreknowledge of the movements of the Saturnians who would certainly finish the two lovers.

The Old Man's previsionary powers were revealed to Tim and Rosalia. The Old Man asked them to see 'things' on the long wall covered with black curtains. While they were waiting for things to happen, they were passing through a peculiar state of mind; they felt that a part of them was drifting away; yet, in the centre of the drift and dreaminess another part of them seemed tremendously alert. They saw on the curtains the end of Osparas on the Emerld Lake, the hazy image of the institute in confused flames at first, and then Osorno erupting, the terrible flow of lava, the buildings crumbling and vanishing, people trying to escape, the earth swaying and splitting open. Describing the prevision of that event seen on the curtains, a view of the future caught in the present, Tim says, " ...(but) I knew beyond any doubt and question that I was seeing what would happen, what was already happening in some different time order."[12] It was through the mystical powers of this old possessor of wisdom and master of Time that Tim entered a different order of Time. It can be said that while his Time One observer—the conscious self—was drifting away under the influence of the Old Man's yogic power, his Time Two observer was unaffected and alert; Tim was gradually lifted out of passing time and enabled to enter his Time Two realm. Rosalia who had earlier contemptuous opinion about this Old Seer had to change her opinion when thoroughly convinced of his rare gifts and mastery over Time.

Before presenting the second vision before Tim and Rosalia, the Old Man said, "It is what could and may happen, not yet what will happen. So it is a vision of a vision—out of any order of time yet—among possibilities. But it is what they would like to bring about. Watch now."[13] There appeared the images which were jerky, confused and shadowy, but they could see great cities in ruins, landscapes of utter desolation, the dead in rotting heaps. This was the Old Man's vision of a possibility being shown on the curtains—a possibility of the total devastation of mankind and its civilization which was the aim of the Saturnians. The Old Man had taken upon himself the charge of averting such disaster to mankind; he had the powers to destroy the sinister empire of the Saturnians. Nevertheless, the old humanitarian needed the help of Tim in this task. He was all praise for women and artists, whom he called Uranians, because the planet Uranus works through them. The Uranian principle which is basically feminine is one of the construction and peace as opposed to the Saturnian principle, which is the masculine principle, of war and destruction. He was specially gifted through his full and right knowledge of Time to bring about the rule of the Uranians by defeating the designs of the Saturnians. This wise man's apocalyptic view of life in the universe is expressed thus:

> ...One great design clashes with the other. What is invisible and bodiless moves the visible and embodied like a piece on a chessboard. But the game is in five dimensions. Very complicated, but then it's a very complicated universe we're in—even this little corner of it.[14]

Because he was a time-traveller, this multidimensional universe was not such a Sphinx's riddle to him as it was to Tim, Rosalia and others. He obliged Mitchell and Tim with a third vision in which they saw the Saturnian chain on the globe. His words and actions convinced them that what they had taken to be the whole of life was only a thin section of it and that only in this so-called 'real' life there was a charade element, and that behind the earthly reality there was another deeper reality and behind that another reality and yet another and another. These realities could be grasped in different orders of Time. This novel reaffirms Priestley's belief that life's reality can be grasped only through the right understanding of Time. *Saturn Over the Water* has an edge even over the apocalyptic novel *The Magicians* so far as the old yogic personality lends others a vision of possibilities. The novel does not depend upon any Time theory in particular; it artistically exploits different theories according as they suit situations and events. For example, if the Dunnian Serialism is found in the operations of the consciousness of Tim and Rosalia sitting before the black curtains, Ouspensky's concept of the fifth dimension as eternity, the sphere of possibilities, is illustrated by the 'curtain scene', and behind the actions and utterences of Mrs. Baro there is the *ESP* concept. Thus, this novel records a solid development in Priestley's career as a novelist of multiple Time and as one who 'sees' the fullness and meaning of life through Time as a mode of consciousness. The stress is on the expansion and enrichment of consciousness.

If *Saturn Over the Water* was intended to present a yogic timeless view of life, *The Thirty First of June* attempted to portray the world of creative imagination which exists outside time.

The Thirty First of June (1961) looks, on the surface of it, like a story of fun and fantasy, as if meant mainly for children. It is this surface look that makes John Atkins remark, "It is a Romp set in a typically Priestleyan world of timelessness, or rather of various inter-locking time scales."[15] A romp it appears to be because of the eccentric setting, bizarre action, flat characters and devices like magic used as a means of describing the irrational and the unusual. But, underneath the story, there is a serious theme: it illustrates Priestley's belief that imagination too has a reality just as dreams have a reality of their own but of a different kind. This view is expressed by the enchanter Malgrim: "Whatever is imagined must exist somewhere in the universe."[16] Priestley turns this view into an artistic presentation by manipulating the different Time dimensions. There is a smooth sailing, forward and backward, from the medieval world to the twentieth century. Magic is used as a device to knock down the barriers of Time—past, present and future—and to show the oneness of life in a timeless dimension. The tricks the two illusionists, Marlagram and Malgrim, play are the tricks of Time played through magical powers. The reader has to suspend his disbelief willingly in order to reach what lies behind the make-believe world.

The action of the novel takes place not in the actual world and in clock time but in the world of the imagination of the painter called Sam Penty of an advertising firm in London and in timeless time at the preternatural level. The Princess Melicent falls in love with Sam Penty seen in her magic mirror, and Sam sees her in his vision and falls in love and takes her as a model for his painting. They yearn to see each other. The action unfolds on a day which the author calls 'Lunaday', otherwise called 31st of June. The novel alternates the scenes of the medieval Arthurian world and the modern twentieth century London until there comes the scene where people of both the worlds are presented together. The real and the imaginary are put together side by side with a view to showing life in its true nature. The Arthurian capital of Paradore symbolises the world of imagination, while London represents the modern world and its material progress. The two contrasting worlds, namely, the Arthurian world represented by King Meliot and his royal retinue and the twentieth century world represented by Dimmock, the managing director of the advertising firm, and his men represent different values in different times. If Sam, Dimmock and Plunket are enabled by the magician, Malgrim, to pass through the 'wall' into Paradore, the other magician Marlagram—both the enchanters are rivals—manages to bring the Princess Melicent into London in order to unite the lovers but fails in his efforts.

Priestley's views of Time are explained at length by Malgrim. This enchanter assumes a Universe of six dimensions. The sphere of imagination is the sixth dimension which is the world of other possibilities; the meeting of the lovers living in different times becomes an actualised possibility in the consciousness of the painter. The novel emphasises that reality can be understood only with reference to the Time dimension in which it is realised; there is no absolute and universal reality just as there is no absolute and universal Time. The world of so-called reality is confined to world time, while what is called unreal or imaginary is outside world time. This enchanter speaks to Sam about the relativity of Time in the following words:

> I leave real life for imaginary life—and meet you. When you go back with me—as I trust you will shortly—then

> you will leave real life for imaginary life, to meet the Princess. Which is real, and which is imaginary, depends upon the position of the observer. It could truthfully be said that both are real, both are imaginary.[17]

Talking about the third sphere, that is, the realm of the imagination where other possibilities exist, the enchanter observes that there "are parallel times, diverging and converging times, and times spirally intertwined".[18]

The 'wall' is certainly symbolic of Time through which Sam and his friends dart into the medieval time and the Arthurian characters come into the twentieth century London. The inner world of consciousness is suggested when Sam, waiting for the Princess to come for the betrothal ceremony, hears the enchanter Malgrim's voice, "Go down to the darkest corner of the dungeon."[19] After a harrowing time of puzzlement and panic at the hubbub of the Crammed Foods Exhibition of June 1961 Sam found himself on the Crowmwell Road, and Priestley gives the readers a peep into this central character's thoughts at that time:

> ....He had not come from Paradore to find Melicent, there was no Melicent, no Paradore, he had dreamt it all,... All that had happened, he began to feel, was that he had let his imagination play around that Damosel Stockings job too long....[20]

This is a clear proof of Sam's free wandering in the colourful and romantic world of creative imagination and of his return to the world of passing time. The novel gives an artistic expression to Priestley's belief that creative imagination combines power and will to create a higher reality in a higher dimension of Time, to give 'a local habitation and a name' to that which exists in the realm of unrealised possibilities.

If the first three novels of this mellowed phase present life in a rather bizarre and fantastic atmosphere, *Lost Empires* and *It's an Old Country*—the other two works of this period—are set against a solid realistic background. Nonetheless, the wisdom of life, projected through the novelist's Time-philosophy, is dominant in all these novels.

Lost Empires (1965) is an autobiographical novel like *Bright Day* and *Saturn Over the Water*. Richard Herncastle, a celebrated English painter in his seventies, looks back on the golden days of his youth when he was only twenty, working as an assistant to his maternal uncle Nick, a master illusionist of the time in the Variety Theatres, and re-lives that colourful past. Ensconced between the walls of the old English music-halls this novel 'is set back in the golden world' of the pre-1914 England, the world dearest to Priestley. The work has the haunting beauty of a 'lost world', the Edwardian world of fun and laughter, as found in *The Good Companions, Let the People Sing* and *Bright Day*. The story triumphs over passing time. Richard Herncastle speaks of non-passing time when he says to the novelist, "Have you noticed the way the past comes curving back to you, as if you were not getting further and further away from it, but coming nearer to some of it?"[21] Richard, touring all over England as a youth of twenty in the company of co-artists of the Old Variety and Music Hall theatres called Empires, had an adventurous time of the wide world. The novel creates the living atmosphere of a world pulsating with life which is not lost to Time. The happy and unhappy relationships between the stage artistes, the attractions and quarrels between the sexes, their love and hatred, joys and tears, and trusts and suspicions are all effectively presented.

Richard's relations with different females ran at different levels. His relations with Julie Blane were never above 'sex-acts', while he was 'spiritually' related to Nancy. Time is an important element in the novel. The Dick-Nancy relationship (Richard was endearingly called Dick) is an excellent instance of FIP—future-influencing-present. Dick's relationship with the enchanting girl Nancy was of the spirit, and hence, of a nobler order of existence beyond the realm of Time. Richard describes at length the character of his love with this girl in a philosophical way. He says that the magic of her personality made a conquest of his heart and mind completely when he saw her first on the stage; he felt he was gripped by some inexplicable excitement. Talking about his love at first sight he says, "I believe this excitement did not help to create my future relationship with Nancy, but that the relationship, which already existed in some larger time, made itself felt to me, in my immediate narrower time, in the form of this strange excitement: the future was influencing the present."[22] He describes another occasion when the future cast its spell on Richard's present. It was in the army Recreation Hall at Surrey. He was unusually thrilled by the orchestra music, felt it was coming out of a lost world of gaiety. Now a soldier, he felt that the music was responsible for the excitement, as it was rocking him back to his Empires, but afterwards he realised that this was due to the fact that he was going to see—this he never expected—his dear Nancy on the stage. He felt sure that the coming event was casting not only its shadow but also its light in advance. During both these occasions Richard had wandered out of passing time into a future dimension of Time. Reliving the soul-lifting romantic moments he had spent with Nancy, after Sir Alec's party, half a century ago, this Septuagenarian artist says, "Our high spirits together created that great blue bubble, a world unmapped and outside solar space and time."[23] Thus Richard recognises the timeless quality of their relationship. Now their youth is gone but that sunny time has not gone! At the end of the novel the same faith in the timeless character of life is affirmed again by Richard Herncastle who, pointing to his granddaughter Meg capering cheerfully in front of a gramophone playing a pop tune, says to the novelist, "Yes, that's Nancy as she was—all over again."[24] Thus the ending of the novel is symbolic: it shows that passing time goes on passing but the true quality of life remains for ever outside the domain of Time's change.

The novel deals with various tricks that Time plays on the human mind. They may be considered in some detail. The well-known illusionist uncle Nick entertained his audience in different places with his illusion acts. This stern-looking showman with penetrating pensive eyes was not only a shrewd psychologist but also one who knew the true nature of Time. His success as a master magician was due to his "manipulation of different times". [25] While he operated on the stage in one

Time dimension, the audience's mind operated in another. He had grasped the importance of slow time in the mind of the audience, while he was working very fast on the stage. That was his speciality. His well-known role was that of the Indian magician called Ganga Dun. His magic box excited awe and wonder everywhere. A pedestal about four feet high was brought onto the stage and a white box was placed on the top of it. A stage girl called Cissie played the Hindoo maiden who climbed into the box. While the lid of the box was slowly closing, the box was lifted off the pedestal, securely roped, then fastened to the hook, let down from the flies. The box remained in mid-air for a few moments. There was a roll on the side-drum. The scowling magician Ganga Dun fired a pistol three times at the box, which was then lowered and opened, all its sides falling down, and was plainly seen to be empty. There was a chord from the orchestra. While the audience was observing the box with its slowly closing lid making them feel that the girl was still settling down into it, the girl had already got out of it, through a hinged flap on the bottom of the box, into the pedestal. The trick of making the Rival magician vanish depended again on the device of slow time and fast movement. Similarly 'The Vanishing Cyclist' and 'Magic Painting' performances followed the principle of manipulating two different time-dimensions simultaneously. The Mrs. Foster-Jones event particularly spotlights Nick's skill and ability in manipulating different time-dimensions. The plan of giving the slip to the police who had come all prepared to arrest Mrs. Foster-Jones, a leading suffragette, worked wonderfully, mainly because Nick handled the manipulation of two different time-dimensions in a unique fashion: the police headed by Detective Inspector Woods had time to look but not think because while they had their mind moving in slow time the exchange of coats behind the screen, between Mrs. Jones and Julie Blane, who was specially trained for the act, was too fast for any one even to think of it.

The relative nature of Time is experienced by Richard on two occasions. When caught red-handed in each other's arms Richard and Julie were caned by Julie's man Tommy Beamish and Ted till they bled profusely, and Richard felt that the moment of danger for his life would never end. "And time seemed almost to stop."[26] He recalls another occasion when time seemed growing long. It was when in the Recreation Hall at Surrey he chanced upon Nancy, who had become just a sweet dream for him after her departure from the Empires. The moment the performance came to an end, Richard urged by a blind impulse, pushed his way through the crowd to the entrance door at the back of the stage to meet her; he had to wait there till she came out. Soaked in rain and feeling cold with rivulets running down his back, he was standing there. He describes his travail in these words: "I was behind that door for the longest hour there can ever have been."[27] If he felt in the earlier instance that time had come to a stand-still owing to that moment of danger, in this case he felt the hour stretch the longest owing to the fear, anxiety and uncertainty his mind was passing through. Thus these two incidents focus on the relativity of Time with reference to the kind of experience one is undergoing at the moment.

This novel of multiple Time-dimensions has a wise man, a Time-traveller, just as the other novels too of this phase have at least one each. That wise man is the Old Hindu who does not appear in the novel but is described by Nick. Recalling the 'bloody horrors' predicted by this old man he had met at the London Coliseum, Nick said to Richard, ".... I'm not easily frightened, but he gave me the cold shivers. Fire, fury and bloody murder everywhere, and he talked about it all as if he was a kid at a magic lantern show."[28] Nick recalled these predictions on two occasions. The murder of Nonie and the outbreak of the First World War convinced him of the truth of these prophetic words. This master illusionist who was capable of using different dimensions of Time for the success of his tricks was greatly impressed by the precognitive powers of some men like the Old Hindu who are capable of entering the eternal "Now", an experience at once alien to those that hardly look beyond passing time.

The Epilogue tells about the death of most of the stage personalities Richard Herncastle had worked with some five decades ago. But the way their lives are recreated through the working of Richard's Observer Two in Time Two (in Dunne's idiom) affirms that they are in their own time, not lost to Time. The title of the novel *Lost Empires* seems an understatement of the motif of the work, if it is remembered that nothing of the Empires is lost and gone. The picture emerging from the novel is one of the timeless quality of life.

It's an Old Country (1967) practically brings Priesteley's career as a Time fictionist to an end, though he still continued to write works like *Snoggle* (1971) and *The Carfit Crises* (1975) which have Time as an important element. Though this novel is mainly concerned with the portrayal of England as an old country with her distinctive ways and values, Time enters the work as an enigma particularly as baffles the consciousness of the central character, Tom Adamson.

This also is a search-novel like *Saturn Over the Water*. Tom, a lecturer in the University of Sidney, came to England to find his long-lost father in fulfilment of the promise he had made to his mother before her death. He met a number of men and women who had known his father Charles Adamson, and pieced together the bits of information he got from them to form a picture of his father who had left his family thirty-three years before—Tom was a kid of three then—to live with another woman. In the course of his quest Tom was cheated by his crafty cousin Chas and a professional detective called Crike. Also he committed the folly of falling for the beautiful but basically stupid girl called Helga. Luckily, Dr. Firmius and Judy Marston came to his aid in time of crisis. Through the timely and bold efforts of Judy's aunt, Alison Oliver, Tom found his father at long last. The novel has a happy ending with the decision of the lovers, Tom and Judy, to get married.

This search-novel gains in depth owing to the drama that goes on in the consciousness of Tom under the influence of Time, which seems to take different shapes and colours on different occasions. The action of the novel progresses in a double dimension: Tom's search necessitates his going back to the past of his father's life over three decades and more, and at the same time the discovery of his own self—this is not a conscious pursuit—which takes place in the present. The novel is largely a record of what goes on at different levels of Tom's consciousness; everything is observed through Tom's eyes as his consciousness is at the centre of the work. John Atkins aptly makes the following remark about Time in the novel: "Again, the apparent vagaries of time in the lover's consciousness become the centre of interest."[29]

Time appears in a variety of ways in the novel. Some moments are rich, suggestive and even mysterious, while others are empty and tedious. A rare ecstatic moment experienced by Tom, waiting in a little dingy room of the London office of the Blue Caribbean for a telephonic reply from its Avonmouth office regarding his father's whereabouts, is described in these words:

> ...he was suddenly held and entranced by one of those spells of happiness, undeserved and unaccountable that seem to belong to some other level of being: he might have been sharing the sunlight on the window with a demigod. There was a moment when he seemed to be contemplating infinite possibilities, a hundred, a thousand lives; an incredible breadth and depth and richness of being; just a moment; and then of course the spell weakened, the happiness thinned out,.... No thought of his father, no thought of anybody or anything, had come into it at all; it was a visit out of the blue, probably lasting no more than a minute or so; but he never forgot it.[30]

To Tom his first visit to Alison Oliver's house seemed *deja vu*. Though a stranger he felt curiously at home. His feeling at that time is described as follows: "Yet it was as if another part of himself, hitherto detached, had been there waiting for him to join it. He went downstairs and along the passageway to the sitting room as if this was not the first time but the hundredth time he had done so."[31] Certainly it shows that his conscious self knew nothing about it but his consciousness in a different order of existence and in a different dimension of Time did possess the knowledge of the place.

On another occasion the whole progress of his father-search for months together came to Tom, telescoped into a single instant, and he felt it was there 'still going on'. This clearly underscores the truth that nothing of man's life on this earth is snuffed out by passing time and everything is in its own time. The novelist highlights another peculiar feeling that Tom had, while he was sitting in Dr. Firmius's basement, discussing the whereabouts of his father with the wise old man and his sweet-heart Judy. That feeling is recorded here: "Tom felt something he never remembered feeling before, as if it came out of another existence, a kind of completeness that wasn't new but very old, part of some ancient long-forgotten pattern that suddenly revealed itself."[32] This 'ancient long-forgotten pattern' points to the multidimensionality of life and Time, that is, the true character of life is that it is timeless. There comes a reference to this 'pattern' again on another occasion. Hilda Neckerson, a woman in her fifties, who had once loved Tom's father with all her heart, could feel behind the minutes and hours 'an underlying hidden pattern' which is felt at rare moments by all, but only outside passing time.

Contrary to these rich and significant moments there are poor and futile moments, too. A few of them can be considered here. For example, when Tom was engaged in conversation with a County Conservative Women's Group in his cousin Leonara's house, and was bored with their hollow and stupid talk, there was a girl of eighteen who was equally bored with the company of those 'society snobs' and remarked that when stuck in such company she felt she was going up the 'wall'. She asked Tom what time it was. There came no reply from Tom who was greatly puzzled at the question. Priestley's own despairing voice is heard: "Yes, indeed—what time was it?" Here the girl's reference to the 'wall', immediately followed by her query about time, is not without significance. To Priestleyan readers the 'wall', here used metaphorically, definitely means passing time lying like an insurmountable barrier across man's journey of life. The reason why people talk of 'killing' time, interestingly, comes through Tom's experience. Tom felt it a torture to kill twenty-four hours, till

8-30 the next evening, to meet Helga, the great golden witch. He was trying hard how to get rid of the hours, how to shovel them into the incinerator where they belonged! To pass time in a state of anxiety and uncertainly or fear and doubt is always painful, because Time does not exist in itself; it is related to one's state of mind as a mode of experience. Thus Tom's experience of time in this case points to the relative nature of time. The Helga-time (the time Tom spent with Helga) shows how baffling it is sometimes to make any sense out of a situation. Because of Tom's irresistable infatuation with Helga, his moments of excitement seemed endless. He followed Helga, entranced by the Helga-atmosphere, from one exciting party to another till he landed in utter disillusionment and gloom, finding himself a fool enthralled by a bewitching but vacuous girl. However, when his exciting time had come to an end, he tried to puzzle out that mad affair in terms of Time only to meet with a formidable failure which he describes thus:

> Afterwards, Tom could never recollect properly, make any shape and sense out of, this Helga-time. He never asked himself to remember any of it while it was happening. Then, immediately it was over he wanted to ignore the fact that this time had ever existed. And then, long afterwards, when he no longer felt he'd simply been a fool, when he really wished to know what he'd done, thought, felt, while in pursuit of Helga, the time refused to be sorted out into days in which certain things happened: it remained a blur of a mish-mash. He had spent longer than a week but less than a fortnight trying, it might be said, to juggle with large coloured jellyfish.[33]

Thus it is shown here that Time played tricks with Tom's consciousness. It may be said that Tom's Observer One in Time One failed to analyse the enigmatic experience his Observer Two had had outside passing time.

Like the other novels of this period, this fictional work also has a wise man, a Time-traveller, that is, Dr. Firmius. He played an important role in helping Tom reach his goal of discovering his father. Firmius had enriched his consciousness through conscious efforts. He prepared this Australian lecturer for the fruition of his efforts by advising him to bide his time with patience and allow things to take their own time to happen. Firmius's words of wisdom flow from his right understanding of Time. This old philosopher's view of life defies that of the positivist, and he perceives a pattern of things which is outside chronological time. He recognises three kinds of Time, more or less on the lines of what is said about it by the magician Malgrim in *The Thirty First of June*: the First time is linear time generally thought to be the conveyor-belt carrying men to their grave and oblivion; the Second time is where men recompose their lives with some help from others who have shared them out their memories of the First time; and the Third time is where they have to live with what they have imagined. Firmius has a streak of the mystical combined with his intellectual equipment as a student of Time and Reality; he has a wider length of Time One at his command, and can, therefore, see the future in the present. This Time-traveller's wisdom comes from a deeper insight and intuition than are ordinarily given to mortals: his world of Reality is outside clock-time and begins where the sciences end. His argument that nothing that happens once can go into oblivion convinces Judy first and then Tom. He wants this Australian lecturer to discover for himself "the profound difference between efforts of memory and the sense of living time, of everything still happening in its own place".[34] This philosopher's view of life and Time agrees with the apocalyptic view of the trio of magicians in *The Magicians* who believe in the eternal 'Now'. If, for Proust, memory is the channel through which one recaptures the 'lost time' and arrives at life's reality, Firmius holds that it is through consciousness that one can relive the past; in other words, one can have the 'sense of living time' as nothing is lost, and everything is in its own time. Firmius's description of the Ashtree Place is witty and at the same time symbolistic: the top of the house where Chas is living represents energy and the sensuous life; the middle part represents beauty, sex and imagination and Helga lived there; but only in the basement is found wisdom and that is where Firmius lived. The suggestion is that while all things like beauty, sex and energy must change and vanish in passing time the only imperishable and timeless thing is wisdom because it is deep down in man's consciousness, which is outside linear time. This old man of vast knowledge and profound wisdom could have told Tom where to find his father, but, in that case, this Australian lecturer would not have discovered his own identity. The congratulatory telegram from the Ashtree Place on Tom's discovery of his father's whereabouts was a clear proof of Dr. Firmius' foreknowledge of the happy turn events would take for Tom.

While putting his views of life and Time through the lips of Firmius and yet doing so in comformity with the laws of literary art, Priestley has called the reader's attention to the different shapes and colours Time takes under different circumstances in the consciousness of man, and this is accomplished through the presentation of the drama that goes on in the inner consciousness of Tom. This novel, dealing as it does with varieties of Time vis-a-vis human consciousness, brings out Priestley's unique gift as a writer of multiple Time and its wisdom.

NOTES

1. John Atkins, *J.B. Priestley*, p. 191.
2. *The Magicians* (London: William Heinemann Ltd., 1954), p. 69.
3. Paul Brunton, *A Search in Secret India* (New Delhi: B.I. Publication Pvt. Ltd., rpt. 1985), p. 162.
4. *The Magicians*, p. 72.
5. *Ibid*., p. 98.
6. *Ibid*., p. 75.
7. *Ibid*., p. 94.
8. *Ibid*., p. 102.
9. *Ibid*., p. 104.
10. *Ibid*., p. 189.
11. *Ibid*., p. 195.
12. *Saturn Over the Water* (London: Heinemann Ltd., 1961), p. 280.
13. *Ibid*.
14. *Ibid*., p. 287.
15. John Atkins, *J.B. Priestley*, p. 192.
16. *The Thirty First of June* (London: Heinemann Ltd., 1961), p. 51.

17. *Ibid.*, p. 52.
18. *Ibid.*, p. 53.
19. *Ibid.*, p. 144.
20. *Ibid.*, p. 151.
21. *Lost Empires* (London: Heinemann Ltd., 1965), Prologue, p. xi.
22. *Ibid.*, p. 29.
23. *Ibid.*, p. 82.
24. *Ibid.*, p. 308.
25. John Atkins, *J.B. Priestley*, p. 168.
26. *Lost Empires*, p. 172.
27. *Ibid.*, p. 299.
28. *Ibid.*, p. 34.
29. John Atkins, *J.B. Priestley*, p. 168.
30. *It's an Old Country* (London: Heinemann, Ltd., 1967), pp. 176-77.
31. *Ibid.*, p. 205.
32. *Ibid.*, p. 166.
33. *Ibid.*, p. 109.
34. *Ibid.*, p. 200.

6

Priestley's Technique of Writing

The basic difference between drama and fiction as forms of literature lies in the way their 'Idea' is communicated: fiction—a novel or a story—is 'narration' and drama is 'action'. A dramatist presents things as happening while a novelist narrates things as having happened. Form is something that belongs to the original idea. Ideas find, for their expression, forms proper to them. As Anatole France observes, "An idea is of value only because of its form."[1] Structure is an observable shape underlying the work, and technique is the method by which the idea is unfolded or communicated. Technique includes age-old devices like fantasy, realism, symbolism, flashback, irony, etc. as well as structural aspects such as plot, character and language.

Priestley was a master of both drama and fiction. When asked by John Atkins how he decided whether an idea should be developed as a play or a novel he replied, "I happen to dislike plays that have a number of short scenes with varied backgrounds, and if I have an idea that seems to demand this, then I turn it into a novel and not into a play."[2] On the whole he is consistent with this principle of selecting the form, though there are two exceptions, *Music at Night* and *Ever Since Paradise* which present their action in a number of shifting scenes.

First the technique of his Time-plays and then that of his Time-fiction will be examined.

Priestley was a man of the theatre. He felt the pulse of the audience and had a remarkable sense of the stage. His plays create a 'dramatic experience' which according to him should be the ultimate object of a dramatist. 'Dramatic experience' is "the simultaneous double response",[3] one that is the result of the dramatist's successful creative working on two levels: the level of life and the level of the theatre. The plays already analysed and examined in the earlier chapters fulfil the two-fold demand of dramatic art: they are dramatic, that is, they are capable of creating an emotional response; and theatrical, too, that, they are capable of being staged under theatrical conditions. Priestley's Time-plays are a proof of his bold experimentation with ideas as well as form. He was one of the very few playwrights of his time who "tried to introduce new methods and a new approach into a tired tradition".[4]

The following methods in the Time-plays enabled Priestley to give a creative rendering of his views and theories of Time. It should be noted that none of these techniques are exclusively used. In fact, some of them overlap.

Realism: Priestley happily combines in himself the hard-boiled realist and the high romantic; he was never a starry-eyed idealist. If his social comedies like *Cornelius* and *When We Are Married* contain more of realism and less of idealism, his Time-plays exhibit more of the visionary stuff, but it is nonetheless tempered by his sense of realism. He wrote plays with the Time problem for his generation of the thirties who had a poignant sense of loss caused by the First World War.

Walter Ormund's (*I Have Been Here Before*) feeling of despair at his wife's conduct leading him to the brink of self-destruction is realistic and convincing. Equally realistic is the change we find in Ormund under the influence of Gortler's philosophy: a life-hater, to begin with, deeply disgusted with pleasures in passing time, emerges as a life-loving optimist. The picture of the unhappy conways, caught through the prophetic vision of Kay, contains a stark realism, a grim reality of life shown in serial time. The details of Johnson's life (*Johnson Over Jordan*)—his various weaknesses and despicable desire for the pleasures of the flash, his lust of money, etc.,—stage after stage are deeply marked by psychological realism, and help the audience appreciate the true value of life outside linear time. *Music at Night* is consistent with psychological realism and offers a convincing portrayal of the inner drama of the characters under the influence of music which released their consciousness to operate in different dimensions. When Priestley finds the realistic method incapable of depicting the deep-down world of man consciousness he takes recourse to preternaturalism.

Preternaturalism: Most of these Time plays place things outside of the natural, objective world and passing time. If *Desert Highway* dramatises a distant past through the Interlude, *Summer Day's Dream* treats a future possibility and *They Came to a City* deals with man's desire for a timeless order of life. In all these plays Time moves at preternatural levels. If we have in *Time and the Conways* a dramatic rendering of an unrealised possibility through Kay's reverie establishing Dunne's serialism, we find the preternatural technique used for presenting most of the action in *Johnson Over Jordan* outside chronological time. The play makes use of music, mask, dance, ballet and megaphone to show the journey of Johnson's consciousness in a timeless dimension; here the whole pageantry, scene after scene, gives a deeply satisfying, glorious and enduring picture of life's reality which is timeless. The little scenes dramatising the desires and speculations of the characters move at the preternatural level of psychological time; the Jungian unconscious operates outside world time. In some plays Priestley uses fantasy as a means to create an atmosphere or situation in which certain things of man's world of desires and imagination are ably dramatised.

Fantasy: Priestley's fantasy-world does not create a Puck or a Peter Pan. It may sometimes create a world of strange but imaginative ideas. Though his fantasy-creation is at a remove from the actual and natural, it is never improbable. When Priestley feels that a realistic method is inadequate to establish the timeless quality of life, he introduces fantasy. All his Time-plays and Time-fiction do embody an element of fantasy in one way or another. Generally he blends fantasy with irony to satirise the positivistic philosophy which sees nothing beyond linear time. The Interlude in *Desert Highway* jumps back twenty-six centuries. The change of Time-dimentions is used to establish the theme that the essential quality of human life has not changed with the passage of temporal time. *People at Sea* has a 'microcosm of society' which is a kind of fantasy-world; Diana and Valentine, a pair of long-estranged lovers, are fed up with their empty life in passing time and find significance and meaning only in a timeless order and decide to marry. Fantasy in *They Came to a City* comes home to us in no uncertain manner. The play creates the atmosphere of a make-believe world throughout. The fantastic setting and behaviour of the characters put the action of the play in a bizarre light and non-passing time; the whole atmosphere adds to the dramatic effect of Priestley's poetic vision of life's multidimensionality which can never be grasped in linear time. The fantasy-world of a timeless experience sharpens the edge of Joe's remark on those to whom life means only passing time: "Some of 'em'll laugh and jeer just because they don't want anything different.... Some of 'em, poor creatures, are so twisted and tormented inside themselves that they envy and hate other people's happiness."[5] But with this testimony of Joe's before us, dare we call his timeless experience, just fantasy?

Summer Day's Dream has, as the title itself suggests, fantasy-stuff (being only a slight-variation of *A Midsummer Night's Dream*). It presents a future possibility, a fantasy world as the stage and setting for its action; it is a view of what will happen twenty-five years after the holocaust of the Third World War. The world of peace and freedom from the tyranny of ticking time enjoyed by the old Stephen Dawlish and his family is presented as an ironical comment on the mechanical, mercenary life of modern civilization in linear time. Sometimes fantasy is blended with irony for greater effect.

Irony: Priestley uses irony as a method of showing incongruities born of 'appearance and reality'. There is a very poignant dramatic irony in Act III of *Time and the Conways* which is due to the foreknowledge the audience possess from

Kay's prophetic vision of the Conways twenty years later. Everything in this last act is found in a different light because of 'the savage ironies of Time'. The playwright is not just playing a Time-trick by reversing Act II and Act III but is putting effectively the whole view and quality of the work in Act III by the device of dramatic irony. In *Eden End* one can notice a biting irony in Stella's deep disappointment in her pursuit of happiness in passing time; but the sweet-sad memories of her past bring her comfort and Delight. The prodigal daughter Stella's life illustrates the irony of the human condition in linear time as explained by her father Dr. Kirby: our Observer Two in Time Two is not responsible for whatever happens to Observer One in Time One which pays the price and suffers. The honest and sincere efforts of Robert in *Dangerous Corner* to find out the truth end up ironically when he himself falls victim to the outcome of his own relentless act of truth-finding, all of which takes place at a might-have-been level. There is a stark irony in the failure of Diana and Valentine (*People at Sea*), who have lived long in a world of pleasant sensations and brain-fuddling stuff, to rid themselves of the tyranny of Time; Professor Pawlet, a positivist philosopher in the play, comes to terms with life in an ironical way by destroying a product of forty years of intellectual labour, a massive piece of writing on reasoning, after his realisation that life is multi-dimensional and nothing is destroyed by Time (as expounded by Dunne). The fact that a deep sense of frustration and despair should grip Walter Ormund (*I Have Been Here Before*) contains a ring of irony; he is sick of life in linear time. Likewise, there is a biting irony in the relationship of Oliver Farrant and Janet in the same play. Because of ignorance of their mutual relationship in earlier lives they are at their wit's end when confronted with the fact of their being irresistably drawn to each other, and consequently their talk creates an intense dramatic irony.

'Appearance and reality' in *Johnson Over Jordan* produces ironical situations and ironical truths. There is a calm, wise and beautiful face behind the horrible masked face of the

Figure: the 'reality' of life behind Tyrant Time is shown to be beautiful and serene.

Priestley adopts an ironical attitude in showing the funeral service performed by the clergyman in the hall of Johnson's house where his dead body is placed at the same time as Johnson's consciousness is journeying in a timeless order from one stage to another. There is a tragic irony again in Johnson's discovery that the youth he has stabbed to death is his own son and the girl he has chased in a fit of carnal passion is his own daughter, and that they are 'masks and shadows and dreams' resulting from his wrong understanding of life due to his misconception of Time. Similarly we find the author's ironical attitude in *Summer Day's Dream* which contrasts the restless, mechanical life of modern men governed by the cruel command of tick-tocking clock time with the simple ways of the English backwater where there exists no tyrany of Time; the play shows an ironical change not only in the feelings and perceptions of the three representatives of modern civilization but also in the happy conversion of Irina, a stiff and cold Russian lady, into a warm romantic soul that falls in love with Christopher.

All these examples of irony prove that Priestley uses the device of irony with a perfect sense of its dramatic effect in order to highlight how rich and deep is the dimension of Time Two existence and how meagre and dull is man's living in Time One (linear time). Also Priestley uses chronological-looping, which is called 'split-time' device, to achieve actualisation of certain possibilities.

Chronological-Looping: Priestley uses 'split-time' not as a mere trick but as a means to convey his Time-philosophy. This method helps him dramatise some unrealised possibilities. If the split-time device is used in *Dangerous Corner* to act out a might-have-been, it actualises a future possibility in *An Inspector Calls,* while this chronological-looping in a number of short scenes in "Ever Since Paradise" helps expose layers of complex human personality in a timeless dimension. *I Have Been Here Before* creatively employs the Ouspenskian theory of Eternal Recurrence which too has an element of circularity

—time-looping—but of a higher order: the theory of Circular Time helps Priestley make a profound metaphysical proposition into a play. Memory, desire and imagination are dramatised in *Music at Night,* the play almost demolishes clock time by putting the action on a mental plane; a timeless order of the human condition is depicted in the light of the Jungian unconscious. To show the timeless character of reality the playwright splits chronological time at the end of Act I of *Time and the Conways,* makes room for Kay's vision through Act II, and resumes clock time again at the beginning of Act III. The Interlude between Act I and Act II of *Desert Highway* devides chronological time and again loops it. Some very significant Time-symbols are used to create briefly an effective atmosphere of life's reality.

Symbolism: Priestley uses in some of these plays certain Time-symbols: they suggest the enigma and mystery of Time either in things or situations. The chiming of the clock thrice in *I Have Been Here Before* is symbolic. The first chiming in Act I at the arrival of Gortler is symbolic of the Time Problem that is in the offing; the second ringing of the clock is at the entrance of Janet; it chimes again at the coming of Oliver Farrant as if it were expecting him. Certainly the chiming is symbolic of ominous events going to happen.

In *Johnson Over Jordan,* as we have already seen the Figure with a painted horrible face is Time, a great grand illusion of life. Professor Pawlet's (*People at Sea*) act of tearing off the manuscript of his work on reasoning is expressive of his realisation that linear time is not the only time, and life exists multidimensionally. *Johnson Over Jordan* has, besides the Figure, some other symbolic things and situations. Jungle Hot Spot with its lures for Johnson symbolises the world of the senses which he has not succeeded in throwing off though he has moved out of Time One existence; the Inn at the End of the World stands for the Delightful 'peak moments' of Time Two life which has no touch of his earthly life. Johnson's departure, at the end of the play, towards the blue space and the shining constellations symbolises man's exit from his earthly existence, his Time One life. The city in *They Came to a City* is a symbol of a timeless order; the wall stands for world time, the door in the wall for a way through Time to true happiness in life which lies only beyond passing time. The stone monument in *Desert Highway,* buried in the earth, which was worshipped in ancient times by different races, is certainly a symbol of Time, of the continuity of man's life on this earth. The title of the play *The Linden Tree* is significant in that it carries a deep symbolic meaning. It stands for the tree of human life that continues from generation to generation, in family and society, in spite of Time's changes. Likewise, the peaceful English life of the spade and plough symbolises the truly happy and meaningful life, freed from the relentless tick-tock of clock time. Thus those symbols and symbolic situations contribute significantly to the overall treatment of the Time problem. Also flashbacks are used to recapture 'lost time', to show that nothing is lost to Time.

Flashbacks: This method mainly involves the Dunnian Serialism: Observer Two moves back and forth in Time, and the remembrances of past events constitute a double world in these works—the world past and the world present move together deepening the effect of the action. Stella in *Eden End* relives, through reminiscences, her childhood and youth in such a way that the gap of nine years since her departure from home is annihilated. The flashbacks of the lives of Stella, Lilian and Wilfred present their past, all living into the present. Similarly the flashbacks of the Conways in *Time and the Conways*—especially the happy and unhappy remembrances of Carol and Kay—put the first act of the play in a double world; the past is ever present, not a bit of it has sunk into oblivion. There is a recreation, through flashbacks, of the romantic courtship of Valentine and Diana in *People at Sea*. The double-world—one in passing time and the other of the ever-living past—created and held in balance by the flashbacks of the Lindens lends an additional dimension to the play *The Linden Tree;* the sudden burst of laughter of Dinah, whose Observer Two has before it the really happy days of the family years ago, brings about a sudden change in the atmosphere: the warm flashbacks shared by all the three Linden children introduce a sweet-sad atmosphere. Rex's remembrance, at the game of 'Black Sam', of how he had cheated Joe Sykes, a farmer, in Cumberland, takes all the family back to their past. If Mrs. Linden's memories of the happy days revive the days when her children were 'Kids', the Elgar concert played on the 'Cello by Dinah tolls the Professor back to the pre-1914 Edwardian golden world'. *Music at Night* has a fine sprinkling of flashbacks. The memories of Lady Sybil, Mrs. Amesbury, David and Lengel, Chilham and others bring alive their past years; through the operations of their unconscious—here is the Jungian Collective Unconscious at work—the different stages in the story of man's life on this earth are dramatically presented, and linear time stands totally expunged. The reminiscences of the couple Paul and Rosemary in *Ever Since Paradise* constitute a living record of the various stages of their relationship in the past which has always existed in their consciousness. Thus the flashback technique is turned to good account by Priestley in presenting life's mystery, charm, magic and meaning outside clock time. If flashbacks shift the characters to their past, music can take them to their past as well as to the world of imagination. Music plays an important role as a device in Priestley's works.

Music: In some of his plays music is used to introduce a change in time dimensions. This device works remarkably in *Music at Night*. All the ten characters, including the music maestros, David and Lengel, are shown as coming under the influence of the three movements of music. The music lifts them out of passing time into either their past or their world of imagination. Music comes as a turning point at the end of Act I of *Time and the Conways*: Kay, sitting at the open window, hears her mother sing Schumann, and the effect is so dramatic that her Observer Two begins to operate in Time Two, that is, her inner self leaps twenty years ahead as the music goes soaring away. Time-shifts are introduced by music in *Ever Since Paradise*. For example, Rosemary is lifted into a daydream on hearing soft music being played in the background. We have Johnson in *Johnson Over Jordan*, who goes through a mystic experience on account of music which elevates him to a level where he feels the multidimensionality of life. Similarly Professor Linden is rocked back into his golden Edwardian world by the music made by his daughter Dinah.

Just as these various methods are employed as parts of dramatic technique for creating 'dramatic experience' in the plays discussed above, more or less the same methods are used in the works of Priestley's Time-fiction to present life outside clock time.

In three of his novels with Time as a major element Priestley uses the first person narrative technique. They are *Bright Day, Lost Empires* and *Saturn Over the Water*. The rest are narrated by the author. Priestley uses fantasy, flashback, satire, irony, time-shift as some of the devices to convey his Time-philosophy; these methods fall well, as constituents, within the broader compass of the narrative technique. These methods are not exclusively used—this has been seen in the plays as well—but almost all of them may be found working well together in some of these novels. How effectively these methods put across Priestley's concepts of Time to the reader are examined in the following pages.

Fantasy: The fantasy in Priestley's novels is associated with 'magic'; it moves in a timeless dimension. *Adam in Moonshine* depicts Adam's adventures, his moonflights with three girls in a romantic escapade which take him out of passing time. The timeless moments of Adam's experience heighten the effect of the romance. As in this novel, there is a double world in *Benighted* also. The *Benighted* travellers, caught up in the fantastic and weird atmosphere of the Femms's house, feel that time has stopped and they are in a different dimension. Fantasy enters *The Magicians* in a subtle way. The magic powers of Wayland create snow in July with white flakes everywhere, which at once lifts Ravenstreet's consciousness into non-passing time, a nobler and broader dimension. The details of the world created by Sam Penty's imagination in *The Thirty First of June* are the stuff of fantasy, a fay-like creation. The story *The Other Place* creates a timeless fantastic world in which Lindfield wanders for some time. The fantasy-creation—

spreading flower-beds and soft green grass full of sunlight—is a timeless order of existence; the non-passing time of the fantasy-world here suggests the multidimensional character of life. *The Statues,* a futuristic short story shows an actualisation of Walter Voley's precognition of a distant possibility; the colossal statues of the city of London of centuries later come from the fantastic creation of a highly imaginative and intuitive mind. The imaginative world of the couple, Luke and Betty, in *Night Sequence* develops against a fantastic backdrop. Priestley takes recourse to fantasy in a good many stories of the story-collection *The Other Place* because he finds fantasy conducive to the operations of the subliminal mind in a timeless order, which are depicted here.

Satire and Irony: If Priestley adopts a satirical attitude in depicting the mad materialism of modern civilization represented by Sepman, Mervil and his group of 'merchants of death' in *The Magicians,* he adopts an ironical attitude in the same novel in showing the tragic death of Sepman and his wife and the defeat and humiliation of Mervil and his gang. The wicked designs of these people, whose motto is to grab the maximum from passing time before it runs out, are exposed by the magicians, great Time-travellers. The ironies left behind by Time in the lives of the Alingtons in *Bright Day* set off, by contrast, the optimistic account of life that flows through David and Bridget's children outside temporal time. There is a happy irony in the change of attitude that occurs in Gregory owing to the right knowledge of Time he receives from Mrs. Childs (the former girl Laura). Similarly there is biting irony in that the formidable Saturnians should eat humble pie at the hands of the Time-traveller, the Old Man on the blue mountain in *Saturn Over the Water.* Also *It's an Old Country* has, at the end, an ironical change in the attitude of the central character Tom, a professor of Colonial economic history, who at first refuses to credit Dr. Firmius's Time-philosophy but at last comes to believe in the old scholar's view of reality outside temporal time, the one that can be recognised only in non-passing time.

Flashback: The technique of flashback is used very effectively in those fictional works in which Time is a powerful element. This method puts Priestley's people, and the significant events of his plots, out of the purview of clock time, helps him present an integrated view of the human personality of his characters, which can be grasped only outside passing time. The flashbacks of Richard Herncastle in *Lost Empires* recapture his bustling past spreading over five and half decades, in particular, the memorable period of his youth, which he spent in the English music-halls; his past comes curving back to him in all its livingness, showing that nothing of it has been lost and that the true quality of life is found to be outside the fourth dimension. The flashbacks of Gregory Dawson in *Bright Day* constitute the very crux of the plot. Once the Schubert Trio in the hotel lounge in Cornwall triggers off the memories of the past—Gregory's Observer Two begins to work—the novel begins to move in a different dimension: the flashbacks go on weaving a significant texture of Gregory's past and present in a timeless order. Gregory experiences a strange and mysterious beauty in reliving his past because his mind gets released from passing time while doing so; the flashbacks enable Gregory to hear 'the music of experience' as it is freed from Time's tyranny. Timmy Tiverton in *Let the People Sing* goes through his past again through the flashbacks of the events and situations he went through some three decades before as a music-hall comedian; it is through flashbacks of that golden period that he 'sees' his dead wife sweet Betty. Priestley recreates by this technique Margaret's (*Benighted*) happy days soon after her marriage with Philip and she is lifted out of her present and rocked back to those sweet days of the past. It is again by this flashback method that in the same novel Penderel's whole past since his childhood is telescoped in his mind while he is locked in a deadly fight with the monstrous maniac Saul and is profusely bleeding and sweating; his mind moves in a timeless dimension. Similarly in *Faraway* William's flashbacks of his childhood bring that happy time alive before him with the warm world of Christmas cakes and sweets, and his mother's love and affection for him. Priestley successfully uses this technique to establish his point that nothing is destroyed by time, that everything exists in its own time in the eternal 'now'.

'Time-shift' Method: Priestley very often switches from chronological narration to the 'time-shift' method in order to express the timeless character of life. This method breaks time, and again joins it, and therefore it is also called 'Chronological-looping'. The *ESP* phenomena like *FIP*, precognition and retrocognition, the apocalyptic description of things, the yogic method of prediction, etc. fall within the scope of the 'time-shift' technique. William in *Faraway* has precognitive powers: sitting in the smoking room of the Lugmouth Hotel, discussing the proposed trip to the South Seas with Ivybridge and Ramsbottom, he finds himself lifted into a queer experience; he 'sees' the future through the diaphanous curtains of Time, wanders into a new Time dimension. This sort of experience is generally marked by a feeling of 'shiver' or cold creeping through the blood. The old man Candover in *Let the People Sing* is capable of precognition and retrocognition. He 'sees' the fall of Bagdad under Hulagu, a past event of human history (as interpreted by Kronak in the novel); he prophesies the blood and horror of the Second World War, a future event. Similarly, in *Bright Day,* Dorothy and Jock are seen to be gifted with the powers of precognition; the visions of Mrs. Baro and the Old Man in *Saturn Over the Water* are described by splitting chronological time and again joining it. It is by this time-shift method that Priestley shows what happens in 'time-alive' twice exercised on Ravenstreet by the magicians in the novel *The Magicians.* Again it is this method that is employed to highlight the multiple vision of Time in *Jenny Villiers* in which the reader finds the author interlocking different Time-scales. Similarly different Time-scales are adopted in the short story *Look After the Strange Girl.*

The variety of methods Priestley has adopted have helped him put the plots of his works at a preternatural level on a number of occasions, which has, in turn, widened the scope of his art to express his Time-philosophy creatively. It is to be noted that there are some points of difference between the way these methods are used in the plays and the way in which the same methods are employed in the fictional works. As works of art Priestley's Time-plays are more successful and satisfying than his works of Time-fiction. Methods like fantasy, irony and satire are more pointedly and precisely used in the plays, while they lose their effectiveness in the narrative mould in Priestley's hands. For example, the fantasy in *People at Sea, Desert Highway* and *They Came to a City* is strikingly effective in creating the intended atmosphere, while the fantastic scenes in *Benighted, The Thirty First of June* and *Jenny Villiers* lose pointedness and colour perhaps because of their tending to be too bizarre at a preternatural level of Time. The same thing can be said with regard to the other methods used in the two different forms. Brevity is the soul of dramatic art, and perhaps this fact accounts for the difference between the effectiveness of these methods when used in the plays and that of the same methods when used in the novels of Priestley. No less remarkable is the influence of Time on the structure of Priestley's Time-plays and Time-novels.

Structure consists mainly of plot, character and language.

Structurally also Priestley's Time-plays are more satisfying than his Time-novels. The plays we are considering fulfil Percey Lubbock's idea of a well-made book: "the well-made book is the book in which the subject and the form coincide and are indistinguishable—the book in which the matter is all used up in the form, in which the form expresses all the matter".[6]

The way Priestley conveys his ideas and theories of Time in these plays is never dull because his characters are never mere talkers but doers, they are emotionally alive in evoking an emotional response from the audience. His people do not simply go on discussing things in an intellectual, polemical way as most of the characters in Shaw and Galsworthy do; they are emotionally involved in presenting their ideas in the form of chiselled dramatic dialogue on the stage. This point finds suitable expression in Priestley's own words when he was explaining how the Time problem made a willing ally of him as a dramatist: "The Time problem that fascinated me was part of the life I wanted to bring into the Theatre. I had no hope of handling it intellectually, on the level of debate, as Shaw would have done; but on the other hand our whole complex of feeling about Time, whether we are fascinated or irritated by the problem itself, makes willing ally of any dramatist capable of presenting an action, a series of theatrical situations, that will release the emotions."[7]

Priestley's Time-philosophy has guided the plot construction of the plays taken up here for discussion. These plots are of two types: simple and complex. The simple plots consist of rather a limited number of characters and the action progresses mostly uninterrupted. The complex plots have rather a large number of characters and situations, and the action moves back and forth in Time, interruped by shifting scenes. Whether simple or complex they are 'serious' and so constructed that they successfully dramatise Priestley's ideas and views of Time.

I Have Been Here Before is an example of a simple plot. The Ouspenskian Spiral Time is at the background and directs the course of the plot to a desired end which brings out Priestley's distinctive vision of Time. The exposition is convincingly presented. The Ormund couple are staying in the Black Bull to have rest; they are childless, and so unhappy; the husband is a restless, worried business tycoon. The arrival of Oliver Farrant and then of Gortler to the same inn creates a problem. The irresistible infatuation of Janet with Farrant and their flirting further complicate the lives of the couple and the lover. The Second Act reveals the inner turmoil and the conflict in the mind of Walter Ormund. The conflict within Ormund, representing Everyman, goes on thickening. It reaches a climax when he unsuccessfully attempts self-destruction. The mounting tension and tragedy is resolved by Gortler in Act III which shows a complete change of Ormund's course of life under the enlightening guidance of Gortler, a Yogi who has understood the mystery of Time. We see how the Time theory, used creatively in the play, directs the action. Priestley's use of this Time theory avoids the tragic end of the work which would have otherwise ended as a run-of-the-mill love-triangle tragedy.

The course of the plot of *Eden End* shows Time's influence on it. If Stella had kept on wooing Fasrrant, Lilian's life would have been ruined, and the Kirby family would have fallen into a greater ruin. The muddle—you may call it a tragedy—is averted only because Dr. Kirby makes Stella realise that her past is not dead and that it is futile to pursue happiness only in passing time; she recognises the true quality of life, which stretches outside linear time; decides to leave the place with her husband Charles Appleby and to live as best they can. *Time and the Conways* has a comparatively simple plot. The action moves in chronological time in Act I and Act III, but it takes a leap twenty years ahead (to deal with a future possibility) in Act II and it is all projected through the prophetic vision of Kay. The play establishes that the true character of life lies not in the single track linear time but in timeless Time, in multidimensionality. Happy and unhappy scenes are woven together to show how life moves in serial time. *Dangerous Corner* moves on two levels of Time: the present and the might-have-been. To dramatise a might-have-been—a possibility—the playwright splits time, and the action of the plot begins to move in a different Time dimension, and again the action is put back in clock time at the end of Act III. The events of the might-have-been part of the play—bracketed between the stoppage of passing time with the self-destruction of the husband in the radio play at the beginning of Act I and the return of passing time at the end of Act III—take the plot out of the fourth dimension; the idea of circularity is deftly handled. Similarly, *An Inspector Calls* use the 'split-time' device to advance a future possibility. If the might-have-been in *Dangerous Corner* brings to the fore the deep-down dark world of human nature, the twist of time's tail just before the end of *An Inspector Calls* turns the play into an effective play with a valuable moral; the events that would have made it a thriller take a different colour when the stuff of illusion is turned into solid reality by looping split-time. Similarly serial Time has influenced the plots of *People at Sea, Desert Highway, The Linden Tree, Summer Day's Dream* and *Johnson Over Jordan.*

The events of Act II of *Desert Highway* assume a sharp and ironical meaning because the action of the plot is split by the Interlude; the theme that human life has remained basically unchanged is effectively articulated. *The Linden Tree* moves in a double dimension. The past world of the Lindens and their present one are meaningfully reconciled. The Professor recognises the essentially unchanging quality of life in his timeless moments; the generation gap is bridged through Professor Robert's right understanding of Time. The long-separated lovers, Valentine and Diana, in *People at Sea* are brought to meet and stay in the stranded ship; their encounter under odd circumstances and the reminiscences of their romantic days are introduced to bring about a change in the course of events, which in turn change these characters.

Music at Night and *Johnson Over Jordan* are serious plays; their plots are very complex. In fact these plays are an attempt at dramatising a highly poetic vision of life. *Music at Night* puts its action almost outside chronological time. The events in the lives of sixteen characters, six dead and ten living, are presented in a timeless dimension and directed towards the realisation of a metaphysical and moral theme: individual minds are interconnected and they are partakers of the collective unconscious which operates outside chronological time. Act I dramatises the mental adventures and varying moods of a group of men and women attending the musical concert at Mrs. Amesbury's house. This act shows in short scenes, the acting out of Chilham imagining himself as a detective, Ann dreaming herself as the beautiful white queen of the South Sea Island, Sir James Dirnie's might-have-been, David Shiel's courtship of Sybil as of years ago, Peter's reverie and Bendrex's Edwardian world. Under the effect of the 'second movement' in Act II clock-time gives place to psychic time, dramatising the gloomy moods and thoughts of the characters; the action of the play moves back and forth at a preternatural level. The third movement in Act III depicts the universal consciousness operating in all the characters, and the fourth dimension is annihilated, making room for a timeless dimension. Consequently, the action of the play turns complex.

Johnson Over Jordan also has a complex plot. Act I, after showing for a while the funeral ceremony of Johnson, moves on to dramatise the journey of Johnson's consciousness from Time One to Time Two; in scene after scene, this central character is seen passing through happy and unhappy moods, emotions and thoughts, he goes on meeting a number of people he had lived with in Time One and also fictional characters like Don Quixote and Pickwick. The action progresses in more than one dimension and immensely benefits by dance, music and masks. Johnson's encounter with the officers of the Universal I. Co., his meeting with Jill and then with his mother-in-law, with Charlie and the policeman and at last with the Figure, make the action move back and forth in different dimensions, dethroning Tyrant Time and, consequently, the plot becomes much too complex. Act II conducts Johnson through a variety of scenes in the Night Club. All through, Dunne's serialism is at work. Act III acquires a new dimension, that is, the barrier between the consciousness of Jill and Freda in Time One dimension and that of Johnson in Time Two and Time Three dimensions is knocked down. The construction of this play in three stages—the dream-like state, the Jungle Hot Spot, and the Inn at the End of the World to be followed by his journey towards 'Paradise'—is, as noted earlier, comparable to that of Dante's *Divine Comedy* with its three parts—Inferno, Purgatorio and Paradiso. This play powerfully establishes the multidimensionality of life in the light of Dunne's serialism. As in his plays, in his fiction also Priestley shows his dexterity in plot-construction which is examined in the following pages.

Susan Cooper is hitting on the head of the most distinctive mark of Priestley's writings when she observes that "his work is in a solidly English tradition".[8] Priestley's concern for the English tradition is reflected in his attitude to the form of the novel in no uncertain words. He regards the novel as one of the vaguest forms of the art of literature and observes that it is "a loose mixed form, half a work of art and half something else".[9] In a frank and forthright way he remarks, "The point of view, the shape, the pattern, the rhythm, these count for something, but not a great deal, and for nothing at all if the fiction itself does not come to life."[10]

Generally, action is dominant in Priestley's novels. He believes in the story, in the construction of a good plot. But this does not mean that for him characters do not count. But the point of the argument is that generally the events, rather than his characters, catch the reader's attention. He admits that fiction in the twentieth century is naturally concerned with ideas and states of mind constituting 'subjective themes' but he firmly believes that "as novelist should tell a story, and if possible a fairly shapely one, no matter how strong his subjective interests may be".[11] But his novels with Time as an important element strike a balance between the action novel and the character novel. They may be said to strike "a gentlemanly compromise"[12] between these types as is said of novels like *Tom Jones* and *Martin Chuzzlewit*.

Susan Cooper, speaking of what Priestley made of the novel which he accepted as a challenge, remarks: "The form of the novel was a challenge; each idea he had for a different approach to the novel was an extra challenge; so throughout his life he has given a large proportion of his talent to the battle with the novel, and the talent grew as a result."[13] All his novels in which Time-theories and ideas play an important role form a distinctive class among his fictional works. Time has definitely influenced the plots, the characters and the language of these works. It is necessary to examine the plots from this point of view.

Priestley's early novels, namely, *Adam in Moonshine, Benighted* and *Faraway* have an absorbing element, viz. that of fantasy, and their fantastic creation puts the plots of these works in a double world: the present in passing time and the past or the future in another dimension. The 'magic' world of these works necessarily puts the events in different time-dimensions. Priestley's idea of 'time-loop', which involves circularity, makes him end the story of *Faraway* exactly where he had begun: the story which begins one evening in Ivy Lodge, William's house in Buntingham, where William and Greenlaw are playing chess, ends after two years, again one evening in the same house where William and Greenlaw are found playing chess. So does *The Good Companions* end where it begins: the novel's plot lies between the description of a foot-ball match on the 'the backbone of England' at the beginning and again at the end of it. This circularity always directs the events of his works to move in a definite desired direction.

Most of Priestley's later novels with Time as a recurring concept have serious and largely episodic plots. The various time scales used in these works make the plots complex. Time is the cementing force in novels like *Bright Day, The Magicians* and *Lost Empires*. A variety of events are forged into a coherent shape by the author's idea of different Time-dimensions.

Bright Day has a 'well-made' plot. All the events and situations contribute to the main theme of showing the quality of life, as revealed by a number of happenings in the career of Gregory, which is not changed by Time. The events narrated by the central character, Gregory, himself take us backwards and forwards in Time. The Dunnian serialism is at the backdrop, and happy and unhappy scenes of the past and the present constitute the plot. The details of things and events relating to the Allingtons, the Blackshaws and the Nixey couple and others at Bruddersford dovetail into the main story of Gregory and his career. The author deliberately introduces certain scenes which are intended to bring out the timeless character of human life. For example, we have a scene, almost at the end of the novel, where Dawson meets Mrs. Childs (former girl Laura) whose words, and explanation of Time, lend him an awareness of life's wisdom and his duty to himself and the human society about him. The past is captured by flashbacks and the novel clearly establishes how a man's dispassionate attitude to his past can cure his present, and also how his present can help him see his past in a better light.

Jenny Villiers uses different Time-scales and often they are interlocked. The half-awake and half-dreaming self of Cheveril moves in the borderland of reality in his encounters with Jenny, an actress of a century ago, who comes alive before him. His present and the past of the actress and her colleagues are presented in a timeless order. The use of different Time-dimensions puts the action at different levels. The actual time of the plot is one night but the fictional time spreads over generations; the plot takes place in Cheveril's consciousness in different vagaries of Time. With a constant shift in Time-dimensions there is a constant change in the action. The events do not follow the logic of 'before and after' but an inner dynamic of Cheveril's consciousness, which acts as the unifying principle.

The Magicians has in it two strands of action: the scheming activities of Mervil and his gang ending up in humiliation and grief, and the events that lead to a happy change in the central character, Revenstreet. The past events of Ravenstreet's life are presented as happening in his consciousness, while those relating to characters like Sepman and his wife, Mervil and his 'cut-throat' gang take place in linear time; naturally the action spreads in various dimensions. The Dunnian serialism of Time working through the yogic, apocalyptic vision and wisdom of the magicians directs the course of the plot connected mainly with the story of Ravenstreet's life. The 'time alive' experience which Ravenstreet enters twice, through the magical powers of the 'indomitable trio', breaks the chronological flow of time. To show the timeless character of consciousness, Priestley makes use of *ESP* also. The minds of Ravenstreet and Philippa are connected across a vast physical distance, and the Time-traveller Perperek links himself invisibly to Ravenstreet and directly speaks, though not seen physically, to Philippa on her death-bed in the hospital. The reunion of Ravenstreet and his long-lost wife Philippa is envisioned by the magicians, and their humane act actualises a future possibility. Thus the plot is so arranged that it successfully encapsulates Priestley's philosophy of unity of consciousness and Time-dimensions. *Saturn Over the Water* shows the powerful influence of Priestley's Time theory on its action. The search theme and the love theme meet with a successful end under the effective guidance of the Time-travellers—the Old Man on the mountain and Mrs. Baro. The Old Man's vision of time past and time present shapes the course of the plot. Mrs. Baro forewarns the lovers of the coming of the Saturnians in search of Rosalia and Tim. If the lovers had not fled from there they would have been caught and killed by the sinister-minded group. Similarly if the Old Man had not vanquished the Saturnians and frustrated their satanic design of wiping out the civilisation of Europe, certainly chaos would have swept over the earth again. Thus the story that would have ended tragically ends in happiness. *The Thirty First of June* presents the drama of what happens in the imagination of Sam Penty, a painter in the service of an advertising company. The plot goes on moving alternately in two dimensions: in the city of modern London in passing time and in the Arthurian City of Paradore in the medieval age. Priestley's concept of imagination as reality of a higher order which functions outside world time directs the course of the novel in a definite way; the interlocking of different Time-scales creates a complex but deep effect of the action on the reader's mind.

The plot of *Lost Empires* derives its substance from the recapturing of the significant past of the central character, Richard Herncastle, who draws the story out of the well of his memory. The time past comes curving back to the narrator and creates an intensely captivating atmosphere in a Proustian way. It is not simply by 'time-looping' or 'flashbacks' that Priestley makes the narrator catch the past but by his ability to put the action solidly in a recreated ethos and atmosphere of the old music-halls. Long stretches of years are telescoped into the fine narrative fabric of the plot. The illusionist Nick's tricks and actions introduce interesting events and episodes like the Mrs. Forster-Jones scene and the famous Indian Magic Box; these scenes are intended to show how Time plays many tricks on the human mind. The murder of Nonie and the outbreak of the bloody First World War are mentioned as an illustration of the Old Hindoo's predictions Nick heard years ago at the London Coliseum. The relationship of Richard and Nancy is a case of Future-influencing-present. The effect of a future event is felt and experienced first and then its cause is revealed. Richard and Nancy have been lovers in the eternal 'Now' and are going to marry at a future date but their mutual attraction—

especially the lover's infatuation—is described as taking place in the present; it is, in this case, not the present that influence the future but the other way round. Thus the plot of the novel comes under the influence of Time-theories, concepts and Time-tricks. If the psychological time of the mental operations of Sir Bernard in the story *Guest of Honour* puts the plot at a preternatural level of action, the use of various Time-dimensions and their simultaneous operations at several places in the story *Look After the Strange Girl* present an unusual and bizarre setting against which a complex plot develops in a deep and mysterious way.

Like the plot-construction of Priestley's fictional works as well as his plays, the characterisation in these works also has come remarkably under the influence of the Time problem.

Priestley's remark, "A novel in which the people do not seem to us to come alive (even though they appear to be almost monsters) cannot succeed as a novel"[14] is equally true of a play. Priestley's characterisation in his Time-plays as well as Time-fiction is going to be examined in the following pages. These works present two types of characters: Flat and Round. Most of the characters in these works, whether flat or round, "stand like giants immersed in Time",[15] much larger and taller than those in space, as observed by Proust about the characters in all Time-works.

Priestley's flat characters in these works are static, calm, and wise, strange in their looks and dress, highly contemplative and capable of moving out of linear time. These people, gifted as they are with precognition and retrocognition, are unpredictable Time-travellers. They do not change but change other people and the course of events in the novel. Their Time-philosophy decides their attitude to life; they are men and women with 'the milk of human kindness' in their hearts for others. Alan (*Time and the Conways*), a municipal clerk, who was called up in the First World War, has seen life whole; his wisdom of life comes from his right understanding of Time as explained by Dunne. He makes his sister Kay optimistic about life by explaining to her that Time destroys nothing. Gortler (*I Have Been Here Before*) is a great traveller in Time, an experimentalist yogi. This German Professor's optimism comes from his firm belief in Ouspensky's Spiral Time. With his superior knowledge Gortler kindles a light in the dark world of Walter Ormund; changes this business tycoon's career, and averts the tragedy in his life. Dorothy and Jock (*Bright Day*), the mystical soul Margaret (*Summer Day's Dream*), Candover (*Let the People Sing*), the Russian Nature Man (*Faraway*), the Old Man on the Mountain and Mrs. Baro (*Saturn Over the Water*), Dr. Firmius (*It's an Old Country*), the magicians (*The Magicians*), the Old Hindoo (*Lost Empires*) and Sir Alaric (*The Other Place*) are Time-travellers and their actions and words certainly change the course of events in these works and the ways and attitude of the people around them. The role of these rare, queer-looking men and women in Priestley's Time works has already been discussed.

There are other characters who are drawn in the round. They change under the influence of different views and theories of Time. They are an appealing lot, "capable of surprising in a convincing way".[16] They display certain distinctive qualities. All of them are unhappy and deeply disturbed souls; they are restless seekers after something lasting beyond passing time. Some pass through a mysterious experience of Time, some have queer intuitions and feelings about life and things, about past, present and future. Kay (*Time and the Conways*) emerges as a much changed character, a staunch optimist after she begins to 'see' life in its multidimensionality under the influence of her brother's explanation of Serialism of Time. Dr. Kirby and Stella are two very interesting characters in *Eden End*. The doctor has grasped the true meaning of life in the light of Dunne's Serial view of Time. The same view is shared by Stella, who at last learns to reconcile herself to what life offers, to get on well with her husband, Charles Appleby. Walter Ormund, Everyman (*I Have Been Here Before*), undergoes a sea-change owing to his understanding of the Ouspenskian view of Time at the hands of Gortler; a life-hater becomes a great optimist; he has now turned the circle of his Time into a spiral which will enable him to evolve his life nobly. Valentine and Diana (*People at Sea*) become reconciled to each other in the light of their recognition of life's reality as one to be found outside chronological time, and decide to marry and turn a new leaf in their lives. Paul and Mary (*Ever Since Paradise*) get on well together when they see their life as a whole, free from Time's tyranny. Gregory (*Bright Day*) begins to look at life from an altogether different attitude: the explanation that comes from the lips of Mrs. Childs (the former Blackshaw girl Laura), that one should see life beyond passing time to know it truly, changes his whole view of life so that he knocks down the narrow wall of time he has built around himself, and comes out a new man with an optimistic outlook; his bright past comes smiling back to him and his gloom melts away. Likewise, Cheveril (*Jenny Villiers*) comes out of the dejection and sense of hollowness born of the dwindling fortunes of the theatre after he has met with, in varying vagaries of Time, Jenny, an illustrious actress of a century ago; the happy past of the theatre acts as a corrective of the painful present; Cheveril emerges as a new man with a bright future for the British theatre and himself. William (*Faraway*) has his spirit of determination and adventure kept always alive by his precognitive power of 'seeing', through the diaphanous curtains of Time, the treasure trove which he and his friends are striving hard to possess. Similarly, there are others like Tim and Rosalia (*Saturn Over the Water*), Timmy Tiverton (*Let the People Sing*), Sam Penty (*The Thirty First of June*), Ravenstreet (*The Magicians*), the expert team in *Summer Day's Dream*, Strenberry (*Mr. Strenberry Tale*), Luke and Betty (*Night Sequence*) who go through a rare, unusual experience outside their temporal existence and come out as enlightened human beings. The experience of timeless Time which all these people go through has a powerful and thrilling effect on their lives; they become wiser and happier. They come to feel that life is wholesome and worth-living. It should be noticed that Time exerts a significant influence, in various ways, on the thoughts and actions of these characters.

A study of diction also seems called for in so far as its patterning contributes to the definition of the theme of a novel or play.

Priestley's Time-philosophy has influenced the language of these works in a distinctive way. The dialogue of his plays has acquired a marked simplicity, straightforwardness and fluidity. The prose style of the novels is marked by a depth and colour which Priestleyan readers do not normally associate with his social novels. Two specimens are quoted below to highlight this point.

(a) Consider the following conversation between Johnson and the Figure:

"Johnson (alarmed):	A funeral service?
The Figure:	Yours.
Johnson:	They think I'm dead?
The Figure:	Yes.
Johnson (Agitated):	And there they are—Jill Freda, Richard—unhappy And I'm here. Oh,—horrible. What a swine I Am!
The Figure:	No, no. A fool perhaps, an average (cheerfully, but gently) sort of fool. (Pauses, considering him) Robbert, I think you'd Better go on to the Inn now.
Johnson (sharply):	I want to go back to my home, to tell them I'm not really dead—to try and comfort them.
The Figure (with you great authority) :	You can't go back. In that world you are really dead. To try and force your way Back there would be to bring evil into your own house. You must take your road. But you can stay a little while at the Inn first.
Johnson:	What inn is this?
The Figure:	Call it, if you like, the Inn at the End of the World. They are expecting you there.
Johnson:	I have no money now. I flung it all away.

The Figure:	You will not need any.
Johnson:	What shall I find there?
The Figure:	I do not know what things have illuminated your mind and touched your heart.
Johnson:	But how do I go there?
The Figure:	That way will do."[17]

Now consider the following sketch of Jock Barniston, a Time-traveller, a sort of yogi, from the novel *Bright Day*:

> .... He was one of those very rare persons—and we probably do not meet more than three or four in a lifetime—who do little or nothing of any consequence, make no effort to attract attention, seem content with the common place, and yet leave with everybody who knows them an enduring impression of integrity and strength, of vast unused powers, of carelessly veiled greatness. In India Jock Barniston would probably have been regarded as an adept of 'Karma-Yoga', perhaps as one who rested easily between two strenuous and glorious lives, merely going through a routine of living for one incarnation.... Through it all he remained cool and amused yet friendly, like a well-wisher sent to us from some other and nobler planet. On any commonsense view of this life he was not to be explained at all, and to this day, though I, like many others, remember him with affection, he remains to me a mystery.... And perhaps he knew already, when he was talking to me on the tram, in December 1912, that before the next four years were out, that body which he had put on like an overcoat to wear among us would be so much bleeding meat in a sandbag; and this knowledge may have made him look even more cool and amused. He was an enigma, this heroic emperor in disguise; I think he came from a long way off, to drink beer and coffee with us, to smoke a pipe and hear our troubles, to vanish in the slaughterhouse of the First World War, and

> then perhaps to make some cool and amused report on us to some authority outside the solar system....[18]

Surely, this is the language that makes all the Time worlds kin.

Words are no intractable material to this master of stage-craft and stage dialogue, who can fashion them into a pliable instrument for his purposes. Likewise, Priestley's authorial voice in his Time novels never tends to be turgid; all his views and theories of Time are fleshed out in smooth-flowing language.

As an original thinker about Time and man's need to explore life's limitless possibilities through non-clock dimensions of Time, Priestley had to forge his own idiolect, his own idiosyncratic rhetoric, his own coinages to serve as "objective correlations" for what he, and he alone, saw: expressions like "sunlit-plain", "the eternal morning", "magical moments" (Priestley's idiolectal counterpart of Joyce's epiphany' and Thomas Wolfe's 'pinpoints of time'); sometimes he had to borrow an expression of someone else's coinage which served his purposes 'to a T', such as Proust's "music of experience".

His expressive metaphor to signify the journey of a man through 'inferno' is "Hot Spot Jungle"; something in his scheme that comes nearest to Dante's Purgatorio—the stage preparatory to a pilgrim soul's launching into Paradise—is the "Inn at the End of the World" (*Johnson Over Jordan*). A familiar word like 'shiver' gathers a special metaphoric significance in the hands of Priestley, when he uses it as indicative of the change of Time-dimension. At times, such wordsmithy (It is not without propriety that Susan Cooper called Priestley a 'wordsmith') is unpretentiously plain, like *The Other Place* signifying the timeless world.

Priestley had to create his own mythology, too: his "Saturnians" (*Saturn Over the Water*) are those who wield power over the consciousness of men ('water' here being the ancient symbol for consciousness, not the Christian one signifying grace); his "Uranians", on the other hand, are Altruists, Humanitarians.

NOTES

1. Quoted by Harrison Owen, *The Playwright's Craft* (London: Thomas Nelson & Sons Ltd., 1940), p. 21.
2. John Atkins, *J.B. Priestley,* p. 235.
3. J.B. Priestley, *The Art of the Dramatist* (London: William Heinemann, 1957), p. 39.
4. John Atkins, *J.B. Priestley,* p. 229.
5. *The Plays of J.B. Priestley*, Vol. III, p. 200.
6. Percy Lubbock, *The Craft of Fiction* (London: Bradford and Dickens, rpt. 1957), p. 40.
7. J.B. Priestley, *The Art of the Dramatist*, p. 51.
8. Susan Cooper, *J.B. Priestley,* p. 158.
9. J.B. Priestley, *Literature and Western Man* (London: Heinemann, 1960), p. 223.
10. J.B. Priestley, *Midnight on the Desert*, p. 208.
11. Susan Cooper, *J.B. Priestley,* p. 45.
12. Edwin Muir, *The Structure of the Novel* (London: The Hogarth Press, rpt. 1957), p. 28.
13. Susan Cooper, *J.B. Priestley,* p. 81.
14. J.B. Priestley, *Literature and Western Man*, p. 224.
15. Miriam Allott, *Novelists on the Novel* (London: Routledge and Kegan Paul Ltd., rpt. paperback 1965), p. 255.
16. E.M. Forster, *Aspects of the Novel* (London: Edward Arnold & Co., rpt. 1953), p. 75.
17. *The Plays of J.B. Priestley*, Vol. I, p. 314.
18. *Bright Day*, pp. 53-54.

7

Priestley's Achievements

It has been shown at length that Priestley was a wizard of Time. An assessment of his contribution to Time Literature will be helpful in assigning him his rightful place among Time-writers.

Time had never been treated as a serious problem on the English stage before the advent of the twentieth century. Though Shakespeare was the most Time-haunted writer of the Elizabethan age, he never treated the Time problem on the stage. Marlowe's Faustus conjures up the face of Helen, a paragon of beauty of a bygone day, but his drama does not involve any serious idea of Time. The Jacobean and Caroline drama, the Restoration drama, the eighteenth century comedy and tragedy and the nineteenth century poetic plays show no evidence of any serious concern with Time: their business almost ends with its treatment as one of the three unities of drama. It was only in the twentieth century that the problem of Time came to be grappled with and its mystery sought to be unravelled; it came to be treated as a theme on the stage, too. The twentieth century English drama, rich and varied as it is, combines into its fabric several strands. Besides the dominant realistic plays—plays of ideas—of Shaw and Galsworthy, it has Synge's cynical comedies; the comedies of manners by Coward and Maugham; the war-theme plays of Zangwill and Munro and Shariff; the bizarre and fantastic plays by Dunsany and others; the plays of James Barrie, a Time-haunted playwright;

and the Time-plays of Priestley whose Time-philosophy distinguishes him from others.

Time appeared in two kinds of drama: the fantastic and the philosophical. The dramas of Barrie, Lord Dunsany, Reginald Berkeley belonged to the fantastic trend involving the time-element. These playwrights did show a keen interest in Time, no doubt. But none had plumbed the depth and mystery of Time as a metaphysical experience in terms of dramatic art. Their treatment of it was basically one of technique and hardly involved profound Time-vision. It was, however, given to Priestley to explore metaphysically the 'Waters of Time', to engage philosophically with Time in relation to human consciousness and its effect on human behaviour. Like his works of fiction his Time-plays also are based on a well-founded Time-philosophy which derives its composite elements from various Time-theories and concepts.

Priestley's first play *Dangerous Corner* appeared in 1932. By then he had become an established essayist, critic and novelist. His writings had covered a variety of themes and interests; they were a proof of his awareness of the real and the ideal. Enough realism had appeared in his two novels: *The Good Companions* had dealt with both the bright side and the dark side of rural England, of course in a comic light, and *Angel Pavement* was a solid realistic work depicting tragic-comic figures against the grim realistic setting of industrial London. When Priestley chose to write plays in a spirit of challenge and with a love of experimenting with form and technique, he decided to give something at once new to the English stage. Then naturally he had to break away from the popular realistic social drama practised by Shaw and Galsworthy and others, and, at the same time, to keep away from the mere sentimental and fantastic stuff of the Barrie trend. The Time-problem, buzzing as it had been in his mind for long, prompted him to write plays in which Time would be either a major problem or an important idea.

A glance at the themes and techniques of Priestley's plays, with Time as a dominant thing in them, will show his originality and distinctive contribution to English drama. It should be noted that he did not write out of theories; they were rather the source of his inspiration. His plays and novels are artistic products, rather than illustrations with the merest veneer of art. The split-time technique is part of his wider application of Dunne's Serialism. It is used in *Dangerous Corner* to dramatise a might-have-been, in *Time and the Conways* to show a future possibility, in *Desert Highway* to present the unchangeable pattern of human history, in *An Inspector Calls* to bring out the element of interconnectedness in human affairs, and in *Ever Since Paradise* to express the subtle and complex Man-Woman relationship outside passing time. Serial Time is used, in one way or another, in a maximum number of his Time-plays. Serial Time is employed to show in *Eden End* the essential quality of life outside passing time; to present, in *Time and the Conways,* a long view of Time, which is necessary for accepting the changing scenes of joys and sorrows of life with equanimity as does William Blake; to highlight, in *People at Sea,* the discovery of self-identity outside passing time; to dramatise, in *Johnson Over Jordan,* the progress of consciousness after death in order to establish the continuity of life through consciousness in different dimensions of Time; and to suggest in *The Linden Tree,* a solution to the problem of the generation-gap through taking life as a whole, not by taking a three-sectional view of the four-sectional existence. Likewise, the Ouspenskian Eternal Recurrence is employed to show in *I Have Been Here Before* how men, through a knowledge of their earlier lives, can develop their present lives nobly, turn circular time into spiral time and at last escape from the wheel of Time. Jung's theory of the unconscious is at the background of *Music at Night* which highlights the true nature of personality in tune with the playwright's belief that individuals such as Jones and Brown are illusions and individual selves are partakers of a universal consciousness which is timeless; here music is used to raise consciousness to a higher level where it operates in different time-dimensions. The mirror-image in *The Long Mirror,* like the Platonic cave-image, shows the shadow-show of life; the mirror represents passing time; things outside the mirror are not reflected in it but they are not out of existence; also those that are outside passing time do not cease to be, but will exist in another dimension.

Most of these plays, which saw hundreds of productions in England and abroad and gave the audience an altogether alien dramatic experience, unknown in the theatre, and lent them a new awareness of life, appeared between the early thirties and the early forties of this century. They contain a primarily poetic vision and display human life as a blend of the spiritual and the earthly; they depict what goes on in the soul of man in relation to the different time-dimensions. Therefore, Allardyce Nicoll rightly includes Priestley among the subjective playwrights of Europe like Strindberg, Sutton Vene, and Paul Osborne who put their soul's adventure on the stage. Certainly Priestley is one of those remarkable dramatists who were not satisfied with the application of reason to all aspects of human existence, and wanted to revive the long-lost dominance of man's inner spirit. His Time plays truly illustrate Allardyce Nicoll's observation about subjective dramatists that their plays are a record of "the development of a dramatic style wherein the matters of the spirit are brought into close association with ordinary life...."[1]

The essential stuff of Priestley's Time plays is consciousness. His is a metaphysical, and not a psychological, approach to the nature and function of consciousness. He focusses on the correspondence between consciousness and Time; shows the continuity of personality through the continuity of consciousness in different orders of existence and dimensions of Time. This distinctive mark of his Time-works is clearly seen in plays like *I Have Been Here Before, Johnson Over Jordan* and *Music at Night.* Certain moments, which he calls 'magical', experienced by characters like Kay, Janet, Stella, Oliver Farrant, Walter Ormund and Johnson are shown as related even to their earlier births and to the things that will happen in future.

It is singularly remarkable that English drama acquired a philosophical dimension for the first time in its history in the hands of Priestley. While Shaw and others were turning social and political ideas into dramatic art, Priestley succeeded in turning the Time-philosophy—a more challenging task—into Time-plays and thus in giving his audience a peep into enduring realities behind the curtain of Time. G. Wilson Knight rightly observes: "These plays witness a unique identification of metaphysics and drama."[2]

Another important feature of these plays is that they present a profound philosophy in a simple language. Priestley's primary concern being humanity, he wants to share with his audience what he intensely feels and thinks in regard to Time and its influence on the human mind and personality. It was an act of innovative thinking and experimentation on the part of Priestley that in these plays he made a meaningful departure from realism in the heyday of the realistic social drama of Shavian tradition. The visionary, the poet, in him "would not be limited by the chatter and scenery of realism or cabined by the confines of the immediately perceptible world".[3]

Priestley shares a kindred spirit with T.S. Eliot in that both made serious efforts to translate the unknown in terms of the known, the imperceptible world into the perceptible, though they differ in their approach to the goal. Discussing this point, G.L. Evans points out how they share a common ground. If Eliot shows in his poetic dramas like *Murder in the Cathedral* the spiritual and religious realities behind the realities of the common world of men, Priestley shows the mystical and magical realities behind the realities of this world. Both Eliot and Priestley in their dramatic experimentation moved away from the realistic social plays which merely sought to project theatrical images of social forces. Priestley's objective was "to convince that the magic and the mystery swirl about us, that to be aware of it is to be aware of the oneness of humanity".[4] He realised this objective to the satisfaction of his age. All his Time plays from *Dangerous Corner* to *Summer Day's Dream* centre round the working of consciousness at different levels and in different orders of Time; they successfully establish the oneness of humanity.

Priestley followed no school and no movement in literature. He was highly individualistic. Though he owes a lot to Time theorists like Dunne, he did not accept them blindly.

For example, he accepts only three 'selves'—three series—from Dunne's theory of a series of dimensions *ad infinitum*, and adds the idea of Intervention to Ouspensky's theory of Eternal Recurrence to turn Circular time into Spiral time. He is, thus, very original in his approach to ideas, themes and form. Discussing the contribution made to the English stage by the group of Time-plays, in which Priestley's creative imagination is at its best, J.C. Trewin opines: "By 1940 Priestley had become an acknowledged leader of the stage, with more solid work to show in ten years than many dramatists in a life-time."[5] Priestley had first-hand experience of theatrical requirements and the psychology of the audience. He never experimented with the form and technique of drama in a dull and dry intellectual manner but in the light of his rich experience as a working dramatist and producer. Again, J.C. Trewin observes that the distinctive quality of Priestley as a dramatist lies in his experimentation, not in the "manner of the out-and-out intellectual who loses all touch with the theatre, but in the manner of a wary and experienced dramatist who, though he desires to cheat realism, will not do anything merely foolish".[6]

Priestley's Time plays with their profound poetic vision of life in relation to Time and his optimistic philosophy set English drama free from the hackneyed realistic conventions and introduced flexibility in presenting scenes and characters outside the chronological time-track. The philosophical dimension of Time opened up by these Time plays and their novelty of form and technique constitute the core of Priestley's contribution to English drama.

An assessment of Priestley's contribution to Time-fiction, too, is quite essential to have a just and whole view of his contribution to Time literature in English.

Time has been treated in more than one way in English fiction. John Henry Raleigh, a modern critic of the novel, recognises three kinds of Time in the English novel: cosmic time which is cyclical, historical time which is linear, and existential time which is vertical. If Hardy's Wessex novels have cosmic time, indicating the cyclic character of nature, the eighteenth and nineteenth century novels, except *Tristram Shandy,* contain linear time, and twentieth century 'time-fiction' has existential time. Older novelists like Richardson, Fielding, Dickens, Trollope and Thackeray did not have either a metaphysical or yet a really serious psychological concern with Time. With them Time was mainly linear, progressing from the past through the present into future; for them the idea of Time was bound up with the idea of progress. The concept of Time as a straight line breaks down with Hardy and Henry James. The sense of the past becomes dominant with Hardy's Wessex characters, and nature in the land there symbolises cosmic time which is cyclic; Time in Jame's works becomes 'personalised' and internal, with the potential infinity of the past impinging on the present. Jame's concept of psychological time led to the modern psychological fiction.

The fictional time of a novel is not of great importance but the way in which it is treated is important. It assumes significance if it gives the reader a changed temporal rhythm and lends the work a depth and colour. There are, mainly, three ways in which Time is treated in fiction. The first method is that of maintaining an even flow of narration. In this method, even though long periods of time are covered and time is speeded up, time seems to pass smoothly. *War and Peace* and *Henry Esmond* are good examples of this method. The second method is found in dramatic novels like *Wuthering Heights, A Tale of Two Cities* and *The Return of the Native* in which time moves sometimes speedily and sometimes very slowly. The readers feel that they are witnessing scenes as in a theatre, some moving very fast and others dead slow. These novelists can, thus, manipulate its progress. The third method is that of slow motion. Here the moments are expanded and every minute detail is squeezed out. This method is at the centre of the psychological novel and is popularly known as the "stream-of-consciousness" technique which is based on slow-motion effect. "The writers of psychological fiction where the physical action is subordinated to the mental or emotional activity, slowdown the speed of the novel."[7] In this kind of fiction Time is intensely subjective and private, and is removed from the public clock. The "stream-of-consciousness" novelists raised the psychological novel to unprecedented heights.

The twentieth century has seen the dominance of Time in two types of fiction: science-fiction and Time-fiction. Science-fiction was introduced by H.G. Wells with his novel *The Time Machine,* and then followed a torrent of science-tales which used Time as a linear entity, extending it into the future. Though imaginative and entertaining in their own right and capable of giving the reader an 'escape route' from the dull routine of day-to-day affairs, science-fiction-tales had no serious purpose; they were shallow and superficial in depicting the affairs of men. The writings of this class dealt with Time-travelling and all manner of Time tricks, with the result that men were reduced to machines.

Time is the nucleus of psychological fiction. Time-fiction, derogatorily labelled 'Time-school-fiction' by Wyndham Lewis, is based upon Bergson's *la durêe,* which is a psychological theory of Time. Bergson's *la durêe* puts forth the view that chronological time is unreal, and reality can be found only in psychological time, in man's inner sense of duration. Articulating his belief in a constant remoulding of human personality by experience, Bergson observes that consciousness is a process of endless accretion, so long as the mind and senses are functioning, and that consciousness is "the continuation of an indefinite past in a living present".[8] Out of this line of thinking about consciousness came the preoccupation with Time which is central to the psychological novel. T.S. Eliot expressed the Bergsonian view of Time in poetry:

> ...the pattern is new in every moment
> And every moment is a new and shocking
> Valuation of all we have been.[9]

Virginia Woolf puts the same Bergsonian concept of 'duration' in her famous statement: "Life is not a series of gig-lamps symmetrically arranged; life is a luminous halo, a semi-transparent envelope surrounding us from the beginning of consciousness to the end."[10] From Dorothy Richardson onwards all psychological novelists got their inspiration from

Bergson's view of Time. The moment of significance, termed 'epiphany' in Joyce, was the 'moment of illumination' in Virginia Woolf and became 'pin-points of Time' in Thomas Wolfe. The 'slice of life' of nineteenth century realistic novels was replaced by 'Slice of Time' in Time-fiction.

Priestley sees little literary or philosophical value in science-fiction and holds no high opinion about the psychological novel either. Regarding science-fiction he feels that as these works do not come out of the depth of consciousness, the immortal gift which man possesses, the wonder and the mystery of the universe and of the inner world of man are miserably missing. Time, treated only on the temporal plane, though undoubtedly in a fascinating way as in W.H. Hudson's *A Crystal Age* and W. Olaf Stapledon's *Last and First Men,* ceases to be the ancient enigma and becomes vulgar; the reader is cheated out of a strange and thrilling experience. Philosophically too this class of writing is of no value because it offers no help in solving the Time problem.

Priestley is a non-Bergsonian writer of multiple Time. Though he has used psychological time in a number of his works, he markedly differs from the exponents and practitioners of this school of fiction on key points. He is opposed to the enormous emphasis placed by the Bergsonian theory of 'duration' on psychological time. He feels that Bergson puts all sorts of different experiences in the hold all of his *durêe.* He regards psychological time as only one kind of Time, and it cannot be the last word in solving the problem of Time. The basic limitation of the Bergsonian theory, Priestley rightly thinks, is that it hardly goes beyond the world of the senses and mind. Priestley believes in the existence of dimensions other than the meagre earthly existence which is chained and cribbed by passing time. Therefore, he goes to other Time theorists like Dunne and Ouspensky and Jung, who help him look at Time from different angles, and adroitly exploits their theories to the advantage of his art.

Priestley's Time-fiction made a bold departure from the Bergsonian psychological fiction just as his Time-plays did from the realistic social drama. His emphasis is not only on the importance of consciousness in arriving at 'reality' but also on the orders of consciousness. He recognises the function of consciousness at three levels: the conscious, the unconscious and the superconscious. These levels correspond to three orders of Time: Time One, Time Two and Time Three. In his works of Time-fiction Priestley displays a greater degree of freedom and flexibility than in his Time-plays; here he does not bind himself to any particular Time theory; in fact, in some works like *Jenny Villiers* he combines two or three theories for greater effect.

As a Time-fictionist Priestley is a writer of multiple Time. His commitment being to life rather than to art, he works in different orders of consciousness which necessarily involve different dimensions of Time. A glance at the themes and technique of his works of Time-fiction will give an idea about the depth and range of his world of multiple Time.

The Dunnian Serialism is at the background of *Faraway, Bright Day, Let the People Sing* and *Lost Empires*. These novels establish the multidimensionality of Time and, thereby, of life. These works recreate the past through flashbacks and show that nothing of it has been lost to Time and everything is in its own time. William (*Faraway*) experiences his childhood and adolescent days again and also sees the faraway island through the diaphanous curtain of Time. *Bright Day* goes on weaving its plot with Gregory's past and present into a timeless fabric; Gregory's reminiscences restore his Edwardian 'sunlit plain' which brightens his gloomy present; he hears the 'music of experience' in a Proustian way through recapturing Time in its 'purity'. Timmy Tiverton (*Let the People Sing*) finds his smiling past come alive to him and this music-hall comedian in his fifties shakes off his 'winter' and again beams with the joy of 'spring'. *Lost Empires* depicts the 'eternal morning' of Richard Herncastle, a septuagenarian painter, whose Edwardian England of bustling music-halls comes curving back to him. The Ouspenskian idea of imagination as a reality is shown in *Jenny Villiers* and *The Thirty First of June*. If the veteran playwright Cheveril meets in his reverie a well-known actress of a century ago and his encounters with her fill him with optimism for the future of the theatre, Sam Penty, a painter of an advertising firm, imagines for a model an Arthurian Princess, and the novel connects modern London with medieval Paradore; Penty's world of imagination creates a timeless order in which past and present merge; in these novels, the consciousness of the living and that of the dead are depicted as part of one all-pervasive consciousness which is timeless. *Jenny Villiers* is a rare technical tour dẽ force. It combines Serial Time, the Ouspenskian concept of imagination as a reality and the Jungian Unconscious into an artistic whole which produces a radically new view of human personality presented outside unidimensional time. *The Magicians,* presenting an apocalyptic view of life, combines Serial Time with the *ESP* concept, which mainly consists of precognition and postcognition; the work creates a composite picture of human existence at different levels of consciousness; the three magicians, master Time-travellers, possess the profundity of Oriental mysticism. *Saturn Over the Water* deals with opposite forces: the good and humane and wise are represented by the Old Man on the mountain and Mrs. Baro, while the wicked and sinister forces are represented by the Saturnians; at last the world is saved from the clutches of the saturnians by the wise and enlightened group, who are Time-travellers. If the wise men in *The Magicians* save modern civilization from 'Sepmanism', the Time-travellers in *Saturn Over the Water* save it from an imminent extinction at the hands of misanthropes. Priestley employs a technique by which he can combine several Time theories and concepts for projecting a timeless reality of life as is effectively brought off in these two novels. The wise and noble souls form quite a large group in his works. The Old Man and Mrs. Baro (*Saturn Over the Water*), the 'indomitable trio' (*The Magicians*), Dorothy and Jock (*Bright Day*), the Old Hindoo (*Lost Empires*), the old Candover (*Let the People Sing*) are Time-travellers and act as vehicles of the universal consciousness; their unconscious is capable of jumping back to the past or ahead to the future not only of individual lives but also of the world.

The stories *The Other Place, Look After the Strange Girl, The Statues* and *Night Sequence* have Time as a dominant element and display a novelty in the technique of narration. The *ESP* concept works in *The Other Place* and *Night Sequence.* Dr. Alaric produces a myseterious effect on the mind of Lindfield; he releases the consciousness of the latter by concentrating his attention on a black pebble-like stone; Lindfield enters another dimension; he spends only three and a half minutes of clock time but feels that he has spent a whole day there.

Night Sequence shows how a couple called Luke and Betty enter the consciousness of Sir Edward and his niece Julia who have gone out of earthly existence in Time One; the consciousness of those in Time One and that of the dead are part of one world mind which is outside clock time. Like *Jenny Villiers,* the story *Look After the Strange Girl* adroitly interlocks various dimensions of Time; the consciousness of the three characters in the story functions in a timeless order. *The Statues* is a fantastic futurist story in which the London of five centuries later is envisioned by Walter Voley; Walter's consciousness is released from Time One dimension and leaps to a distant future.

Apart from a rich variety of themes and the originality of techniques these fictional works contain certain deep and mysterious moments which Priestley calls magical moments. Priestley describes such moments that everybody does experience sometimes; it clearly shows that during those moments men enter another dimension of Time and are given a peep into another dimension of life. For Priestley life is mysterious and its reality is caught only in such 'magical moments'. Generally such moments are signalled by a 'shiver' or cold, suggesting a change of time-dimension. Adam (*Adam in Moonshine*) feels lifted out of passing time into another dimension while in the company of Helen in moonlight. The 'shiver' felt by Penderel (*Benighted*), all of a sudden, while walking with the girl Gladys, indicates a shift from one time dimension to another. Ramsbottom (*Faraway*) feels something of a sudden cold creeping through him when he enteres another dimension of Time, his past, under the spell cast on his consciousness by the Old Russian Nature man. In *Bright Day,* Joan passes through a queer feeling of cold, all of a sudden, while strolling with Gregory; this was a moment which gave her a peep into the future tragedy of the Alingtons. Likewise, William's consciousness (*Faraway*) catches sight of a future possibility, the discovery of the island; he too feels that something cold is plucking at his spinal cord; this is a shift of time-dimension. A variety of moments are described in *It's an Old Country*. Priestley calls some moments rich and some 'empty', others mystifying ones and so on. These come from different experiences of Time as felt by consciousness. This discussion of Priestley's themes and techniques, and of the kinds of Time he treats vis-a-vis consciousness clearly establishes that Priestley is unique among the Time-writers and that his contribution as a Time-fictionist is one of rare distinction and originality.

These works of Time-fiction, so far discussed, stand out as a class by themselves. They show the effect that Time has on the consciousness and behaviour of the characters. Further, they evidence the fact that Priestley is a novelist of moderation, unlike those of the psychological school. In Priestley Time and space are well-balanced, whereas Time is a monster in the 'stream-of-consciousness' novels.

Priestley takes care to avoid the kind of obscurity born of too much of 'turning inward' which is found in novels like *Ulysses* and *Finnegans Wake*. Too much stress on the 'moment' as a time-unit in the psychological novel has thrown the novel-form out of gear. Writers like James Joyce and Virginia Woolf shift the thrust of psychological analysis from the character to the 'moment' which becomes a highly personalised projection of the author's mind and the result is not a happy one. "So the characters become mere projections of the author, as for instance can be clearly seen in *The Waves* where all six characters are different aspects of Virginia Woolf which she had tried to separate."[11] Priestley's Time-novels are free from this blemish of the author's personality blotting out the distinctive identity of the characters.

Judged by Edwin Muir's observation about the dramatic novel and the character novel, that "they are rather two distinct modes of seeing life: in Time, personally, and in Space, socially".[12] Priestley's works like *Bright Day, The Magicians* and *Lost Empires* bear out the fact that he has seen life both personally in Time and socially in space and, therefore, the picture emerging from his Time-fiction is one of balance. These works include the best of both, the dramatic novel and the character novel. Priestley believes in moderation, not in extremity of any kind. He is a traditionalist so far as he fits subjective themes into an objective narrative mould, but a progressive writer in respect of themes and ideas and their treatment from a philosophical view of Time.

Priestley's Time plays gave English drama a new direction by adding a philosophical dimension; established the supremacy of man's inner spirit over his reason; broke away from the beaten track of socialistic tradition. Equally original and valuable is his contribution to English fiction. His Time novels and short stories treat life in multiple Time. Priestley as a writer of Time fiction is a non-Bergsonian. His works of Time-fiction deal with different levels of consciousness in different orders of Time. Priestley's achievement as a Time-writer needs to be thoroughly discussed with a view to fixing his place among others of his kind.

It is surprising that Priestley is accused of escapism. If Heywood Broun, an American columnist, commenting on two of his Time plays, dismissed him as one of "these escapists",[13] James Agate, speaking of *I Have Been Here Before,* sarcastically remarked: "Our author likes to play at the Game of Recurrence and Intervention because it gives people a second chance...",[14] which amounts to charging Priestley with being an escapist. This is an unjust criticism. Priestley, on the contrary, is one of those writers who accept, with courage, the challenge of existence. It is his firm belief that man can really be himself only outside clock time and in moments of intuition when he feels linked to some mighty universal mind. To give people an awareness of the nobler dimensions of life is no act of escapism. It needs to be clarified how we interpret the word 'escapism'. Escapism is of two types: vulgar escapism and creative escapism. Things like overstimulation of sex, scenes of violence and fight as found in cheap thrillers, and an overdose of fantasy for fantasy's sake as noticed in some science-fiction writings are examples of objectionable escapism. Priestley's Time works are inspired by a profound belief that men can enrich and expand their lives only if they can look beyond chronological time. His is a positive-oriented healthy attitude to life, not one of a coward who, being incapable of facing the grim and harsh realities of life, wants to run away from the world. All new ideas do introduce some kind of fantasy in a creative way. Priestley feels in his very bones that Time as an idea is of the greatest significance to humanity. A fitting reply to this charge is contained in Priestley's own definition of good literature: "...it is necessary for all of us to do some escaping, and I have always held that in all good literature there is a certain satisfying balance of sharp criticism of our common life and an escape from it."[15] His Time-philosophy is not a life-denying nihilistic view which traces the inexorable march of life towards death. His Time-works speak volumes for his commitment to life, his staunch belief in the worthwhileness and wholesomeness of human existence. Therefore, certainly Priestley is not an escapist in the way some critics regard him as such.

In some quarters Priestley was even called 'Jolly Jack Priestley'. This criticism is double-edged: it suggests an excessive optimism on Priestley's part as well as his writing on too many things. His jovial picaresque novel *The Good Companions* was responsible for his being called 'Jolly'. This left-handed compliment stuck to Priestley despite the fact that he wrote really serious works like *Time and the Conways, I Have Been Here Before, Bright Day* and *The Magicians*. 'Jack' was used in the sense of 'Jack of all trades'. As John Atkins reads, this criticism suggests that Priestley has thinned out his talent by spreading it too wide; that is, by attempting too many forms. By implication, it accuses him of trying out too many ideas and of careless writing. Priestley explained why he tried fiction and many different forms: "because I had a lot of ideas that would not leave me in peace and because I could not resist the challenge."[16] It was in his very nature to receive ideas in all their abundance as they came from all quarters to him. He never considered himself a meticulous craftsman in fiction like Henry James or Conrad. But his Time plays like *Eden End, Time and the Conways* and *Music at Night* bear evidence of the fact that a lot of planning, thinking and contemplation had gone into the making of them. To him life was much greater than art. For that matter, Shakespeare is not a meticulous craftsman in the sense that Ben Jonson is. But who can mirror more of life than Shakespeare? This is not to suggest that Priestley stands equal to Shakespeare, but that what he loses in terms of art is made good by what he depicts of life. Susan Cooper raises the question which Priestley's readers might ask, and answers it herself: "If Priestley had worked only in one field, would the narrowing of focus have turned him into the unalloyed, hundred-percent artist that he has not in fact become? Unlikely—for the nature and range of an artist's work must always depend upon his personality, and in the last analysis Priestley is probably more concerned with the condition of man than with the condition of literature."[17]

The third charge brought against Priestley is that of pessimism which is as myopic as that of excessive optimism. He was described as a 'prophet of gloom', a charge largely based on the impression of "exuberant pessimism"[18] derived from the wartime novel *Blackout in Gretley* (1943). However, his works like *Eden End, Time and the Conways, Bright Day, The Magicians, Saturn Over the Water* and *Lost Empires* are no doubt touched with a certain amount of gloom; they have a haunting atmosphere of melancholy. But this melancholy-element adds a strange charm to these works. Priestley's pessimism is not the Hardyan type of passimism; it is born of a deep concern for the purpose and value of life which is emphasised in all his Time-works. The happy ending of all his plays and novels proves that he was never a pessimist with a deep distrust in life. The Time-works are a proof of his belief in the ultimate triumphing of life over Time and change. Of course, Priestley's grumpy face and his admission to being inclined to pessimistic moods in loneliness must have lent unwittingly some credence to this criticism, but it was an unjust charge, nevertheless. Priestley's own words should set at nought the charges of optimism and pessimism both taken in a wrong sense: "I dislike novelists who try to win popularity—or to retain it—by writing out of a sort of mechanical cheerfulness and optimism; but I equally dislike a determined gloom and pessimism, which happen to be more fashionable now in literary circles."[19]

A more serious charge is as regards the diction of Priestley's Time-plays. If the general opinion in the thirties was that he had no poetry in him, critics, like Ashley Dukes, observed: "he chooses a poet's subject and handles it in prosaic form...."[20] This kind of criticism stems from an expectation that the Time theme required poetic language. Some think that lack of purpose and seriousness was the cause of this alleged lack of poetry in him and that, his values being just to entertain the average audience, he compromised his commitment to values. Again this is a false charge. On the contrary, he was earnest and serious in the treatment of the Time problem which, he feels strongly, concerned the whole of mankind. An answer to this charge is found in his views regarding the theatre and dramatic experience. According to him the most important thing in the theatre is dramatic experience which is achieved by the audience as a result of the dramatist's successful working at a double level: the level of life and the level of the theatre. The real world and the fictional world meet in the theatre. A successful creation of dramatic experience has the poetry of the theatre, whether the plays are in verse or prose. A really poetic drama, according to Priestley, is one in which emotion and imagination are at the height of creation, and a drama, though written in prose and realistic convention, can be a poetic drama provided it appeals to the poetic sensibility of the audience. Poetic language is, he feels, 'heightened speech' marked by a higher imaginative quality, and not necessarily verse. He tried a bit of verse in *Johnson Over Jordan* and *Music at Night* which he never called poetry, and perhaps he felt that verse did not suit his purpose.

Priestley's reply to this charge comes from him in unmistakable terms: "But though I experimented with dramatic form, I was still working within the tradition of English realism. Too much of enrichment of speech would have destroyed this realism."[21] Moreover, he believed that verse for the stage was out of tune with the twentieth century ethos. Priestley is happy to find in good modern plays at least moments of the poetry of the theatre which, "like fruit that has fought for its juices against frost and rain, they (the plays) have wrung out of our harshly prosaic circumstances".[22] Seen in the light of Priestley's definition of the poetry of the theatre, his Time plays do possess plenty of moments of poetry. Therefore, the charge may be dismissed as untenable.

Another charge is that Priestley has used the stage as a platform for expressing his ideas. Two things need to be considered here. First, was Priestley a dramatist of ideas? If he was, did he use the stage for propagating his ideas? In the first place, he was certainly not a dramatist of ideas in the sense Shaw and Galsworthy were. His are not "discussion plays" at all. In the words of David Hughes, "to call him a dramatist of ideas crushes much of the breath out of his plays".[23] Though there cannot be a work of literature without some central idea in it, that idea need not necessarily be a social or political one to be treated as in a Shavian play. Priestley's Time plays do have philosophical ideas but they need no propagation through the instrument of the stage. These plays should not be judged by the yardsticks of realistic social drama, though Priestley brought even metaphysics within the compass of the realistic convention. That Priestley's motto was not didactic is made clear in his own words: "I would never have dreamt of trying to use the Theatre to convert people to some particular view of Time I held, nor of turning the playhouse into a lecture hall in which I would explore the intricacies of the problem."[24] Still a most surprising statement comes from A.C. Ward: "Ideas are the most exciting of adult playthings, but they hardly are so in J.B. Priestley's hands."[25] This kind of criticism results from the usual practice of looking at twentieth century dramatists more or less in the light of realistic social ideas dramatised by Shaw and his followers. This comment does not hold true at least of Priestley's Time plays which stand as a class by themselves in the history of English drama; they stand unique for concentrating on man's inner experience of non-passing time, and not for ideas relating to Time in the external world of man.

Like the plays, Priestley's novels too are not exempt from unfair and unsympathetic criticism. David Hughes thinks that the instant success of *The Good Companions* did Priestley an injustice equal to that success, making critics brand him "as a solid traditionalist who made an attempt, in currying public favour, to drag our bright progressive literature back into the mists where the jolly spirits of Fielding, Smollett and Dickens eternally dance."[26] This criticism is clear evidence of the fact that the novels with Time as a dominant force which Priestley wrote after the *The Good Companions* were not seriously considered by critics. In fact all his works of Time-fiction are a clear proof of his progressive thinking on the survival and real progress of mankind in the modern world, and a record of his untiring experimentation with the form and technique of the novel. Of course, he is a traditionalist in a good sense: he believed in telling a story, describing events and delineating characters in various ways, and never sought to subordinate the novel-form to ideas and states of mind, as did some of the modern psychological novelists.

Priestley's place as a Time-fictionist was overshadowed by his fame as a Time-philosopher of the English stage, and moreover he has suffered at the hands of academic critics who have all along denied this professional writer his due and legitimate place. It is really surprising that a balanced critic of A.C. Ward's eminence should say that "None of his (Prietley's) later novels surpassed *The Good Compnions* and by 1950 his stature as a novelist had dwindled",[27] when better works like *The Magicians* and *Lost Empires* and *Saturn Over the Water* had been produced. Priestley's fictional characters too are wrongly judged. It is alleged that "even in his most serious novels he seldom tries to penetrate far into their consciousness",[28] This is another way of calling him a traditionalist. The depiction of what goes on in the consciousness of Ravenstreet (*The Magicians*), Gregory Dawson (*Bright Day*), Richard Herncastle (*Lost Empires*) and a host of others disproves this statement. Moreover a writer should be judged by the principles of his own writing, not by those followed by other writers. Priestley is not a psychological writer and therefore, should not be judged by the yardsticks which we apply to the 'stream-of-consciousness' school of fiction.

The last charge is that Priestley's writing is too simple. Priestley's own reply to a young writer who complained of simplicity in his writing may be quoted as an answer to this charge: "But I've spent years trying to make my writing simple. What you see as a fault, I regard as a virtue."[29] To Priestley simplicity of expression was an article of faith. He declares that art to him was never synonymous with introversion and obscurity. He deliberately aimed at simplicity and not at complexity such as is found in writers like Joyce and Virginia Woolf who dig rather too much into the mind in the name of depth psychology. He rejects the idea of literature as a cerebral activity. Ivor Brown's words hit the nail right on the head: "He has written for the general reader and not for the intellectual specialist.... If he turns to mysticism, he does not mystify, and the fact that his thinking is restless has never inclined him to be obscure. He deals in theories without being the abstract or the baffling theorist."[30]

Without a comparative view regarding the achievement of a writer, it is not possible to fix his place among others. Priestley's distictive achievement as a writer of multiple Time comes out only in comparison with that of other major English and non-English Time-writers.

James Barrie uses, in plays like *Dear Brutus, Mary Rose, Peter Pan* and *Admirable Crichton,* the split-time device to create a 'might-have-been dream world' but Priestley uses the same device in *Dangerous Corner, Music at Night* and *Ever Since Paradise* to dramatise the inner world of the characters and in *Time and the Conways* to give a dramatic rendering of a future possibility. Time in Barrie is largely temporal: in *Mary*

Rose, Peter Pan, and *Dear Brutus* linear time is either arrested or reversed, and Barrie does not work in any deep philosophical dimension. In Priestley human life is observed outside clock time; he shows the influence of Time on the consciousness of his characters and time as experienced by them as a condition of existence. Barrie lacks depth, while Priestley is profound in his contemplation of Time; Barrie is sentimental in his fantasy-creation, whereas Priestley is never so because he does not totally sacrifice realistic norms for the sake of a poetic world of make-believe. "One feels that Barrie squandered a fine talent upon unworthy material, while Priestley's whole imaginative being is at full stretch, and his technical virtuosity working with his imagination."[31] Lord Dunsany's macabre fantasies *A Night at an Inn, If* and *The Gods of the Mountain* also blend the fantastic and the realistic as Barrie's plays do, involving the time element. *If,* like *Dear Brutus,* dramatises the 'second chance' theme with the difference that while Dunsany's play is built on the premise that accidents shape man's destiny, Barrie's play shows character as destiny. The same theme is put in a different philosophical light by Priestley in *I Have Been Here Before* and *They Came to a City.* Walter Ormund of the former play undergoes a total change in his very view of life and becomes a 'new-born' man under the influence of Gortler's enlightened view of Time as a multidimensional entity, and the recurrent tragedy is avoided. The characters in the latter play, however, get a chance to peep over the wall of passing time and then enter a timeless order of existence; Priestley makes a fine symbolistic play out of the 'second chance' theme; the play is endowed with a unique richness because of fairyland atmosphere which belongs to the deeper consciousness, with linear time totally expunged. Reginald Berkeley's *The World's End,* which deals with the theme of the second chance on the lines of *Dear Brutus,* seems shallow compared with Priestley's plays dealing with the same theme. Benn W. Levy's *Mrs. Moonlight,* depicting a woman who keeps her figure and looks for ever arrested at a particular age by virtue of some magic power, stands close to *Peter Pan* and *Mary Rose.* Levy's treatment of Time is linear and hence superficial compared with Priestley's treatment of multiple Time.

Priestley stands superior in his vision and treatment of Time to Shaw too. The central stuff of *I Have Been Here Before, Music at Night* and *Johnson Over Jordan* is the continuation of life beyond death through consciousness in different dimensions of Time, and the distinctive quality of these plays can be grasped better by comparing them with Shaw's great and ambitious drama *Back to Methuselah*. Priestley's plays concentrate on expanding and enriching consciousness till man reaches the superconscious stage at which he can see 'himself wholly and realise the 'reality' of life. Priestley believes that even while existing in the material body man can achieve immortality through consciousness which continues from one time-dimension to the next. Shaw's play, spanning a vast stretch of linear time from a distant past to a far-off future deals with the evolution of the Life Force in the process of the onward historical march and it is "one long concentration on the breaking of the opacity shutting man from the immortality, or eternal life, which is his birthright."[32] The process of man's development in Priestley's plays is spiritual and philosophical and it is to be achieved in multiple Time, while it is basically rational and spiritual in Shaw's play and it is to be achieved in linear time as made clear in Lilith's Epilogue.

The plays of Priestley's predecessors, except Shaw, deal with a kind of 'wish-fulfilment' on the stage. Their main concern is not Time as a spiritual or philosophical experience, as in Priestley; they concentrate on the fantastic and the supernatural as against the natural. The supernatural is absent from Priestley, whose main concern with Time is philosophical.

Coming to fiction, we find that there are a larger number of novelists than dramatists who were haunted by Time. Here Priestley is compared only with the major contributors.

If H.G. Wells' *The Time Machine* depicts a man who projects himself into the future with the help of a machine, his *The Shape of Things to Come* has something of a prophecy. No doubt, Wells presents a new concept about Time, describing it as the fourth dimension, but his works lack depth and colour because they do not treat Time as a condition of living, and as an experience of existence vis-a-vis consciousness. But Priestley's Time novels deal with the effect of Time on the human consciousness at different levels and in different dimensions of Time; they are, therefore, deep in their meaning and message. A comparison of *Bright Day* with Arnold Bennett's *The Old Wives' Tale* brings into bold relief the distinctive quality of the former. "The flow of time governs background as well as characters"[33] of Bennett's novel, a monumental work of realism in English fiction. But the fundamental difference between these novels is that Bennett's Time is the single track chronological time, while Priestley's is multidimensional Time moving at different levels of Gregory's consciousness. Bennett shows his characters—the three sisters in particular—as victims of Time and his novel breathes pessimism, whereas *Bright Day,* written around the Dunnian idea of Serial Time, delivers the message that nothing is destroyed by Time and everything is in its own time; and the novel ends on a strong note of optimism.

If Aldous Huxley's novels having the Time-element in them, like *Eyeless in Gaza, After Many a Summer* and *Time Must Have a Stop* show a distrust of materialism and a respect for the spirit urging modern man to seek solace in religion, Priestley's novels of wisdom like *The Magicians, Saturn Over the Water* and *It's an Old Country* condemn the 'rat-race' in today's world and show the remedy to modern man's 'anguish and fever' to lie in the right understanding of Time. Priestley's novels establish that life is multidimensional and consciousness continues from one Time-dimension to the next endlessly whereas Huxley's Time, being linear, ends at the death of Uncle Eustace, the central character of *Time Must Have a Stop* though his disembodied consciousness continues fighting against absorption in the universal consciousness; Huxley finds no possibility of contact between the dead and the living, while Priestley shows a possibility of inter-communication between the living and the dead at the level of consciousness demolishing the barrier of Time, in his novels like *Jenny*

Villiers and plays like *Johnson Over Jordan* and *Music at Night*. If *The Magicians* depicts the mad race of Sepman and his business associates for grabbing the maximum from passing time before it 'passes away', *After Many a Summer* harps on the futility of long life. The basic difference is that Huxley's American millionaire, horrified by the ugly changes caused by linear time, turns to mystic eternity, while Priestley's Ravenstreet gains a true understanding of life through the gift of a timeless view of it conferred on him by the 'indomitable trio' of magicians who can move in various dimensions of Time.

A brief and critical comparison of Priestley with the psychological novelists also is necessary in order to have a better appraisal of his achievement as a fictionist of multiple Time. The moment is the most important thing with psychological novelists, especially with those of the "stream-of-consciousness" technique. Dorothy Richardson's *Pilgrimage* minutely records the moment-to-moment impressions of the heroine Miriam Henderson's mental world. Though James Joyce uses Viço's theory of cycles in the development of man in *Ulysses* and takes the Homeric *Odessey* as the framework for the novel, his emphasis is on a psychological digging into the consciousness, moment by moment, of Leopold Bloom, Molly and Stephen Deaedalus. *Finnegans Wake,* the most experimental novel ever written, is a long concentration on the consciousness of H.C. Earwick, dethroning clock-time. Like Joyce's novels, the novels of Virginia Woolf also emphasize the 'moment' and reduce external action in clock time to the minimum. The past is shown as impinging upon the moments of the Ramsays in *To the Lighthouse* and Clarissa Dalloway and Peter Walsh in *Mrs. Dalloway.* There are two basic differences between these 'stream-of-consciousness' novelists and Priestley. In the first place, consciousness in Priestley is not confined to the period between the two ends of earthly life—birth and death—as in Joyce, Virginia Woolf and their followers; in some of Priestley's novels, like *Jenny Villiers* and *The Thirty First of June,* and stories, like *Look After the Strange Girl, The Other Place* and *The Statues,* consciousness goes 'before and after' earthly existence to earlier lives and the events to come in future. Secondly, the past that is ever-present in 'the moment' in these psychological novels is Bergsonian, that is, it is ever accruing into the moment, while the past in Priestley's works is Dunnian, that is, it appears in a series of dimensions.

One great distinctive quality of Priestley's Time-fiction is that it is not obscure. Psychological novels, particularly those of Joyce and Woolf, are tainted by an element of obscurity which results from an overstressing of 'personalised time' and intricate allusiveness. W.J. Harvey points out how these writers have tried to get over the danger of subjective time, upsetting the balance in their works: "It is interesting to notice that the more centrally a novel is located in a subjective consciousness, then the more the novelist has to compensate by stressing not objective, natural time (the passing of the seasons, the organic rhythms of growth and decay, etc.), but simple mechanical time. Thus Joyce is concerned throughout *Ulysses* to emphasize 'the dance of the hours'; thus Big Ben booms throughout *Mrs. Dalloway*;..."[34] Priestley does not fall a victim to this danger. Works like *Bright Day, The Magicians, Jenny Villiers* and *Saturn Over the Water* and *Lost Empires* maintain a balance between the world within and the world without, which are, all the while, interacting in consciousness. Moreover, the novel as a form of literary art, seems to burst at the seams in the hands of Joyce and Woolf, who ambitiously fill it with too many things from a variety of subjects and disciplines. This unhappy feature is pointed out by S. Diana Neill in her observation about Joyce's novels, which is true of other psychological novelists also, if in a lesser degree: "Yet for all that it is impossible not to feel a certain hollowness at the core of his creation...he (Joyce) lacked most of the more obvious qualities needed to give great delight in fiction."[35]

Both James Joyce and Priestley have used cycles of Time, but their concepts of Time-cycles are different. Vico's cycles in Joyce are basically the repetition of cosmic time, though they are claimed to be "all-inclusive, embracing human experience in its entirity".[36] Priestley's Ouspenskian Eternal Recurrence shows the recurrence of the same events and the same persons with the same individual consciousness as found in *Jenny Villiers, The Other Place* and *Look After the Strange Girl,* yet, he believes, the course of events can be changed through intervention.

Furthermore, the past as treated by Priestley is different not only from the past as it is treated by the 'stream-of-consciousness' novelist discussed so far, but also from the past, as part of biological time, continued through inherent genetic traits of a personality from its ancestors as shown in Virginia Woolf's *Orlando* which moves on two time levels, and also from the historical past of Mrs. Woolf's conception, carrying the racial and cultural traits of man, and being present in a contemporary personality, as illustrated by *Between the Acts.* In works like *Jenny Villiers* and *Look After the Strange Girl* Priestley's emphasis is on the singular importance of a free movement of consciousness not only through the different selves of one and the same personality in different dimensions of Time, before and after Time One existence, but also through those of other lives. In short, Woolf's Time in the above-named two novels is biological and historical while Time in Priestley is spiritual and philosophical.

Similarly, Priestley, being a writer of multiple Time, differs from the non-English Time-fictionists like Thomas Mann, Marcel Proust, William Faulkner, Thomas Wolfe and Kafka. Priestley's *Bright Day* and *Lost Empires* are Proustian in so far as they recapture the past through 'flashbacks', but the basic difference is that these works use the Dunnian Serial Time, while *Remembrance of Things Past* recaptures the purity of 'lost time' through a voluntary exercise of memory in calling up significant moments of the past. Mann's *Magic Mountain* displays the relative nature of Time psychologically by showing how the inmates of the Sanatorium are unaware of the passage of Time, being isolated from the outside world, and Hans Castorp becomes aware of time only when he returns, like Rip Van Winkle, to the plains; Priestley, on the other hand, uses the *ESP* concept in *Jenny Villiers* and some stories in which the consciousness of the characters is released from them and wanders into their earlier lives in different dimensions of Time while clock time is reduced only to a few hours or minutes. Faulkner's *The Sound and the Fury,* told by the three Campson brothers, spreads over four days of fictional time but covers, psychologically, the entire emotional history of the Campson family which at the same time symbolises the emotional history of South America; the past in the novel is so obsessive and oppressive that Faulkner is charged by Sartre with having "decapitated time, deprived it of its future, that is, its dimension of deeds and freedom...."[37] In *Bright Day* and *Lost Empires* also the past is a dominant influence, but the characters are not deprived of their future, of their will and power to act; on the contrary, Gregory and Richard, the central characters of these novels, emerge full of hope for a meaningful future at the end.

Priestley stands distinguished yet on another ground: his treatment of certain rare moments which he calls 'magical' is entirely different from the way in which such moments are treated by others. Proust calls them 'eternal essences' which, liberated as they are from temporal attributes, help him discover his self from the passage of time; for Joyce such a moment is 'epiphany' which is a sudden spiritual manifestation; for Virginia Woolf it is 'illumination of being'; for Thomas Wolfe, a Proustian in recapturing 'lost time', such moments are gleaming 'pin-points' of time which are of two kinds, suspended moments and all-embracing moments; Kafka creates a kind of nightmarish time-continuum which in turn creates a 'temporal vacuum'. All these writers visualize various effects of Time on the human mind in the light of the Bergsonian *durée*. Priestley's 'magical moments' are unique because they give a peep into the flow of consciousness 'before and after' early life in Time One—in the Dunnian idiom— and they are not psychological but metaphysical in character; his 'magical moments' give a peep into the Great Unknown which no writer of the psychological school has dreamt of.

The discussion in the foregoing pages establishes how distinctive Priestley's contribution to Time-literature is. In the first place, he is a writer of multiple Time. Secondly, he is the only major writer of the twentieth century who has dealt with the Time theme in two major forms of literature: drama and fiction. He made a bold attempt as a dramatist to depart from the popular realistic stage and to offer something remarkably original to the English stage, namely, the treatment of the Time problem which drew the attention of the audience to the inner world of man and gave them the kind of dramatic experience which was exhilaratingly new in the theatre.

Priestley's achievement as a Time-dramatist is two-fold: he has treated a number of themes against the background of his Time-philosophy and displayed great technical virtuosity in treating those themes. He is not a follower of any school or writer; his allegiance, first and last, is to life.

As in drama so in fiction too, Priestley has made a solid and lasting contribution and his place in Time-literature is certainly enviable. He has enriched English fiction with his Time-works which are remarkable for the novelty of both ideas and technique. It was singularly original and brave on his part as a fictionist to tread new ground, in so far as he chose to write in a non-Bergsonian way, at a time when the Bergsonian psychological fiction had become synonymous with Time-fiction. No other fictionist of Time has looked at Time and its influence on man from as many angles as Priestley did. He is undoubtedly unique as a writer of multiple Time. As a literary artist—as a craftsman—Priestley may not be as great as Joyce or Woolf or Faulkner, but considering the fact that his primary concern was with life rather than literary art, and that to him understanding life and solving its problems through the right understanding of Time was much more important than anything else, it can be said that his place among English writers of Time is certainly one of eminence. In so far as he added a philosophical dimension to Time plays and Time-fiction in English, he has no equal.

Priestley was not just a popular entertainer but a writer with a profound philosophy. Priestley belonged to the age of Bernard Shaw, G.K. Chesterton and H.G. Wells, though he arrived late by two decades. Like them he also was a social phenomenon rather than an artist, and "a sage who knew all the answers, who wrote about any and everything".[38] Priestley has a message for mankind. It is not any impracticable sublime sermon coming from a starry-eyed idealist, but one that has a basis in reality. He pleads for a good and noble life. Behind his fervent plea there is a genuine concern for the survival and progress of the human race. His warning against irresponsible living comes clear and sharp:

> It is here, in the world we have made, we really begin to "live with ourselves", and reap between these heavenly heights and hellish depths what we have sown.[39]

Priestley's view of life and the Karma doctrine come very close: we cannot absolve ourselves of the fruit of our action; we are responsible for what we are and will be responsible for what we are going to be; as we sow, so shall we reap. He stresses that men should learn to make their lives sublime by suffusing themselves with love, imagination and emotion and understanding, which will lift them out of the meagre and dull life in Time One existence into higher orders of Time. Faith in the continuance of life after death will fill them with optimism and inspire them to do only good, beautiful, noble and humane deeds and they will not be hell-bent on accomplishing their desires by hook or crook before their time 'runs out'. Priestley's Time-philosophy, which is the sustaining power behind his Time-works, lays a singular stress on the expansion and enrichment of consciousness so that man will be able "to kindle a light in the darkness of mere being"[40] (to use the words of Jung, who spells out the goal of man's life on this planet in those words). His optimistic view of life outside unidimensional clock-time makes one feel that man is not a helpless victim of the process of 'becoming', but he has the making of his life in his own hands—through a proper understanding of Time.

Though Priestley's poetic vision of life, as expressed in his Time-works, embodied itself in 'the other harmony' of prose, we may, quoting William Blake's poetic words about the Bard, pay our tribute to this sage-like Time-traveller as follows:

> Hear the Voice of the Bard!
>
> Who Present, Past and Future sees.[41]

NOTES

1. Allardyce Nicoll, *World Drama* (London: George G. Harrap & Co. Ltd., 1968), p. 773.
2. G. Wilson Knight, *The Golden Labyrinth* (London: Phoenix House Ltd., 1962), p. 387.
3. Ivor Brown, *J.B. Priestley* (London: The British Council & the National Book League Longman, Green & Co., 1957), p. 25.
4. Gareth Lloyd Evans, *J.B. Priestley: The Dramatist* (London: Heinemann Ltd., 1964), p. 147.
5. J.C. Trewin, *The Theatre Since 1900* (London: Andrews Drakers Ltd., 1951), p. 226.
6. *Ibid*., pp. 230-31.
7. A.A. Mendilow, *Time and the Novel* (New York: Humanities Press, rpt. 1972), p. 126.
8. Leon Edel, *The Psychological Novel 1900-1950* (Ludhiana, India: Lyall Book Depot, 1965), p. 29.
9. T.S. Eliot, *Four Quartets* (London: Faber and Faber, 4th Impression, 1946), p. 18.
10. Walter Allen, *The English Novel* (London: Penguin Books, 1970), p. 344.
11. Giorgeo Metchiori, "The Moment as time-unit in fiction", *Critical Approaches*, ed., Shiv Kumar and Keith Mckean (New York: McGraw-Hill Book Company USA, 1968), p. 225.
12. Edwin Muir, *The Structure of the Novel* (London: The Hogarth Press, 1928), p. 63.
13. J.B. Priestley, *Rain Upon Godshill* (London: Heinemann Ltd., 1939), p. 64.
14. Gareth Lloyd Evans, *J.B. Priestley: The Dramatist* (London: Heinemann Ltd., 1964), p. 119.
15. J.B. Priestley, *Rain Upon Godshill,* p. 63.
16. J.B. Priestley, *Margin Released,* p. 176.
17. Susan Cooper, *J.B. Priestley: Portrait of an Author*, p. 211.
18. David Hughes, *J.B. Priestley: An Informal Study of his Work*, p. 17.
19. J.B. Priestley, *All About Ourselves and Other Essays* (London: Heinemann Ltd., 1956), p. 257.
20. Gareth Lloyd Evans, *J.B. Priestley: The Dramatist*, p. 44.
21. *Ibid*., p. 42.

22. J.B. Priestley, *The Art of the Dramatist* (London: Heinemann Ltd., 1957), p. 28.
23. David Hughes, *J.B. Priestley: An Informal Study of his Work*, p. 127.
24. J.B. Priestley, *The Art of the Dramatist*, p. 50.
25. A.C. Ward, *20th Century English Literature 1901-60* (Bombay: B.I. Publications Pvt. Ltd., rpt. 1986), 133.
26. David Hughes, *J.B. Priestley: An Informal Study of his Workup*, pp. 16-17.
27. A.C. Ward, *20th Century English Literature 1901-60*, pp. 71-72.
28. Nionel Stevenson, *The History of English Novel,* Vol. XI (New York: Barnes & Noble INC., 1967), p. 309.
29. J.B. Priestley, *All About Ourselves and Other Essays*, p. 33.
30. Ivor Brown, *J.B. Priestley* (London: The British Council & National Book League Longman, Green & Co., 1957), p. 6.
31. Gareth Lloyd Evans, *J.B. Priestley: The Dramatist* (London: Heinemann Ltd., 1964), p. 26.
32. G. Wilson Knight, *The Golden Labyrinth,* p. 349.
33. Walter Allen, *The English Novel,* p. 321.
34. W.J. Harvey, *Character and the Novel* (Ithaca, New York: Cornell University Press, 1965), pp. 105-06.
35. S. Diana Neill, *A Short History of English Novel* (London: Jarrolds Ltd., 1951), pp. 323-24.
36. John Henry Raleigh, "The English Novel and the Three Kinds of Time", *The Novel,* ed. Robert Murray Davis (Englewood Cliffs: Prentice-Hall INC., New Jersey, 1969), p. 250.
37. Petrica Drechsel Tobin, *Time and the Novel—The Geneological Imperative* (Princeton: Princeton University Press, New Jersey, 1978), p. 112.
38. John Atkins, *J.B. Priestley—The last of the sages*, p. 41.
39. J.B. Priestley, *Man and Time,* p. 304.
40. *Ibid.*, p. 308.
41. William Blake, "Hear the Voice of the Bard!", *The Golden Treasury,* Selected by F.T. Palgrave (New Delhi: Oxford and IBH, n.d.), p. 315.

Bibliography

(A) Primary Source

John Boynton Priestley's Works

Drama

Collected Plays: Vol. I-III, London: William Heinemann.

The Roundabout, London: Heinemann, 1933.

Duet in Floodlight, London: Heinemann, 1935.

Spring Tide, London: Heinemann, 1936.

Mystery at Greenfingers, London: Heinemann, 1937.

The Long Mirror, London: Heinemann, 1943.

The High Toby, London: Heinemann, 1948.

Bright Shadow, London: Heinemann, 1950.

The Rose and the Crown (One Act Play), London: Samuel French, 1947.

Treasure on Pelican, London: Heinemann, 1953.

Try it Again (One Act), London: Samuel French, 1953.

A Glass of Bitter, London: Samuel French, 1954.

Mr. Cattle and Mrs. Moon, London: Heinemann, 1955.

The Glass Cage, London: Heinemann, 1957.

Fiction

Adam in Moonshine, London: Heinemann, Popular Edn., 1952.

Benighted, London: Heinemann, 1951.

The Good Companions, London: Heinemann, rpt. Nov. 1933.
Angel Pavement, London: Everyman's Library rpt., 1962.
Faraway, London: Heinemann, Cheap Edn., 1950.
Wonder Hero, London: Heinemann, 1933.
They Walk in the City, London: Heinemann, 1936.
The Doomsday Men, London: Pan Books Ltd., 1947.
Let the People Sing, London: The Book Club, 1940.
Black-out in Gretley, London: Heinemann, 1942.
Daylight on Saturday, London: Heinemann, 1943.
Three Men in New Suits, London: Heinemann, 1945.
Bright Day, London: Heinemann, rpt. 1949.
Jenny Villiers, London: Heinemann, 1947.
Festival at Farbridge, London: Heinemann, 1951.
The Other Place (Short Stories), London: Heinemann, 1953.
The Magicians, London: Heinemann, 1953.
Low Notes on a High Level, London: Heinemann, 1954.
Saturn Over the Water, London: Heinemann, 1961.
The Thirty First of June, London: Heinemann, 1961.
The Shapes of Sleep, London: Heinemann, 1962.
Sir Michael and Sir George, London: Heinemann, 1964.
Lost Empires, London: Heinemann, 1965.
It's an Old Country, London: Heinemann, 1967.
The Image Men, London: Heinemann, 1969.
Snoggle, London: Heinemann, 1971.
The Carfit Crisis (Stories), London: Heinemann, 1975.

Criticism

The Figures in Modern Literature, London: John Lane, 1924.
The English Comic Characters, London: John Lane, 1925.
George Meredith (E.M.L.), London: Macmillan, 1926.
The English Novel, London: Earnest Benn, 1927.
Thomas Love Peacock (E.M.L.), London: Macmillan, 1927.

English Humour, London: Longman, 1929.

Theatre Outlook, London: Nicholson & Watson, 1947.

William Hazlitt, London: Longman (for British Council), 1960.

Literature and Western Man, London: Heinemann, 1960.

Charles Dickens, London: Thames & Hudson, 1961.

Essays, Autobiographical and Other Works

Brief Diversions, Cambridge: Bowes, 1922.

Papers From Lilliput, Cambridge: Bowes, 1922.

I For One (Essays), London: John Lane, 1923.

Open House (Essays), London: Heinemann, 1927.

Apes and Angels (Essays), London: Heinemann, 1928.

The Balconinny (Essays), London: Heinemann, 1929.

Delight (Essays), London: Heinemann, 1949.

Thoughts in the Wilderness (Essays), London: Heinemann, 1957.

Essays of Five Decades, London: Heinemann, 1969.

The Moments and Other Pieces, London: Heinemann, 1966.

Postscripts (Talk on BBC), London: Heinemann, 1940.

The Art of the Dramatist (Lectures), London: Heinemann, 1957.

Midnight on the Desert (Autobiography), London: Heinemann, 1937.

Rain Upon Godshill (Autobiography), London: Heinemann, 1939.

English Journey (Travel), London: Heinemann, 1934.

Journey Down a Rainbow (with Jacquetta Hawkes), London: Heinemann, 1955.

Margin Released (Autobiography), London: Heinemann, 1962.

Man and Time, New York: Aldus Allen Books, 1964.

Over the Long High Wall, London: Heinemann, 1972.

Outcries and Asides, London: Heinemann, 1974.

Particular Pleasures, London: Heinemann, 1975.

(B) Secondary Source

Aiyer, P.S. Sivaswamy, *Evolution of Hindu Moral Ideas*, Calcutta: The Calcutta University, 1935.

Allen, Walter, *The English Novel,* London: Penguin Books, 1970.

Allott, Miriam, *Novelists on the Novel,* London: Routledge and Kegan Paul, rpt. Paperback, 1965.

Atkins, John, *J.B. Priestley—The last of the sages,* London: John Calder, 1981.

Aurobindo, Sri, *The Life Divine,* Pondicherry (India): Sri Aurobindo Birth Centenary Library Publications, Vol. 19, 1970.

Barrie, J.M., *The Plays of J.M. Barrie,* ed., A.E. Wilson, London: Hodder and Stoughton, 1948 (Peter Pan, Dear Brutus, Mary Rose).

Bennett, Arnold, *The Old Wives' Tale,* Harmondsworth: Penguin Books, 1954.

Bernard, Theos, *Hindu Philosophy,* New York: Philosophical Library, 1947.

Blake, A.G.E., *A Seminar on Time,* Charles Town, USA: Claymont Communications, 1980.

Brown, Brian, ed., *The Wisdom of Hindus,* Delhi: Heritage Publishers, 1973.

Brown, Ivor, *J.B. Priestley,* London: The British Council & The National Book League Longman, Green & Co., 1957.

——, *The Priestley Companion,* London: Heinemann, 1951.

Brunton, Paul, *A Search in Secret India,* New Delhi: B.I. Publications, rpt. 1985.

Cleugh, M.F., *Time and its Importance in Modern Thought,* London: Rupert Hart-Davis, 1958.

Cooper, Susan, *J.B. Priestley—Portrait of an Author*, London: Heinemann, 1970.

Davis, Robert Murray, ed., *The Novel, Englewood Cliffs,* Prentice-Hall, INC, USA, 1969.

Dunne, J.W., *An Experiment with Time*, London: Faber and Faber Ltd., 1934.

——, *The Serial Universe*, London: Faber and Faber Ltd., rpt. 1945.

Durant, Will, *The Story of Philosophy*, Part I, New York: Simon and Schuster, 1942.

——, *The Story of Philosophy*, London: Ernest Been Ltd., 1946.

Edel, Leon, *The Psychological Novel 1900-1950*, Ludhiana (India): Lyall Book Depot, 1965.

Eliot, T.S., *Four Quartets*, London: Faber and Faber, rpt. 1946.

Evans, Gareth Lloyd, *J.B. Priestley—The Dramatist*, London: Heinemann Ltd., 1964.

Faulkner, William, *The Sound and the Fury*, London: Chatto & Windus, 1974.

Ford, Boris, ed., *The Pelican Guide to English Literature*, Vol. 7, The Modern Age, Penguin Books, 1964.

Forster, E.M., *Aspects of the Novel*, London: Edward Arnold and Co., rpt. 1953.

Frank, Eric., *Philosophical Understanding and Religious Truth*, New York: Oxford University Press INC, 1945.

Fraser, G.S., *The Modern Writer and His World*, Baltimore, USA: Penguin Books, 1970.

Furness, R.S., *Expressionism*, The Critical Idiom Series, No. 29, London: Methuen & Co. Ltd., 1973.

Gascoine, Bamber, *Twentieth Century Drama*, London: Hutchinson, University Library, 1967.

Grossvogel, David I., *Limits of the Novel—Evolutions of a Form from Chaucer to Robbe-Grillet*, Ithaca and New York: Cornell University Press, 1968.

Harvey, W.J., *Character and the Novel*, Ithaca, New York: Cornell University Press, 1968.

Hastings, James, ed., *Encyclopaedia of Religion and Ethics*, Vol. XII, Edinburgh: T. & T. Clark, 1934.

Hentschel, Irene, *Introduction to Time and the Conways,* London: Heinemann, 1950.

Hudson, W.H., *An Outline History of English Literature,* Bombay: B.I. Publications Pvt. Ltd., 1978.

Hughes, David, *J.B. Priestley—An Informal Study of His Work,* London: Rupert Hart-Davis, 1958.

Hume, R.E., trans., *Thirteen Principal Upanishads,* London: Oxford University Press, 1934.

Huxley, Aldous, *Brave New World,* Harmondsworth: Penguin Books, rpt. 1969.

——, *Eyeless in Gaza,* Harmondsworth: Penguin Books, 1968.

——, *After Many a Summer,* Harmondsworth: Penguin Books, 1971.

——, *Time Must Have a Stop,* New York: Sundial Press, 1947.

Jeans, James, *The New Background of Science,* Cambridge: The New University Press, 1947.

Joyce, James, *Ulysses,* London: The Bodley Head, rpt. 1958.

Kafka, Franz, *Castle,* trans. Willie and Edwin Muir, New York: Knopf, 1956.

Klein, Holger, *J.B. Priestley's Plays,* London: Macmillan Ltd., 1988.

Knight, G. Wilson, *The Golden Labyrinth,* London: Phoenix House Ltd., 1962.

Kumar, Shiv and McKean, Keith ed., *Critical Approaches,* New York: McGraw-Hill Book Co., 1968.

Leggett, H.W., *The Idea of Fiction,* London: George Allen & Unwin Ltd., 1934.

Lubbock, Percy, *The Craft of Fiction,* London: Bradford & Dickens, 1957.

Mann, Thomas, *Magic Mountain,* trans. H.T. Lowe-Porter, Harmondsworth: Penguin Books (Penguin Modern Classics), 1971.

Mendilow, A.A., *Time and the Novel,* New York: Humanities Press, 1972.

Meyerhoff, Hans, *Time in Literature,* Berkeley and Los Angeles: University of California Press, 1960.

Muir, Edwin, *The Structure of the Novel,* London: The Hogarth Press, rpt. 1957.

Narasimha Murthy, M.G., ed., *Stories British and American,* Bombay: Orient Longman Ltd., rpt. 1987.

Neill, S. Diana, *A Short History of English Novel,* London: Jarrolds Ltd., 1951.

Nicoll, Allardyce, *British Drama,* London: George G. Harrap & Co. Ltd., rpt. 1964.

——, *World Drama,* London: George G. Harrap & Co., 1968.

——, *The Theory of Drama,* London: George G. Harrap & Co., 1931.

Owen, Harrison, *The Playwright's Craft,* London: Thomas Nelson & Sons Ltd., 1940.

Palgrave, F.T., ed., *The Golden Treasury,* New Delhi: Oxford & IBH, n.d.

Poulet, Georges, *Studies in Human Time,* Eng. trans., Elliott Coleman, Baltimore: The Johns Hopkins Press, 1956.

Proust, Marcel, *Remembrance of Things Past,* Vol. I, trans. C.K. Scott Moncrieff, New York: Random House, 1934.

Radhakrishnan, S., *The Brahma Sutra,* London: George Allen and Unwin Ltd., 1960.

——, *Indian Philosophy,* Vol. II, London: George Allen and Unwin Ltd., 1946.

——, *The Bhagavadgita,* London: George Allen and Unwin Ltd., 1948.

Reynolds, Ernest, *Modern English Drama,* London: George G. Harrap & Co., 1949.

Russell, Bertrand, *History of Western Philosophy,* London: George Allen and Unwin Ltd., 1954.

Shakespeare, William, *The Complete Works of Shakespeare,* ed., B. Hodex, London: Spring Books, 1961.

Shaw, G.B., *Back to Methuselah,* Oxford: The World's Classics, 1945.

Sinha, Jadunath, *A History of Indian Philosophy,* Vol. II Calcutta: Central Book Agency, 1952.

Sterne, Laurence, *Tristram Shandy,* London: The World's Classics, Oxford University Press, rpt. 1941.

Stevenson, Nionel, *The History of English Novel,* Vol. XI, New York: Barnes & Noble INC, 1967.

Thomas, Edward J., trans., *The Song of The Lord,* London: John Murray, 1931.

Tobin, Petrica Drechsel, *Time and the Novel—The Geneological Imperative,* Princeton: Princeton, University Press, USA, 1978.

Tomlin, E.M.F., *Western Philosophers,* London: Hutchinson & Co. Ltd., 1969.

Trewin, J.C., *The Theatre Since 1900,* London: Andrews Drakers Ltd., 1951.

Ward, A.C., *20th Century English Literature 1901-60,* Bombay: B.I. Publications Pvt. Ltd., 1986.

Weber, Alfred, *History of Philosophy,* trans., Frank Thilly, New York: Charles Scribner's Sons, 1925.

Wells, H.G., *The Time Machine,* London: J.M. Dent & Sons Ltd., 1946.

Whitney, William, trans., *Atharva Veda Samhita,* Vol. II, Delhi: Motilal Banarasidas, 1962.

Wolfe, Thomas, *Of Time and the River: Legend of Man's Hunger in his Youth*, New York: Scribner's Sons, 1935.

Woolf, Virginia, *Mrs. Dalloway,* London: The Hogarth Press, rpt. 1958.

——, *To the Lighthouse,* London: The Hogarth Press, rpt. 1955.

——, *Between the Acts,* London: The Hogarth Press, 5th Impression, 1953.

Yaravintelimath, C.R., *Adventures in Time—A Study of J.B. Priestley's Plays,* Dharwad (India): Chaitra Prakashan, 1988.

Ziolkowski, Theodore, *Dimensions of the Modern Novel*, Princeton: Princeton University Press, 1969.

(C) Periodicals

Observer, August 27, 1978.

Observer, April 20, 1975.

Observer, August 19, 1984.

Observer, January 1, 1978.

Drama, No. 115 (Winter 1974).

Drama, No. 112 (Spring 1974).

The Times Literary Supplement, London, Dec. 21-27, 1990.

Reader's Digest, Bombay, Dec. 1990.

Span, New Delhi, Feb. 1991.

Guardian, August 16, 1984.

Listener, No. 112, August 23, 1984.

Author, No. 95 (Autumn 1984).

Spectator, September 1, 1984.

Index